THE KING
AND
HIS COURT

THE KING

AND

HIS COURT

Pierre Viansson-Ponté

translated by
Elaine P. Halperin

with a Foreword by
Janet Flanner

HOUGHTON MIFFLIN COMPANY BOSTON

The Riverside Press Cambridge

Foreword

AT THE AGE of seventy-three, President Charles de Gaulle has recently entered into the sixth year of his Fifth Republic, which has rejuvenated France. From the time of his earliest youth, nothing has interested him like French history. For almost a quarter of a century he has been the single and singular Frenchman who has created his own French history, intermittently but connectedly. He began it as that lone French voice on the London B.B.C. in June 1940, after France fell, when he called upon Frenchmen to fight on with him in the Resistance. Today his most compact and original historical creation is, of course, the Fifth Republic itself, which is like no other Republic France has ever had and is indeed like no other powerful responsible government on earth today. By the special almost sovereign style of his presidency over it, his Fifth Republic has a certain solo quality which makes it unique.

As the Chief of State of France, he is rarely visible in its capital city. Thousands of Parisians have never seen him except facially condensed on the national television screen. His is in a way a private government between him and his

ministers behind salon doors. "Before De Gaulle, France
had many problems. Now she has only one—De Gaulle,"
said M. Raymond Aron, the well-known Paris political commentator, himself formerly a Gaullist. "How can you govern
a country which has two hundred and forty-six different
kinds of cheese?" De Gaulle once ironically inquired, an
oblique reference to France's individualistic, multiple, and
incoherent political system of ten or fifteen parliamentary
parties, which, during the last decade of the Third Republic
and all the years of the Fourth Republic, tossed out national
governments exactly like emptied cheese boxes. President
de Gaulle became the answer to his own question. He governs France as what the French themselves, especially those
who strongly disapprove of his régime, call *un autocrate
bénévole,* a benevolent autocrat.

Fundamentally he is a phenomenon. It has been pointed
out that few French people can have studied the De Gaulle
phenomenon more closely than he himself. General de
Gaulle is that rare exception, a cerebral military man with
remarkable intellectual endowments and special qualities—
with a memory like an archive, dominant gifts as a stylistic
writer and speaker, a cold excellent lucid brain as thinker
and logician. He is paradoxical and complex, liberal and
tyrannical, delegates to others the few items that do not interest him as head of the state, and is implacable. He can
emit intuitive flashes of genius or remain with his ideas
walled behind his pride. He has physical and moral bravery,
vision, creative energy, and is possessed by a strange permanent modern mysticism. He has been an insatiable reader
of certain royalist French philosophers over those lonely
periods of his life when his career seemed lying fallow but
was really taking its deepest roots. In the fourth and most
famous of the earlier books he wrote, *Au Fil de l'Epée,* published when he was only forty-two years old, he listed four

qualities which he considered requisite for an ideal leader
of men, an occupation he was already clearly analyzing: "a
dose of egoism, of pride, of hardness and of ruse." Over the
past year or so in his famous TV speeches, he has finally
ceased egoistically referring to himself in the third person —
as it were addressing himself in public the way courtiers address a monarch. His indifference to physical danger during
his official visits to the French provinces, where he plunges
into crowds to shake hands with the peasants and townsfolk,
so alarmed the secret service men supposed to guard him
against assassination that one of them bravely pointed out
to the General the risks he ran. "Try to get this into your
head, monsieur," the General reportedly replied, very coldly,
"De Gaulle does not interest me except as a historical figure."
He seems beyond the reach of personal sentiment for himself.
It is an emotion he reserves only for *la belle France.*

More than three dozen books on President de Gaulle
have been published in France. The present volume by M.
Pierre Viansson-Ponté tells what the other books on De
Gaulle largely omit. With accuracy, humor, and thus *lèse
majesté,* he describes the hurried ceremonials of the great
formal gala dinners at the Palais de l'Elysées. "No cheese is
served (malodorous) and no fruit (takes too long to peel)."
He annotates the moralistic social rôle of Madame de Gaulle,
the rigid protocol for visitors to the Chief of State himself,
the no less inflexible formality which ties his ministers to
him until he suddenly releases them—by dismissal. Aside
from its penetrating resumé of what happened in and to the
Fourth Republic and what has, or has not yet transpired in
the Fifth Republic, the most intimate material, the most
rare and important, is the roster which Viansson-Ponté has
compiled of character sketches and records of the loyal devoted six or seven dozen leading Gaullists, along with Gaullism's few ambitious traitors. These men by their devotion

or even by their heresies explain the original appeal and also the power today of De Gaulle—followers and believers and also occasional outcast dissenters, at one moment all patriots together in a large yet intimate national movement that formed the present France. It is a roster of modern confraternal Frenchmen capable of what seems like a medieval devotion to a contemporary historical French movement and above all to its chief, who created the history they serve.

JANET FLANNER

Contents

Foreword by Janet Flanner   v
Author's Preface   xiii

PART I: THE RITUALS

CEREMONIALS

1. The Introduction   3
2. The Handshake   7
3. The Invitation   7
4. Gala Evening   8
5. The Official Reception   12
6. The Formal Dinner   12
7. The Intimate or Informal Dinner   14
8. Lunch at Colombey   15

LITURGY

1. The Interview   18
2. The Consultation   22
3. The Appointment   24

4. The Promotion   25
5. The Petition   25
6. The Resignation   26

THE SERMON

1. The Ceremony   29
2. The Trip to the Provinces   31
3. The Trip Abroad   34
4. A Few Words to the People   35
5. The Short Address   35
6. The Oration   36
7. Submersion in the Crowd   37

CATECHISM

1. The Diplomatic Conversation   39
2. The Committee   41
3. The Council of Ministers   42
4. The Press Conference   44

SUNDAY

1. Reading   48
2. The Mail   49
3. Television   51
4. The Social Conventions   52
5. The Country   53

KINSHIP AND RANK

1. The Kings, Good Cousins All   55
2. The Peers   60
3. The Partners   65
4. Konrad, the Friend   73
5. Liege Lords, Noble Seigneurs
   and Gentle Ladies   76

THE LIGHT CAVALRY PARTY

 1. The Old-Time Gaullist   81
 2. The Shock-Trooper Gaullist   86
 3. The Drawing-Room Gaullist   89
 4. The Professional Gaullist   92
 5. The Technocratic Gaullist   94
 6. Women Gaullists   96
 7. Wolves Hunt in Packs   98
 8. Gaullists Also Die   100
 9. Chamber Music   104
10. Military Music   106

PART II: THE DIRECTORY

How To Use the Directory   113
To Understand the Symbols Fully   115
Biographies   124

Author's Preface

"GAULLISM is sometimes a thousand faithful, sometimes the whole country. Everyone has been, is, or will be a Gaullist." This was said by General de Gaulle himself, and he knows whereof he speaks. It is hardly surprising then that there are a thousand and one "Gaullisms." Many attempts have been made to number, classify, and describe them, but each time something happens that necessitates a change in definition or a reversal of opinion.

Today, in 1964, Gaullism is a reality that cannot be denied. An autopsy would reveal that it is neither a doctrine nor an organization but a living experience.

To begin with, there is the General's own experience: his passionate feeling for France, his unembodied and sacrosanct concept of power and the State that rules the Nation, his skill in positive and pragmatic action, plus a tendency to gamble on the grandeur of the country and the infantilism of its children.

Secondly, there is the General's real experience with his faithful, at the very core of which is his concept of loyalty— a feudal bond, mystical and mythical in nature. Gaullism is

first of all a Guild whose members are bound together by
indissoluble ties. For example, a very old companion of the
Liberation who became a relentless enemy, Jacques Soustelle, rebelled, was excluded and exiled, yet he remains a
member of the group, of the family; so do the imprisoned
generals, or any other liege lords guilty of desertion.

As for the Gaullism of the people—the very real experience of the General's relationship to the masses—it resides
in the adherence that gives a legitimacy to power which
public acclaim and the referendum, those symbols of feudal
homage and consecration, confirm. Ademocratic, it is both
"depoliticization" and incantation.

This being so, where and who are the Gaullists? What
criteria does one employ in including one man in the Knighthood and excluding another? The fact is, there are no rules.
Men come and go, the choices are no more consistent than
the results. I have tried to make a compendium. To do so,
I have had to set arbitrary limits. All the men listed in the
"directory" have one thing in common: they shared in at
least two of the three great Gaullist adventures—the Free
French movement or the Resistance, which lasted until the
beginning of 1946; the attempt at reconquest by the R.P.F.
(Rassemblement du Peuple Français), which failed; the Republic today under De Gaulle. But such arbitrary limits exclude many and diversified situations; they cannot mirror
the subtle ties, they leave no room for the original dialectics,
the secret and irrational element that represents the essential
nature of the Guild. Consequently, no firm conclusions or
even tentative ones can be drawn.

Furthermore, one might easily object to many of the
names that have been included, or conversely, demur at the
many omissions. Let no one take offense, for no malice was
intended. This compendium, which also contains a description of the rituals, seeks merely to sketch a few faces, a few

scenes, and provide a little food for thought for everyone, be he friend or foe, who is intrigued by General de Gaulle and by the personalities—often little known or misunderstood—of the men called the Gaullists.

PIERRE VIANSSON-PONTÉ

Part I

The Rituals

Ceremonials

YOU STAND awkwardly at attention like a very raw recruit. You have been warned not to look too serious lest you appear sad on what is supposed to be a happy occasion, but you had better not smile because, after all, this is not a party. Depending upon your temperament or political convictions, you will, when introduced, either make a few unintelligible sounds from which a sharp ear might glean the word "President," or, on the contrary, you will speak up with assurance, enunciating each syllable distinctly, saying, "General, I present my respects."

In the first of these instances, you will receive in exchange either a muttering as inaudible as your own, or a pointedly courteous reply such as, "Delighted to make your acquaintance, monsieur," or "Pleased to see you"—dry, precise, full of reservations and innuendoes whose unspoken meaning is: "You had to go through with this but you don't like it and, believe me, it shows," or "I can pull a face as long as yours, but it's too late, you're cornered and I have the upper hand."

On the other hand a respectful, military greeting which obviously stamps you as an ardent disciple, means that you

will receive a warmer welcome. The General usually pro-
nounces a favored phrase like, "Oh, how do you do, dear
friend," if you are a member of the press, or, "Oh, So and So,
I am delighted to meet you," if there is time.

Should the man be important, a personal remark or allusion will further enhance the salutation and indicate that
the General is well disposed. Thus, in addressing a diplomat
(be he a Paraguayan or a Finn), he might add, "I like your
country very much, monsieur, I'm sure you are aware of
this"; or to a writer or journalist (be he the author of cross-
word puzzles, a manual on arboriculture, a thesis on the relative pronoun in the Roman poets of the early Empire, or
a pornographic novel, it doesn't matter): "I read your work
with pleasure, monsieur"; to someone in the theater, in radio
or television (actor, author, director, producer, etc.): "I
wish I were free to go and applaud you"; to a professor (of
Sanskrit, corrective gymnastics, or comparative law: "I have
the greatest respect for your field"; to a businessman: "Your
activities are most useful to our country," if the volume of
business exceeds a certain figure, he will add: "I might even
say necessary"; to a pretty woman: "Your charm lends honor
to this old house, madame"; to a priest: "Help us with your
prayers, your Eminence, we are greatly in need of them";
to a military man: "Saint-Cyr? What year?" To an elderly
man: "Your experience is valuable to us, you know"; to a
young man: "You are the future of France, monsieur, be
worthy of it"; to a young woman: "You bear within you the
aspirations of your country, mademoiselle. Do not forget it."

At this point it must be said that such greetings are but
one phase of an introduction, not of a conversation. They
therefore call for no answer, even when the interrogative
form is used. Indeed, it would be most unseemly to take advantage and presume to start a conversation. This is neither
the place, the time, nor the occasion. Should you be so bold

as to persist, you will immediately be made to feel the impropriety of your action: a certain empty, vacant stare signifies that you have suddenly become transparent, virtually nonexistent; a special way of moving the lips without uttering a sound makes it plain that the General is no longer listening, that he is already preparing to greet the next person. His performance is so flawless that a very naïve person might turn around expecting to see someone (this has happened), only to realize that there is no one there.

When introductions have been proceeding at a rapid pace for a protracted period (during the hand kissing, for example—see Gala Evening), and the General is very tired, he becomes a little confused in his salutations. Thus he has been known to solicit prayers from fashionable ladies and compliment an archbishop on his charm, to praise bankers for their artistic talent and to hold hoary academicians responsible for the economic future of the country. One brilliant representative of the French press in a foreign capital blushed with surprise when, after his name was announced, he heard a sonorous "How do you do, madame." Neither his name, his very masculine appearance, nor his personal habits could explain the error.

The ceremony described above is obviously part of a personal introduction and occurs only once, when the General meets someone for the first time. His phenomenal memory, reinforced by a filing system consulted opportunely and kept carefully up to date, makes it impossible to be formally introduced twice. Thanks to a conditioned reflex, the repetition of a name immediately conjures up in the General's mind the circumstances of the initial introduction, even if it were a chance meeting or one that occurred twenty years before. If a caller had not been introduced at the Interview, the Invitation, or the Consultation (see these headings elsewhere), he would be treated in precisely the same manner anyway, were this the seventeenth, thirty-second, or eighty-fifth time. The only difference is that the usual "monsieur" would give way to the more familiar "my dear friend," and might, on the fifth or sixth introduction, change to "my dear So and So."

Now we come to another category, the official or (often) the collective introduction. A politician who belongs to a standing committee of a parliamentary or municipal assembly and who is also an important industrialist (he may even have received the Cross of the Liberation) could be "introduced" eight times in the course of a single year. This same man might likewise be part of a delegation from the National Assembly (or Senate), from the local bodies of Paris which are permitted each New Year to present their good wishes. He might also attend the receptions given annually in honor of the standing committees of these bodies; the cocktail parties for the elect of an "economic group" or the annual reception given for the members of the Knighthood.

Should the occasion be less important—a procession of representatives of various branches of the government, or, during a trip to the provinces, of mayors and municipal councillors, a review of the staff of some enterprise or large plant he is inspecting, etc.—the introduction is reduced to a minimum: "How do you do? How do you do? How do you do? . . ." or "Monsieur, monsieur, monsieur . . ." And when the General, reaching down almost to the populace, addresses an athletic team, war veterans, employees, etc., his language is direct and familiar: "Greetings, hello, greetings . . ." or even, "Old chap, old fellow, old chap . . ." Of course, even when the name is given during an official introduction, it remains quite superfluous and no attention is paid to it because the person is either already well acquainted with the General or in all certainty never will be.

2. THE HANDSHAKE

This can be performed quite apart from a formal presentation and may assume either an individual or a collective character. Naturally, at receptions it is individual. Striding back and forth before delegations, or between rows of admirers, visitors, or guests—rows formed spontaneously to meet him—the advancing General extends his hand mechanically at every third step. Sometimes he singles out someone he has either met ten minutes before and has already congratulated or a stranger standing in a strategic place. A policeman in full dress who, together with fifteen of his colleagues, is responsible for security measures during a gala evening at the Palace might (this has actually happened) shake the august hand four times between the hours of ten and midnight. His assignment is to keep a close watch on the Chief of State. Any sudden move will bring him face to face with you-know-who; hence the privilege of shaking hands with the General several times in the course of one evening.

Collective handshakes occur at ceremonies and on official trips. Thrusting his arm, if not his whole body, into the crowd, the General kneads flesh the way a baker kneads dough. He "makes contact," as the saying goes. In fact, in hit-or-miss fashion, he pinches, strokes, taps, rubs a finger here, a palm there. At the end of such days, when he has mingled with several thousand, it is not unusual for him to have a swollen, scratched, even skinned right hand and a painful arm. But it won't be long before there is scarcely a Frenchman between the ages of two and ninety-six who can't boast that one day he "shook the hand of General de Gaulle."

3. THE INVITATION

It's a visiting card always accompanied by a parking sticker to be pasted on the windshield and bearing on the

reverse side precise instructions regarding entrances and
exits and the exact locations for cars that are chauffeur-
driven and those that are not. The tone of the invitation is
peremptory: "General de Gaulle requests Monsieur and
Madame X to be good enough . . ." A far cry from American presidential invitations.

The inevitable question of dress is always designated with
extreme precision, never a vague formula such as "white
tie" or "evening dress," which might plunge some into the
depths of perplexity and cause a catastrophe. Instead,
clearly indicated, "informal dress," "dinner jacket" (rarely),
or "full-dress uniform, decorations."

The lists are accurately drawn up; rarely is there an error,
like inviting a bachelor or a widower to come with his wife,
or divorced couples to attend the same gathering—besides,
divorce is frowned upon. Similarly, the spelling of names is
carefully checked, but the penmanship is middling because
this task is entrusted to a Republican Guard whose handwriting is distinguished only for its waywardness.

4. GALA EVENING

The setting is the unchanging Elysée Palace, Opéra,
Comédie Française, or the Little Theater of Versailles. Unless it is a gala evening held in one or another of these official
settings the General will not attend, regardless of the occasion. He never goes to the Chaillot and only rarely to the
Odéon.

At the Elysée, a gala evening usually follows a large dinner
and begins at ten-fifteen. A long line of cars forms at the
intersection of the Avenue de Marigny and the Champs
Elysées, moves past two mounted Republican Guardsmen,
inches along toward the Palace arcade, and enters the large
illuminated courtyard. The cars stop momentarily to deposit their passengers at the foot of the red carpet, then head

toward the exit of the Rue de l'Elysée or the one at 55 Faubourg Saint-Honoré. As soon as the twelve to eighteen hundred guests have mounted the central staircase, they are caught in such a crush that absolutely no one can escape for a split second, even for some quite legitimate reason.

First comes the cloakroom. Valets snatch away coats and hats and, in exchange, hand over two small metal checks. When it is time to leave, the first of these is collected at the entrance of the narrow passageway leading to the cloakroom and slipped straightaway down a tube to the attendants; whereupon the right garment is placed on a special dumb-waiter and returned to the owner in exchange for the second stub. Woe to anyone who loses his check! But let us render unto Caesar . . . This dazzling system is not the brain child of the present regime; it dates from the Fourth Republic, which undoubtedly accounts for all the confusion.

Then, because of the impossible bottleneck, the queueing up begins in earnest. The dinner over, the General stations himself in the Murat drawing room to receive his guests. And time and time again the same ritual is repeated: the footman, charged with the high office of announcing, softly asks your name, makes sure that the couple preceding you has already been greeted by the General, Madame de Gaulle, and the guests of honor, and, clearing a way, announces you in booming tones which usually do less than full justice to your surname. Thus announced, you advance, and there ensues a curious exchange of salutations with the two official couples—sometimes three, if the Prime Minister and his wife are present to share the honors.

The husband kisses a hand or two—always that of Madame de Gaulle, only sometimes that of a queen or a president's wife. For example, Mrs. Khrushchev's hand was not kissed, but Jacqueline Kennedy's was. You bow as if to kiss the hand of Queen Elizabeth or Her Majesty the

Empress Farah of Iran, but you don't actually do so. Meanwhile, your wife extends her hand to the General, who kisses it, then she lowers it perceptibly to greet the other chief of state. Neither of the two K's kissed a single hand, nor did Chancellor Adenauer, but Prince Philip, the kings of Norway, Sweden, and Morocco, and the Emperor of Iran did. The others, of course, shake hands.

When African chiefs of state are involved, the problem is a little more complicated, the uncertainty greater. People become confused, make mistakes, and end up by kissing the General's hand. The General himself has never been known to kiss the hand of any man, save that of a cardinal or bishop.

All down the line guests are asking each other, "Do we or don't we?" Naturally, the staff has dubbed this routine "the hand kissing."

It's a long wait. The line moves slowly through an endless corridor, into one overcrowded, overheated drawing room, then into another. To allay impatience, refreshments are served, trays are passed. Appetites grow apace as people mill about. Amusing things happen. For instance, a footman artfully plying his trade announces in even tones, "Monsieur le Prince," then, after a pause, "Ringuet." He is introducing the well-known scientist Leprince-Ringuet. Once he was heard to call out "Monsieur Pasteur," then "Madame Vallery-Radot," whereupon, blushing with embarrassment, the distinguished academician Pasteur Vallery-Radot advanced, accompanied by the Abbé Fulbert Youlou, president of the Congo—a very black man swathed in a very white cassock.

Once the formalities of the receiving line are over, or cut short because the General has had enough, people pour into the living rooms. Almost never is there any place to sit. The few chairs available are already taken. Madame de Gaulle

is seated among a circle of friends. Two passable buffets are
set up; by midnight they have been laid waste. Cognac, a
"Spécial long drink," takes the place of whiskey on certain occasions such as receptions for industrialists. For the Russians,
vodka is laid on. If champagne is served it is usually a Taittinger brand, doubtless because the price is right.* The
string orchestra of the National Guard does the best it can.
Gershwin was played for the Kennedys, Prokofiev for Mr.
Khrushchev, Parry for Queen Elizabeth, Beethoven for the
German Chancellor, even Grieg for the King of Norway.

Surrounded by a swarm of unofficial personalities, the
General strolls back and forth. Carrying out their instructions, messengers tap the sleeve of someone who has been
singled out for the privilege of chatting with the host—perhaps a former cabinet member, or an ambassador to the
country of the sovereign who is being feted that night.
There is seldom any entertainment. Occasionally, *Swan
Lake* will be performed on a small stage by some shining
light of the ballet. Only two rows of chairs are set up. The
rest of the audience tries to press forward. Those that are
bored gaze at the uniforms, eyeing the decorations suspi-
ciously. Well, well, the Postal Award! Oh! A medal for
Epidemic Diseases! To say nothing of the man who sports
the commander's scarf of the Nicham Iftikar (a Tunisian
medal), although the entire country knows his extremist
views on Tunisia! Everyone knows that the French adore
decorations.

Precisely at eleven-thirty the General retires. The evening
is over. A special occasion such as the gala at the Opéra or
the Comédie Française may be filmed or televised, but
everyone is aware of traditional protocol and custom, even

---

* The two Taittinger brothers, who own a famous champagne business, have
divided up their duties. One, deputy and the mayor of Rheims, is a Gaullist;
the other, a former president of the Municipal Council of Paris, is a conservative. Their champagne is of no known political persuasion . . .

though the ritual of the receiving line is naturally omitted. After congratulating the performing artists, the General appears in the lobby and remains there for exactly one-half of the intermission time. One or two acts of a play are readily lopped off to enable the General to retire according to schedule.

5. THE OFFICIAL RECEPTION

If an official reception is not followed by a gala evening, it is almost always imbued with Anglomania; held in the drawing rooms, it is called a "cocktail party," believe it or not, and a "garden party" when, weather permitting, it is staged outdoors. The word "reception" is used for a party in honor of some state official rather than the head of a foreign country. However, evening parties for the various branches of the government, parliamentary assemblies, and academic or economic circles (intellectuals, artists, or scientists) tend more and more to become cocktail parties, occasionally even three or four times in a row. As for the military, they are invited for an apéritif after the review of the troops on the fourteenth of July and the eleventh of November; Companions of the Order of the Liberation are given a private reception every eighteenth of June after the Mont Valérien (see the Sermon, the Ceremony). Protocol is much less strict at afternoon receptions where dress is informal. The General chats readily, knowing well enough that later he may have to issue an official denial of his remarks as reported by the press.

6. THE FORMAL DINNER

It always precedes gala evenings and boasts one truly extraordinary moment. The guests, who average about two hundred, are presented with all the pomp and ceremony of the Introduction (see this heading elsewhere), as are those invited later. All are handpicked, selected on a special basis, which means that a man who is neither a deputy nor any other kind of official has no chance of being invited. The table is U-shaped—a grave decision made after much deliberation, and one that put an end to the T-shaped table that had been customary in the days of President Coty. The General of course sits at the head of the U, flanked by the most prominent guests. A red dot on the formal card that is enclosed with the invitation indicates each guest's exact place at the table. Officials responsible for protocol watch for arrivals anxiously. When in doubt they immediately send footmen to inquire: "With or without Madame?" Because if Madame was invited and did not come, the entire seating arrangement has to be altered in order to conform to the rules of etiquette. The din lasts until the last guest arrives. Eight-fifteen is the time indicated on the invitation; the dinner begins no later than nine.

The extraordinary moment occurs when the General sits down. This is the signal for a great crackle and rustle as one hundred or one hundred and fifty men in tails or uniform and their ladies in silk dresses imitate their host. Just as the tall figure at the head of the table lowers himself, the rush begins. Thirty maîtres d'hôtel race in at the same moment with the entrée. Plates are served and removed in record time and with fabulous dexterity. Sometimes they are still three-quarters full, and a few guests have not even had time to so much as pick up their forks. The wines—a white, a red, and champagne—practically never come back twice. No cheese is served (malodorous) and no fruit (takes too long to peel). Dinner is over in an hour. One can always go afterward to Les Halles or the Left Bank to get something hot to eat. The spectacle is pleasing, the entire affair is expedited efficiently, the food looks attractive, but it is not a meal. Well, never mind, nobody comes to gorge or sample a fine cuisine.

7. THE INTIMATE OR INFORMAL DINNER

The table is usually set for twenty or thirty and there is always some special occasion: a medal to pin on one of the faithful or on an important member of the Knighthood, the unofficial visit of a prominent foreigner, an honor to bestow on a governmental dignitary who is being retired or assigned to new duties, etc. Since the dinner is in honor of a certain individual, his entire family is invited—sons and daughters, their spouses, sometimes even the grandchildren. Personal friends (or those presumed to be) are likewise invited, and the same courtesy is usually extended to members of the elect and ultimately of the government itself. If the General has already pronounced a few words before going in to dinner, before pinning a medal on the guest of honor, for example, then there is no speech. If not, then sometimes but not always, he waits until dessert is being served and then utters six or eight phrases in an informal and familiar way, eventually lifting his glass to offer a toast.

It must be remembered that at all times—be it a banquet during an official trip, or a gala or informal dinner at the Palace—the General stuns everyone by the amount of food he puts away. He has always eaten the rather indifferent Palace food heartily—the eternal fish with green sauce, the inevitable chicken, the tough roast. He piles food on his plate and eats it all, gobbles three pieces of bread, takes a second helping of vegetables, polishes off two pieces of cake absentmindedly, and in a flash his plate is empty! Refusing the white wine, he downs with gusto a full glass of heavy red wine. He takes coffee, but rarely a liqueur. To a foreign envoy who complained that he was unable to give up smoking, the General gave his prescription for foregoing the cigars and cigarettes he used to enjoy. "Do what I did," he advised.

"First I announced to my wife, to my associates, to everyone around me that I was going to stop smoking. After that, my word, it was quite easy. Obviously I could no longer do it."

8. LUNCH AT COLOMBEY*

It takes, at best, a little over three hours from Paris. In Colombey the car turns right and climbs the side of a hill. The gates of the Boisserie are immediately thrown open; obviously one is expected. A few more turns and a flight of stairs comes into view. The house is small and rather unattractive—a far cry from Chambord, Chenonceau, or Rambouillet. It typifies a retired officer's estate, and only the presence of a tower, an inelegant one at that, gives it the status of a "château."

In the drawing room, Madame de Gaulle puts her knitting aside for a moment to welcome the guests. She inquires about the condition of the roads, mentions the weather, and even says a word about the General. Then she resumes her knitting, and the clock on the mantelpiece slowly ticks away. At precisely one o'clock, two doors open almost simultaneously. On the right the General emerges from his study, shakes hands, and, in time-honored fashion, welcomes his guests, naming each of them as he does so: "Happy to see you here," or "Thank you for coming." On the left, the door to the dining room is flung open. If there is a bit of a wait before the servant announces "Lunch is served, madame," the General will inquire about road conditions, mention the weather, and say a word about himself. He does not sit down. The guests are then ushered directly into the dining room.

First, the hors d'oeuvres. Total silence. Some stout-

---

* The "château" de la Boisserie at Colombey, in the department of the Haute Marne, is the De Gaulle estate. The General bought it shortly before World War II.

hearted soul will start a conversation with Madame de Gaulle, who responds graciously. They talk about the condition of the roads, about the weather. On good days the General emits a few concurring grunts.

Next the roast. At this point one brave man starts the ball rolling. He turns squarely to the General, coughs to clear his voice, and then plays his trump card: "Fine weather, is it not, General?" (or "terrible weather"). Usually the question remains suspended in mid-air. But the brave man persists, or rather he repeats: "Fine weather for a walk, don't you think, General?" Thoroughly annoyed, the General finally answers: "For your information, my dear friend, I never walk." Silence.

During one such lunch, a leader of the first Gaullist political party, the R.P.F., who was reputed to be a bit too fond of wine, was thoughtlessly asked, "You drink, monsieur, I have been told?" Just as thoughtlessly he replied, "In any case, not here, General." That put an end to the conversation.

But usually the conversation does not take such a turn. Luncheon over, the visitors are served coffee in the living room. The talk is about the condition of the roads, the weather. On special occasions the General takes his guests for a short turn in the park. Soon, he repeats the ceremonious handshaking, "Happy to see you," "Thank you for coming," and retires to his study. There's nothing for it but to drive back to Paris, over three hundred kilometers away.

An invitation to lunch at Colombey is actually a signal honor bestowed only upon a few of the faithful. Generally speaking, the occasion is devoid of political significance.

But to be honest it must be said that this description fits *a* lunch, not *the* lunch, because it is not always so boring or vacuous. In any event, the General receives his guests in such a lordly fashion that the modest setting is easily forgot-

ten. Chancellor Adenauer, received at the Boisserie as a
friend, has had an opportunity to judge, as have many others,
how witty, relaxed, and charming the General can be.
Lunches at Colombey are like the weather of the Upper
Marne: probably the one just described took place on a day
of heavy rainfall.

Liturgy

1. THE INTERVIEW

IT LASTS exactly a half hour—this is strictly the rule. If it lasts longer it is a real event. The request has to be presented to the secretary-general of the Palace or chief of the presidential staff. The summons comes three days or six months following the request, sometimes never. Date and time of day are indicated by letter as soon as the request for an interview has been granted; they are confirmed twenty-four hours before the appointment and again by telephone on the very morning of the day. Cancellation or postponement occur but rarely.

One is cautioned to arrive a little ahead of time but not too early; to bring the summons and also some identification for the sentry; to make sure, unless the person is a very high official, that the licence number of the car has already been given to the guard by the chief of the presidential staff, otherwise the gate of 55 Faubourg Saint-Honoré will remain firmly shut and one will be obliged to enter ignominiously on foot.

First there is the customary check, then the caller is left to cool his heels in a small waiting room adjacent to the offices of the General and his chief of staff. After the visitor just ahead has been ushered into the General's presence, the caller is taken to the office of the aide-de-camp. Then he, in turn, is announced and escorted to the General by the aide-de-camp, who discreetly shuts the door. The tête-à-tête begins. It can assume one of three typical but very different forms:

Monologue. No sooner is the visitor seated than the General begins to talk. He never stops, even though his interlocutor has come to make some request dear to his heart, to explain a situation or the intricacies of a problem, and to sound out De Gaulle. It doesn't matter. The visitor's name, the mere sight of him, some recollection he brings to mind, or the alleged nature of his call—any one or all of these unleash a monologue studded with gracious or pedantic allusions, personal memories, sweeping historical evocations, or caustic expressions of opinion. Sometimes the sole purpose is to prevent the visitor, who dares not interrupt, from making a request, whose nature the General has already guessed or knows and which he does not wish to grant. At other times, he honors a privileged character by thinking out loud or taking him into his confidence. Or again, he might be trying out ideas, formulas, new plans on one individual with an eye to using these later before huge throngs. His thought unfolds, expands, soars. Time passes. The interview draws to an end. One last idea and the visitor is at the threshold. The aide-de-camp is waiting. The visitor leaves. He has not had a chance to utter a single word.

A general, a man of distinction but very modest and somewhat shy, has just reached the door, after listening to a dazzling monologue, when, to his amazement, he hears himself reproved: "You see, dear friend, what will forever keep coming between us is *your* tremendous arrogance." A politician, recounting for the benefit of friends an animated, controversial conversation with the General, remarked: "I told the General thus and so . . . I pointed out to him that . . . I answered him, 'Oh, no, General, you can't possibly say that. You have no right to.' " When De Gaulle read or heard about it, he merely shrugged his shoulders and said complacently, "And to think that he never got a word in edgewise!"

Utter silence. The visitor arrives thoroughly prepared to discuss his business. He offers a brief preamble, followed by explanations. He marshals his arguments, makes his points, outlines his conclusion. The General seems to be listening. He does not interrupt, says absolutely nothing. Has he heard? One may well wonder. To make sure, and because the time is almost up, the caller raises his voice and finally puts several questions to the General. "The circumstances being what they are, will you tell me what you contemplate doing? If my arguments seem conclusive, will you agree to give the necessary instructions? May I hope for a favorable response?" Nothing. Absolutely nothing. Silence.

The visitor coughs and repeats his questions. His tone is more plainly interrogative, more anxious, expectant. But he can't go on forever repeating the same questions in different ways. He waits. Still nothing. After an interminable interval, the General gets up. He says, "Well," or mumbles what sounds like "We'll see . . . I'll think about it . . ." In any event, he makes it plain that the interview is over. He accompanies the visitor to the door. Once there, as if seized with remorse, he makes one unambiguous remark. It is usually a brush-off. To the secretary-general of an important political party who came to complain about the Gaullists and to appeal to him, the General tendered the following crumb: "I am going to tell you what you represent to me, monsieur: an empty coffer into which one puts money which you don't even know how to use. Good day, monsieur."

Dialogue. If it gets started at all it is jerky, elliptical, un-even. The General asks a question, interrupts, asks another, comes back to the first. Often abashed, the visitor embarks upon an explanation, which is promptly cut off by some incongruous remark or by a further request for clarification. It is impossible to have any real discussion, any kind of conversation unless the person is exceptionally determined and experienced. For De Gaulle it's a game that consists either of forcing the caller to contradict himself and be caught off guard so that the breach in his argument can be widened unmercifully, or of squeezing the lemon so hard that it yields up its very last drop and then tossing it all dried up into outer darkness.

In certain instances, if the General wants to charm or dazzle, he gives one a glimpse of his phenomenal memory. A prominent financier called to discuss a rather complicated and important technical problem. With the help of his associates, he had prepared a careful summation of the matter. His arguments were closely reasoned and in perfect order. He committed them to memory and recorded his talk on tape. It covered eleven points and took exactly sixteen minutes. He was ushered in, invited courteously to be seated and to explain his problem ("I am listening to you, monsieur"), and the banker discussed the eleven points according to plan. As he was finishing, the General took over, repeated the eleven points without distortion and in order, and gave his advice on each one equally methodically. As I have said, the case in point involved some very specific technical questions which are not easy to understand. The financier left stupefied with admiration and permanently won over.

Save for these charm tactics and also the numerous amenities that on occasion are part of an interview—for the General, if he chooses, can be pleasant, endearing, humorous, friendly, almost affectionate—the caller usually departs in an anxious frame of mind. He had apparently been listened to, understood. Yet, had he really been heard? There is nothing to prove it. Neither an answer, approval, nor even the tacit acquiescence he had counted on had been forthcoming. He can only tell if there should be evidence of tangible results. Or perhaps, a few days or months later, an official pronouncement, a chance phrase, will suddenly pop up in a public speech and the visitor will recognize his own words, some argument or idea he had advanced which, at the time, he had no reason to believe had even been heard. Such are the vicissitudes and hazards of an interview.

2. THE CONSULTATION

It is akin to the Interview (Dialogue) but differs in that it occurs not because one has requested it but as a consequence of a spontaneous summons from the Palace. Moreover, only experienced experts (or those presumed to be), a very small number of personal friends, and a few high-ranking associates are invited. Naturally, whenever necessary the Prime Minister, members of the government, as well as dignitaries of the regime and a few important officials are consulted on matters relating to their special competence or in order to sound them out.

But the Minister of Agriculture may be invited to discuss an industrial problem of European scope, or a religious matter because he is supposed to represent secularism within the cabinet. The ministers of Justice, the Interior, and the Army are sounded out on matters relating to . . . the ministry next door.

On important questions of policy, summons will be sent not only to the Prime Minister but also, and foremost, to Jacques Chaban-Delmas, who is invited to the Palace far oftener than anyone realizes or than is announced—frequently in the evening after dinner. A former international rugby star, and a general in the Resistance when he was only twenty-nine, Chaban-Delmas is president of the Chamber of Deputies. Whenever there are pressing economic problems, Bloch-Lainé,* Albin Chalandon,† Emmanuel Monick,‡ and Louis Vallon will appear at the Palace—discreetly, because often the current Minister of Finance has not been informed. I do not know whether Maurice Schumann, Ambassadors Alphand (Washington), Brouillet (the Vatican), Courcel (London), Dejean (Moscow), and Louis Joxe are asked because of the offices they hold, but their voices are heard on important questions of foreign policy. The personal status of certain Gaullists, seriously compromised for a while, has since improved. This is true of Roger Frey, Pierre Guillaumat, and Georges Pompidou himself.

New ideas at the moment of their inception are often tried out on the secretary-general of the Palace, Étienne Burin des Roziers, sometimes on the chief of the presidential staff, Georges Galichon, or perhaps on a past or present technical adviser. Both men, their watches in hand, have a private, five-minute meeting with De Gaulle twice a day, morning and evening, to discuss current business—that is, if they have a chance to talk, which is not always the case. Finally, although they have no well-defined expertise, De Gaulle's brother-in-law Jacques Vendroux, his cousin Montalembert, the faithful Palewski and Hettier de Boislambert, his son-in-law Boissieu, are permitted to enter and air their views.

We have mentioned about twenty names, some of them quite famous, others scarcely familiar even to Frenchmen, yet these are the men who constitute the King's Household, his privy council, who belong to the real Gaullist family.

* Head of the bank Caisse des Dépôts—actually the most important commercial bank in France.

† Head of the Banque Commerciale de Paris.

‡ Former president of the Banque de Paris et des Pays-Bas (Paris and Netherlands Bank).

3. THE APPOINTMENT

Even when an appointment is almost a sure thing, plainly predictable, carefully prepared in advance by allusions, soundings, warnings, or formal notice, it remains an uncertainty until the very last minute: for such is De Gaulle's way. If the press should make a premature announcement of an appointment that has not actually been confirmed, the sequel is uncertain. Sometimes a man who has to all intents and purposes been designated for a post and told about it in advance loses all chance of getting it because his appointment might appear to be the result of pressure; at other times, the reverse occurs: "they" think they will embarrass me by disclosing his name, but that won't stop me from appointing him.

Thus, for instance, General Billotte, who had already contacted people, set up his cabinet, and was about to leave, at the very last minute, between Evian and independence, lost his position as the top representative of France in Algeria to Christian Fouchet. Conversely, the names of Michel Debré and Georges Pompidou were spread all over the newspapers long before they had received a firm commitment from their leader, and the appointment of Roger Frey as Minister of the Interior—he had merely been serving as interim minister for several weeks—was facilitated rather than postponed by the publicity given to a decision before it had been officially confirmed.

An appointment is not the result of consultation: it is an order, one that is impossible to wriggle out of. Some men were skillful in drawing attention to their self-abnegation, discipline, and spirit of sacrifice—which the exercise of their present function required—and obtained in return a promise of future reward. A year before Geoffroy de Courcel left the Palace one knew that he would one day become ambassador in London; it was also common knowledge that René Brouillet would go to the Vatican or Vienna. And Christian Fouchet left for Algeria with the promise that he would enter the government upon his return.

4. THE PROMOTION

Rarely is it conferred upon a faithful collaborator with the exception of a few tried and true of the Knighthood, and these are not so much promoted as given key positions. It took Gaston Palewski four years of constant effort and a good deal of friendly cooperation to shake the dust of the embassy in Rome and become a minister. On the other hand, stars appeared in rapid succession on General Fourquet's sleeve because, at the time of the putsch in April 1961, he happened to be the highest ranking officer who was unquestionably loyal and enjoyed freedom of movement.

Let us take the extremely rapid rise of Jean Foyer,* who was promoted within four years from the modest position of adviser to Houphouet-Boigny,† to what was one of the most important positions in the government (in view of the difficulties this regime got into in judicial and police matters), namely, the Ministry of Justice. His rise was due far more to Michel Debré's long-standing influential friendship than to royal favor. But it is nevertheless true that nobody puts on his slippers and stays quietly at home after leaving De Gaulle's house, and that one ceases to move up as soon as one moves away from the sun.

5. THE PETITION

The General does not like them. If a request is made by a commoner or a person of little importance, he rejects it

---

* He had been Keeper of the Seals.
† At that time he was a French minister and today is President of the Ivory Coast.

whenever possible. He consents only if the petitioner is so prominent that he feels it would be wise to be obliging, perhaps in order to extract a promise of future good behavior. But then it is a political act rather than one of intercession in the usual sense.

During ceremonies and trips, when the General comes in contact with the masses as well as with the notables, sometimes even during official receptions, petitions are slipped into his hands, as if he were Louis XIV. At first he tries not to notice the paper, slip, or document. If he is unable to do so, or if he is taken by surprise, he picks it up with the tips of his fingers, as if it would burn him, and quickly tosses it to someone in attendance, usually to Colonel Bonneval, whose pockets are always bulging. It will be read later and answered—everything is answered. But one might as well send the thing through the mail; at least it wouldn't run the risk of being mislaid.

The only petitions that have any chance of success are those connected with the Gaullist saga: a request from the wife of a member of the Knighthood who met death in the ranks of the Free French, from a political enemy crushed under the steamroller of the purge after the Liberation, or, having had to suffer from more recent sanctions, from one of the faithful deserving of the slight help he is requesting, etc. These are occasionally reenforced by a note in the General's own hand, which insures fulfillment of the petition. Other requests are transmitted without comment to the appropriate officials. Nepotism or favoritism is practiced only at the intermediate level of the hierarchy, never at the top.

6. THE RESIGNATION

It, too, is an order and cannot be disputed. Like the Appointment, it is a significant act, full of symbolic meaning.

Furthermore, depending upon the circumstances and the context, it can assume different characteristics—expiatory, admonitory, something to be hushed up or regretted.

The resignation of Antoine Pinay* was expiatory. People were talking far too much about the Pinay loan, the Pinay franc, the Pinay economic recovery, even about Pinay's ideas, his political policy, his plans. The cardboard statue had to be demolished, the emptiness behind the illusion had to be exposed. But Pinay's resignation had a further advantage and satisfied quite a different requirement: It rid the councils of one of the few men who ventured stubbornly and at times furiously to contradict the Chief of State. Some said, "You'll see, in six months nobody will mention Pinay's name any more." A slight exaggeration, but not entirely devoid of truth.

Soustelle's† resignation was admonitory in nature. It spelled sanctions for disloyalty and served as a warning to all those who might be tempted to violate discipline. Rejected, haughtily excluded, the man whose name was acclaimed in Algeria in the presence of De Gaulle, the leader of a newly formed clique, was pushed too far and rebelled. His disciples were forced to come out into the open or break with Soustelle.

The hushed-up resignation: So did Wilfred Baumgartner depart,‡ to the accompaniment of a rustle of courteous letters and compliments exchanged. Why did he leave? Why was he not retained? In any case, the two men separated amicably, like partners who had come to the end of a contract that neither cared to renew, but who remained good friends.

* First De Gaulle's, then Michel Debré's Minister of Finance from 1958–60.
† Jacques Soustelle was one of the earliest partisans of De Gaulle, but subsequently was judged disloyal because he was opposed to the Algerian peace.
‡ Leaving the Ministry of Finance where he had succeeded Antoine Pinay.

Salan's* departure from Algeria was a far more bitter affair, but the homage rendered an "honored liege lord" and the promises, which were never kept, helped him to swallow the affront discreetly.

The sudden dismissal of some of the faithful from their ministerial posts—Edmond Michelet from the Ministry of Justice, Louis Terrenoire from the Ministry of Information—must be placed on the "regretted" list. "My poor friend, the Prime Minister thinks that . . . I am sure you are anxious to make his task and mine easier, and I would appreciate it very much." Whereupon the victim is appointed temporary secretary-general of the Gaullist party or member of the Constitutional Council, which after all does help to pass the time.

Into which of these categories should Prime Minister Michel Debré's resignation be put—a step he offered to take ten times and which in each instance was refused by a shrug of the shoulders, only to find himself dismissed when he no longer really cared to resign? It, too, had expiatory significance: the Prime Minister came only belatedly to believe in peace for Algeria and in the danger of activism;† moreover he paved the way for the violent activities of these extremists by blocking negotiations for such a long time. His resignation was also admonitory in the sense that it symbolized a fresh start, a new policy, the desire for an opening toward the center and a refusal to hold elections immediately. It was, nonetheless, somewhat hushed-up and made to appear regrettable, and therefore epitomizes resignations of every category. Thus Debré's resignation turns a new page upon which may be inscribed some day, if the need should be felt, a recall to political action.

* Leader of the April 1961 putsch, he was imprisoned for life.
† The movement directed against De Gaulle by those trying at all costs to keep Algeria French as well as by extreme right-wing elements who were using the Algerian crisis for their own ends.

The Sermon

1. THE CEREMONY

THE KING is everywhere at home, the president presides wherever he happens to be: this is an immutable principle.

Another characteristic of any ceremony: it is a symbol, and this must be felt and understood. The ideal ceremony takes place in a setting replete with esoteric significance and historical memories that are linked, however artificially, with the occasion; it borrows the spirit from tradition, whereas the rites have to be invented. It must inflame the imagination of the masses, and, at the same time, have meaning for officials, prominent citizens, diplomats, and foreign governments; thus it serves as a link between propaganda and political strategy, between the past and the future.

The archetype of the perfect ceremony was the handing over of the flags of the Commonwealth to the African chiefs (or their representatives) on July 14, 1959, at the Place de la Concorde. Think about it a minute; it had everything.

At the foot of the Obelisk of Luxor, which was surrounded by a gigantic, conch-shaped raised platform, six hundred choir members intoned "The Invocation" and then Gossec's "Hymn to the Supreme Being":

Hatred for kings arouse the country,
Begone, vain desires, unjust pride of rank,
Corrupting luxury, base flattery
More deadly than tyrants . . .

In a single stroke that day, after Berlioz's "Marseillaise" and to the tune of the "Hymn to the Year II," before the notables, the assembled multitude, and an immobile army, the attempt was made to conciliate all political systems, to exorcise the ghosts.

Another shrewd stroke was the proclamation of the Constitution on September 4, 1958, the anniversary of the founding of the Third Republic, at the Place de la République. Ingenious too was the idea of a Franco-German march from the Mourmelon camp, in the presence of Chancellor Adenauer, to be followed by a mass in the Rheims Cathedral celebrated by the archbishop. The same can be said about the Little Theater at Versailles, opened in honor of Queen Elizabeth of England, the illumination of the banks of the Seine and the Eiffel Tower (American style) for the Kennedys, the house that Lenin inhabited rediscovered for the benefit of Khrushchev . . . Obviously André Malraux, whose lyricism is given free rein, has stage-managed these evocative scenes. But such stunts are becoming increasingly difficult to put on and consequently more rare. What a pity!

There remain the inevitable monuments to the dead in cities and villages, the absurd pealing of bells "To the Fields," then "To the Dead"; the decorations conferred at the Invalides, the parades on the fourteenth of July and the eleventh of November, sometimes interrupted by the sudden departure of the President of the Republic to review the fleet tied up at Toulon three hours away as well as the Legion and Saint-Cyr on the Champs Élysées. And there is also the Mont Valérien on the eighteenth of June, when the General, taking leave of his suite and of the Knighthood, descends alone into the underground tomb, where repose the ashes of fifteen soldiers and officers killed during fifteen glorious battles waged by the Free French, to commune with the dead in true Wagnerian fashion.

Nothing is left but the dull liturgy of inaugurations—exhibits of automobiles, airplanes, children's wear, even of household appliances. Who knows, maybe soon he will attend exhibits of office equipment or gift-wrapping. He is obliged to show interest in fresh discoveries, new models; there are industrialists to be congratulated, mothers of large families to be decorated. The General has to receive not only a procession of some sixty delegations who come each New Year to offer their good wishes, but also porters from Les Halles who bring lilies of the valley on the first of May, to say nothing of the lambs brought in tribute from the Republic of Angora. In Paris and in the provinces, year in, year out, he has to visit three arsenals, five nuclear centers, ten military barrages, thirty model farms, fifty factories . . . If the idea of a vice-president, hitherto rejected because supreme office is not a thing to be shared, is someday accepted, the incumbent can look forward to a fine list of chores.

2. THE TRIP TO THE PROVINCES

It is the supreme leader's benign duty to call on the simple citizen. This gesture is designed to establish between them a direct and personal bond of allegiance which eventually will become inescapable. It is considered so important that, despite the time it consumes and the fatigue it entails, it is systematically carried out, province by province, down to the very last. Even Paris, where the Chief of State lives eleven months out of twelve each year, must welcome him borough by borough, to say nothing of the suburbs, no matter how red they happen to be.

The wheels are by now completely greased for protocol, method and organization. These trips have been described a thousand times: always the same entourage enveloped by security devices, with advance guards, closed-rank protection, plus flank and rear guards; a program rigidly scheduled, minute by minute, each day of which takes up to ten or twenty pages in a small book marked "secret" that is constantly consulted by ministers, journalists, and policemen; a series of halts between lunch, always at the sub-prefecture, and dinner, always at the prefecture, with menus prepared in Paris three weeks before; a one- to five-minute stop in towns and villages where the municipal council, presented by the mayor, himself introduced by the prefect, barely has time to pay its respects before receiving the stereotyped answer; then the bunch of flowers presented by schoolgirls, handshaking all around, and the slamming of a door while the police, on edge and exhausted, still bustle about; a flying tour of the small, beribboned village; the anticipation of an incident (that never occurs) precipitated by those naughty trade unionists who pretend they are not taken in but come anyway, only to find themselves applauding; the presentation of the judicial and administrative bodies of the government, of mayors—"Oh, Mr. Mayor, what progress are you making in your water supply?"—local and national representatives; visits to the town hall, the university, the refinery, the museum; mass at the cathedral and the bishop's touching sermon; then the crowd again and always, handled, embraced, aroused, harangued—come snow, rain, or heavy wind.

Habitués of these marathons have a stock of good stories (mostly unrepeatable) and practical jokes (mostly in poor taste). A common practice is to lean out of the window of car number twenty-one or thirty-seven just as the procession is about to get underway and obligingly tell a fat policeman standing stiffly at attention about some imaginary disarray in his clothing, pretending to warn him softly so no one can hear: "Policeman, your fly is open . . ." Immediately the poor man begins a frantic dance to rectify the situation and at the same time maintain both his dignity and a semblance of respectful attention. The effect is irresistible. Or a pretty girl is invited to join the procession (this has happened, even in the assigned car of a multi-starred general), only to be deposited in the midst of some wilderness twenty-five kilometers further on. Or one can amuse oneself by managing to shake the General's hand five or six times in a single day; one has only to edge into the first row of a group of army veterans, teachers, or prominent citizens, and, since the face is familiar, it never fails that one's hand is taken in preference to that of others milling about. But none of this is very serious.

Others have used such occasions patiently and scientifically to study "the General's style" and to draw scholarly conclusions from the way the adjectives waltz through his off-the-cuff speeches. Apparently they do not know that the hodgepodge of phrases repeated one hundred times is totally inassimilable or that, prior to publication, it is revised or even completely recast, a task performed in concert with journalists of every political persuasion and officials of the suite. Naturally, this invalidates the observations of experts in grammar and exegesis.

The trip to the provinces, familiar in its slightest detail to all those who watch television and who, at any rate, learn more about their own country this way, remains nonetheless a series of pilgrimages, with the Holy Sacrament, flags flying, devout young girls, the clergy, and pious crowds all roaring republican hymns after the sermon.

3. THE TRIP ABROAD

It is no less carefully planned than the trip to the provinces, although sometimes the details must be left to the discretion of native officials who have no feeling for symbolism. But it is a more serious undertaking.

The shining success that was ever after to serve as a model was, of course, the triumphal visit to West Germany during the summer of 1962. Frankfurt, Hamburg, and Munich made up for the relative coolness at that time of Toulouse, Saint-Nazaire, or Clermont-Ferrand. The workers at Krupp erased the memory of their comrades of Decazeville. One could comment at length on the true import, the deeper significance of this phenomenon, but it would be ungracious to quibble. After all, it was France herself that was being acclaimed beyond the Rhine, and this is of no mean importance.

The trouble is that from now on it will be difficult to reach such heights, yet one can no longer be satisfied with a conventionally courteous welcome. And the General intends to visit many countries, if God grants him life and the people grant him votes; Iran is in the offing as well as the Scandinavian countries. He has return calls to pay on South America, a continent which tomorrow, already today, happens to be central to world conflict; and above all on Africa, from Bamako to Brazzaville and from Yaounde to Algeria, stopping on the way in Tunis and Rabat, and preferably three times instead of once: this will be the climactic gesture on decolonization. Finally, there is the U.S.S.R., but only if the international climate of opinion is favorable and the people can be spoken to directly, in Russian if necessary. Phineas Fogg was not so ambitious. But the seven-year term supposedly ends in 1965. Thus, unexpected vistas are opened to the possibility—officially denied—of a second mandate.

4. A FEW WORDS TO THE PEOPLE

The detailed (and secret) schedule of presidential visits to the provinces contains this notation, a dozen times for each day: "9:32. The General says a few words to the people."

The "few words" are by definition of purely local interest and purpose. Consequently, larger national issues are not mentioned, or only indirectly brought in by allusions to the past. The everlasting formula goes something like this: "The welcome given by your charming town goes straight to the heart of the man who addresses you and who bears the heavy responsibilities of which you are aware. In the majestic shadow of your château [or, "at the foot of your basilica which moves me deeply," or, for want of anything better, "on the banks of this delightful river"], the honor you do me fills me with a sense of your encouragement and support. I will think of it often and, during the hours that still lie ahead, should God grant him life, General de Gaulle will take comfort in this affection displayed by Montagu-les-Herbiers [Vandoeuvre-sous-Domecy, Hérissey-le-Petit]. Long live France!"

Applause, "Marseillaise" (one stanza and the refrain), a few handshakes, and back on the road.

5. THE SHORT ADDRESS

The short address is reserved for small towns or third-rate sub-prefectures. In contrast to the "few words" pronounced at the large village square with the General standing on a level with his audience, the short address is delivered either from a town-hall balcony, at the head of a flight of stairs, or from a podium or rustic platform that is difficult to climb and often unreliable and unsteady.

It lasts from three to six minutes and consists of some topic of local interest, more or less extensive allusions to the state of national affairs, plus an optimistic conclusion about the future, youth, hope. First the salutation: "Pézenas, lovely and noble city, Mr. Mayor and members of the municipal council, with such men at your head I need not fear for your destiny." This is followed by remarks indicating a knowledge of rural affairs and of the art of wine-growing in Languedoc, "Yes, I know all about your concerns." And then, depending upon the current international situation, the General mentions Africa, Europe, the two giants, or the United Nations, "that Thing."

Sixteen times he has used and repeated the same phrases; on ten other occasions he has pretended to confide in the people, the cadence of his phrases falling as smoothly as polished stones. But time is limited and the General returns to essentials—France's regeneration, economic recovery, the great and substantial expectations one has every right to entertain because "of the youth I see among you, so fine, so numerous" [should seditious shouts be heard, he adds, "and so lively"]. Yes, youth will reap our heritage by forging its future when we are no longer here. Yes, indeed. "Long live Pézenas, long live the *département* of Hérault, long live the Republic, long live France." Note that the last two are always named in this order, which is never reversed.

6. THE ORATION

At the beginning of De Gaulle's seven-year term, the prefects and agencies responsible for organizing official trips automatically chose the largest square in the city for the podium from which the General would speak, unless, of course, there was a public building that boasted a balcony overlooking the square. At Strasbourg there is the Place Kléber, at Nancy, Place Stanislas, at Lyon, Place Bellecoeur, at Toulouse, Place du Capitole, at Nice, Place Masséna, etc.

But there were disappointments. As time went on the great central square seemed too huge and more than half-deserted, particularly if the weather was inclement. Those responsible for security, acting in good faith and determined to run no risks, shut out the crowd, admitting to the enclosed area only those who had been carefully screened, invited, and provided with passes that were checked ten times over; even so, they were herded together behind barriers at a respectful distance. On the television newscast the General seemed to be addressing only a few hundred people and this made a sorry impression. Different measures had to be adopted.

Since then, more often than not, a smaller place is selected in preference to the large square. Any expert on mass demonstrations knows that 5000 people crowded together in a space where half the number would be comfortable look like 20,000, whereas 20,000 gathered in a spot that easily holds 30,000 seem like a mere 5000. Nothing is more complicated than trying to assess the size of a crowd.

The setting is vastly improved today and the oration now lasts twenty minutes. The topics are local, regional, national, and international. Addressed to supporters and enemies, young and old, prominent citizens as well as all and sundry, the oration provides an opportunity to launch new formulas, to try out new ideas. It always contains one or two passages on essential matters written expressly for use by the press; in fact mimeographed copies of the speech frequently are distributed in advance. It calls for applause at the right moments and a prolonged ovation at the end. It is expository in content, and often the significance of some vague phrase becomes plain only afterward.

7. SUBMERSION IN THE CROWD

Every time the Chief of State goes on an official trip, all of France is treated to a rather extraordinary and, in some respects preposterous, spectacle. Between the reception at the prefecture and the speech, before or after a ceremony or tour of inspection, during the arrival at or departure from a city, perhaps a foreign one at that, there is always a moment when the General comes into direct contact with the crowd. At such times he can be seen turning his back on a group of officials, pushing aside the police force, and rushing into the middle of the crowd like a soccer player dashing through an opening in the line.

To say that he mixes with the crowd is an understatement: he plunges into it, wallows in it. One can keep an eye on him not so much because of his height, but because he is the virtual center of a whirlpool. Disappearing one place, he pops up another for a moment, then is lost to sight again for a long, underwater stretch, only to surface like a diver at the other side of the street; he breaks away, crosses from one side to the other and dives in again to do another stint. In the narrowest streets of old cities, he has been seen making headway at the rate of three kilometers an hour for thirty minutes at a stretch, while the procession marks time, the bodyguards are seized with panic, and the police force has more than it can handle.

He has been seen to emerge with three buttons missing, uniform torn, hands scratched, military cap askew, but eyes sparkling with pleasure, looking delighted to be alive. This choice spectacle has been given to the people of London, Hamburg, Milan, Algiers, Dakar, Lille, and Perpignan. Algerians carrying knives have been arrested along the route the General was to take, to say nothing of activists armed with loaded revolvers, and even fanatics with hypodermic syringes. He doesn't care, convinced that he leads a charmed life;* he needs this contact with the masses to prove anew his invulnerability, his ascendancy, his immersion in the fountain of youth.

* The author uses an Algerian term, *la baraka,* meaning luck that is a talisman.

Catechism

1. THE DIPLOMATIC CONVERSATION

ANYONE who has had an opportunity, if only once, to attend a conference or diplomatic conversation at the summit between heads of states or governments will be in for quite a surprise. Is it possible? Those basic facts, those truisms that for weeks have been spun out in vacuous editorials of second-rate newspapers, those high-flown phrases explaining a new, insignificant facet of a problem, those pompous and vapid conclusions, so identical with what had been predicted ten times over that they read like caricatures—is there really nothing more to them? Of course there are exceptions, real conversations, and discussions worthy of the name. And one must be able to discern the true meaning behind the façade of words. But generally speaking, a diplomatic conversation seems to be the last refuge of the art of talking without saying anything.

For his part, General de Gaulle is marvelous at making old, worn-out ideas sound new, ingenious, and bold. He also knows how to listen and to respond in such a way as to give his interlocutor the comfortable feeling that he has understood, almost that he has been convinced. His personal ascendancy does the rest. Chancellor Adenauer, with whom he has talked at least twice a year since 1958, senses this more than anyone else. When the aged German Chief of State, mustering his courage, voices reservations, ventures a reproach or a criticism—politely and moderately, to be sure— in short when he takes a position that is quite different from that of his French counterpart, the latter usually reassures him: "I understand your point of view and I will take it into account." "I will take it into account." More than once, taking comfort in this vague response, the Chancellor planned to make capital of his success, only to find himself eating humble pie. And he is not the only one; Macmillan too, and how many others!

Nonetheless, the conversations referred to are the real diplomatic ones. Because there are also the fake ones of the kind required by protocol and included in the schedule of some Scandinavian sovereign or African president. The guest of France would feel hurt if a one-hour tête-à-tête with General de Gaulle had not been scheduled at least twice during his stay. On the other hand, they scarcely have anything to say to each other: There are ministers, experts, and ambassadors to resolve the minor economic, financial, or even political questions that arise in the relations between the two countries.

In such instances, De Gaulle relies on entirely different tactics. A past master in the use of them, he devotes a proper amount of time to banalities and mutual promises of friendship and cooperation, then takes the floor and never stops talking. His is a dazzling monologue in which he alludes to eternal and European Russia clashing with avid Oriental China; the Indies of Columbus merely succeeding in conquering matter and space while our ancient peoples are dedicated to the life-giving things of the mind; Africa awakening from its millennial slumber; the France of Charles de

Gaulle, as absorbed in its past as in its future, compensating for its technological insufficiencies by the boldness of its thought. The visitor will feel that he is not leaving empty-handed, that he has the trust and confidence of the awesome giant of world politics.

2. THE COMMITTEE

It was started during the Debré premiership. The General was irritated by some of the innovations introduced by his Prime Minister. To put it baldly, he was distrustful of several steps taken in important affairs, primarily African. Yet the Council of Ministers was unable to cope with all the problems; it was deemed unwise to prolong and multiply beyond measure meetings of this kind whose purpose was to decide on certain formalities (decrees, appointments), to fix basic positions, but not to work out measures that define a policy or to see to their implementation. Such is the task of the Inter-Ministerial Councils that meet with the Prime Minister, or at the most, when the subject is a major one, of a full Cabinet Council presided over by him. After all, the General can hardly take the place of the Prime Minister and preside over interministerial conferences.

And so he hit upon the idea of committees. The first ones were invested with an official character and their composition and jurisdiction were fixed by decree: the Committee for Algerian, European, foreign, economic affairs, etc. The Élysée became a super ministry, the Prime Minister was short-circuited, the government reduced more plainly than ever to matters of secondary importance, to seeing that orders were carried out.

Later, the game was subtly changed. The committees' preserve was no longer to comprise major problems (or at least not exclusively), but rather those that at any given moment the President of the Republic might decide to take on. Committees were set up to deal with veterans' pensions, the price of milk, or miners' strikes. On the other hand, under the premiership of Pompidou it became possible for the government, as distinct from the presidency, to deal with questions pertaining to Algeria, Europe, the economy. Initially set up as an ostensible means of relinquishing power, the committees actually became a convenient way to control everything; but they are not likely to develop into permanent institutions.

3. THE COUNCIL OF MINISTERS

Anecdotes about the Council of Ministers have provided more than half the text of one book on the General's "sayings." From the usual, "Monsieur the Minister of Foreign Affairs, don't break our ear drums, but please raise your voice a little"—thus interrupting a soporific report by the sterling Couve de Murville—to the furious: "Ah! I was just waiting for them! That's all we need!" hurled at Monsieur Triboulet who was speaking for the veterans, whose minister he is—all this has been recounted ten times over. All save perhaps the heavy boredom of these monotonous meetings that become virtually funereal when the General is not in good form.

"Nobody says a word," a new minister remarked with surprise and disappointment upon leaving one such Palace conference. On the rare occasions when an official communiqué or a commentator really has something to impart, one can be pretty certain that the purport had not been discussed at the Council, but decided in ten minutes by the General and the Minister of Information at the close of the Council meeting. How often have political journalists, lunching with a minister on a Wednesday, the day the Council meets, been amazed at his total lack of information! A short speech, an appointment, a trip, or a fresh approach to some question is announced with fanfare by a government spokesman. The minister knows nothing about it, he hears of it for the first time over the air: "We have been told nothing, the matter was not discussed." That's the rule—nobody says anything.

Nobody, that is, save the General. The ministers, fascinated, listen to his brilliant monologue. Historical memories illuminate the future like flashes of lightning piercing the night. Centuries collide, continents rise up, the peoples of the world clash, while France alone, everlastingly serene, goes steadily on her way. Sometimes bitterness carries the General away. In any event, one is told, we are a generation that has been sacrificed, a generation desperately staking everything on spirit and courage in the face of brute force, or skepticism, "I am criticized because I am not obeyed. But one is never obeyed. Did I myself obey?" or concern, "I will not make a spectacle of my decrepitude. Ah! I'm twenty years too old . . ."

Sometimes still, but rarely, after a triumphal tour of the provinces, a successful trip abroad, or some lucky stroke of fortune, optimism prevails. At such times everything seems, if not easy, at least possible. The same is true when things go badly, when there is a wave against De Gaulle that hits him like a slap in the face. One minister has commented: "He is never as relaxed and determined as when faced with a dangerous situation. And in a crisis he is sublime."

Because decisions are made elsewhere, often before a voice can be raised in objection—each man's opinion is asked only in exceptionally important and serious circumstances: a putsch, a revision of the constitution, a dissolution of Parliament—the Palace conferences consist merely of secrets suddenly and obliquely hinted at, flights of fancy that quickly subside only to end in sarcasm, denunciation, or irony. After the council meeting is over those who attended begin to ask themselves questions; in this "government by the word" the ministers are clearly the prime interpreters. What was he trying to say? Did he really frown? Was it a mistake not to answer him? How he emphasized this blunder, raised his voice in interrogation about that affair! The air was charged with changes to come and, like swallows before the storm, it was best to lie low.

Often one learns more from the interpretation of an attitude than from defensive reasons or formal decrees. For example, several members of Pompidou's government were at first surprised that the General, who, in July 1962, had been most reluctant to consult the country on constitutional reform (he had said, "We'll see next year, at election time"), suddenly seemed more eager the following September and hastily proceeded to stage a referendum. He dismissed all objections with a wave of the hand, even closing his eyes to the threat of a parliamentary crisis. Why the sudden rush? The only event of the summer after Algeria became independent was an attempt on his life at Petit-Clamart. But it was the key to the mystery. The matter came up during one of his monologues to the Council which he had launched in order to cut short a long-winded legal discussion. He said, "There's no time to lose. I have perhaps only two more months to live." These few words tell the story.

4. THE PRESS CONFERENCE

It's the high mass, the major ceremony of the ritual and it has all the pomp reserved for important holidays.

First an underground rumor begins. Those in the know declare that the General will possibly break his silence in the not-too-distant future . . . They are shrewd at guessing the moment when De Gaulle might have something to say for which a television presentation will not suffice because it is too brief and too limited.

Once the announcement has been made, all sorts of speculation begin: he'll say this, he won't say that. Two or three days before the appointed time predictions of his subject, if not of what he will actually say, suddenly become more precise. This does not mean that a light has suddenly dawned but rather, more prosaically, that the Palace press service has begun to distribute to newspapermen the questions they are expected to ask. The television viewers should realize that during a press conference any journalist who asks De Gaulle a question and receives a long, detailed answer has agreed to play the role of accomplice. If a question is really impromptu and spontaneous one can sense it, and the manner in which it is answered is also revealing.

Finally the great day arrives. The huge hall used for galas is set up as a theater of sorts, with one thousand seats. The Avenue de Marigny has been roped off for parking. Security officers are stationed at the entrance to the courtyard, around the Palace, in the drawing rooms. The ministers are seated to the right of the speaker, members of the cabinet and of the President's general secretariat, to the left. Facing them six hundred journalists, and two to three hundred guests —officials, diplomats, parliamentarians, supporters—are seated beneath the thousand-crystaled chandeliers. Television and newsreel cameras are set up on the small stage and also in the four corners of the room. The time is three o'clock. The red curtain parts and the General appears.

The technique of the press conference has undergone an important change in the last year. Previously, questions were asked one at a time and answered immediately. Actually, the General had before him a rough plan of the room with red dots to indicate the approximate location of each of his "official questioners." With the aid of this diagram and after answering one question, he would glance at the section of the audience whence the next question was to come. The pre-designated individual would raise his hand, stand up, and be given the floor.

However, unexpected things happened. Occasionally a

person who would never have been allowed to ask a question caused embarrassment by managing to slip between two official interrogators. At other times, on the contrary, an expected, planted question remained unasked. Amid titters, the General would put on an act and say: "Somebody, I think, has asked me about Ben Bella." But no one was fooled.

All questions are now asked at the beginning, in no set order. Then De Gaulle sorts them out according to the major topics and announces that in view of the various subjects mentioned he will speak in this or that order. Before starting to do so he names the "authors" and asks them to restate their questions. Thus he can be certain that no important topics are omitted, that everything he wants aired has been mentioned.

Television can proceed calmly, shifting its cameras from questioner to speaker, lingering over the audience and the ministers, but managing to avoid André Malraux, who tends to fall asleep at the first exchange and who does not sleep lightly. It's warm and comfortable, everyone feels at home, the cameras drone on and so does the General. Applause breaks out as the General winds up, to the indignation of the newspapermen—the honest-to-goodness ones—who have not come to clap but to listen.

After the final sally, with great formality the General thanks his audience and people begin to disperse slowly and regretfully, commenting on the great man's every intonation. The cloakroom, taken by storm, has more than it can handle. François Mauriac broods over an allusion made by the General, wonders about some reservation he sensed. Late that night the Palace will distribute the entire official text. It has been carefully checked; its style and occasionally its content have been recast. It now becomes the sole official document.

In January 1960, at the mere announcement that De
Gaulle was to talk, barracks were swiftly erected, only to be
pulled down five days later as a consequence of his remarks.
Inspired by pronouncements that had not even been uttered,
the revolt quieted down under the volley of words. In this
respect the press conference is a decisive weapon of the regime.

Sunday

THE GENERAL reads a good deal. To begin with, he reads magazines—including a few German, English, and American ones—and they mount up. Then, he has a large pile of French newspapers and does not like to find them "prepared"—in other words, checked, with articles clipped and pasted, etc. He prefers to get his own impression of the climate of opinion by seeing the page on which a story appears, the amount of space given to it; and he is quite right. He doesn't clip the articles but merely scans the paper, looks it over, crumples it, and goes on to the next, with the exception of *Le Monde,* which is brought to him at the Palace when he drinks his coffee; this he reads carefully, page by page.

As he glances at the papers, skipping here, reading minutely there, only one thought is uppermost in his mind: his image as an historical figure.

A single misquotation, especially if it goes back twenty years, or one recollection of Free France that, in his opinion, is either incorrect or unfortunate, is enough to arouse his ire, and for this his associates as well as the day's callers will pay dearly. On the other hand, an insult, slander, open hostility, or a savage attack leaves him indifferent; these are merely the tactical maneuvers of the moment and therefore not important, not to be taken seriously.

Every book sent to the General with the author's dedication, particularly an author he either knows or knows about, is picked up, looked over, leafed through, but not necessarily read. Every homage elicits a response, usually written in his own hand, often complimentary or reflective. Also, from time to time, because somebody made a remark in his presence that caught his attention, or because he read a review, the General, like all of us, will want some book that people are talking about, some new, popular novel. And so he asks the first person he sees to get it for him; his Court has no library.

Thus, a few years ago, the young wife of a close associate was greatly embarrassed. On two different occasions the General asked her to get him Christiane Rochefort's *Le Repos du Guerrier* (*The Warrior's Repose*), adding: "Be sure to send it to me, I want to read it during my vacation at Colombey." On the one hand, his request was an order and, after she thoughtlessly had said she had read this very risqué book, that she had it at home, it was awkward to pretend that she had forgotten all about it. On the other hand, the young woman and her husband were quite certain that if Madame de Gaulle picked up the book and read a few pages she would criticize the sender very harshly indeed. Did the General think that the novel was a story about military life? Or did he simply want some light entertainment? After lengthy discussion, the couple decided to be cautious and "forget" the request.

2. THE MAIL

Almost all the General's letters are in his own hand, written in the small, clear, military handwriting characteristic of a certain milieu and era. Frequently, the name of the person is written on the envelope by the General and his secretary adds the address.

As for the content, its courteous form detracts not one whit from its vigor or even at times from its liveliness. Of course there are always the more or less banal acknowledgments of a book or a personal note; the warmth of tone is in direct proportion to the degree of the sender's loyalty. But critical and even acid remarks are not at all rare. In contrast to vacuous notes of encouragement or congratulations, such letters are not proudly displayed by the recipients.

But there is, too, quite a different kind of correspondence, and apparently a considerable amount of it: the exchange of letters between De Gaulle and his peers, the chiefs of state. From a habit formed during the war, and emulating Churchill and Roosevelt, he still writes personal, long, and very confidential letters to Chancellor Adenauer, the British Prime Minister, the King of Morocco, or other major figures of lesser stature. In these letters De Gaulle, without giving way to personal feelings, which would be quite contrary to his nature, presents many of his own private opinions and justifies them in straightforward, concrete fashion. He also announces his future intentions, analyzes a situation, reveals his reaction to it just as he would at a fireside chat with a collaborator, associate, or friend.

The lofty concept he holds of his own role and of the importance of the men who, like himself, are responsible to their people and to the entire world for the conduct of affairs leads him to believe in a higher "professional" solidarity of sorts that transcends public attitudes, tactical differences, and political acts.

In this he has met with some misunderstanding, particularly on the parts of Khrushchev and Spaak. Yet he persists, occasionally virtually short-circuiting chancelleries and embassies, going counter to the position of the moment, more often than not anticipating some future eventuality by referring over and over again to the past, sketching one of those huge historical frescoes which inspired Edmond Michelet to speak of him as "a man of the day before yesterday and the day after tomorrow." Recipients of his missives wonder whether he is carried away by the day before or the day after. The impression, however, these letters give (letters which someday will either be added to the fourth volume of his *Memoirs* or perhaps replace it) helps in part to explain the General's considerable personal prestige— the last surviving vestige of the great role he played from 1940 to 1945.

3. TELEVISION

When the evening spent in front of the small screen has been a pleasant one, when nothing has gone wrong with the program that opens with a news commentary at eight o'clock and which the General watches to the very end if he is not otherwise occupied, he says: "*My* television." If he is not satisfied with the commentator's tone, if he is bored or annoyed, then he readily says, "*The* television." And when by chance he flies into a rage, when he feels he has been tricked or made to look ridiculous—that is, he or his regime—he summons the Minister of Information the very first thing in the morning, and, his face red with anger, greets him by saying: "I watched *your* television last night . . ."

De Gaulle was extremely lucky, and he knows it, to have assumed power at the very moment when TV really took hold in France. During the four years of his regime the number of sets has more than quadrupled. Today, when he appears on the small screen, he addresses about ten million Frenchmen—sometimes, thanks to Eurovision, sixty to eighty million or more viewers, whereas in 1958 his audience barely exceeded a few hundred thousand.

Another piece of luck, but one less due to progress than to his own diligence and effort, is his masterly skill in using this propaganda weapon. To be sure, he has at his command the finest technicians, an advantage which other political figures do not enjoy. Nonetheless, compared to the political leaders of whatever party one sees on the television screen during election campaigns, he is a bright star amid seventh-rate supernumeraries. He at least takes the trouble to read his speech beforehand and to commit it to memory. He knows how to deliver it, how to modulate his voice, how to make use of certain mannerisms that end up by becoming more moving than irritating. With the aid of a tape recorder, he practiced at length in front of a mirror. An eminent actor of the Comédie Française gave him lessons in elocution. He learned which gestures and intonations to avoid, the pace and rhythm that would be most effective.

In short, he is a real professional of television, and dramatics are his favorite clime; he is best during a crisis. Millions of Frenchmen are slowly growing old with him—"Look," they say, "he seems tired tonight," or conversely, "Charlie's in good form." Entirely unlike the Big Brother of George Orwell's *1984*, he rather resembles an elderly uncle, "someone you would like for your grandfather," as the *Reader's Digest* once put it. Thus the personal popularity of General de Gaulle is almost entirely independent of his political policies, of his regime; in any case, it is quite unrelated to Gaullism.

4. THE SOCIAL CONVENTIONS

One thing must be said in favor of De Gaulle: he dislikes nepotism and has never dreamed of founding a dynasty. To be sure, he readily cultivates the grandfatherly art, encourages the devotion of his son-in-law Boissieu, supervises the career and progress of his son Philippe, but all this is quite natural. He is not reluctant to attend the marriage of a niece in order to lend honor to the occasion, even if it takes place outside of Paris, and he likes his family to gather at Colombey in the summer and during the Christmas holidays. Toward his brother-in-law Jacques Vendroux, whose affectionate support helped him to endure the difficult years with dignity (years that also posed sordid problems—the symbols of and keys to his independence), he has displayed discreet appreciation. But family life is kept quite removed from the newsreels and television cameras; great care is taken to avoid anything that might remind the public of the large and intrusive Coty family—which is a good thing.

All this is true save in one respect: Madame de Gaulle who never interferes in public life, who is usually modest and unobtrusive, has nonetheless more or less succeeded in carving out her own personal domain. To be sure, she does not intervene in national politics or in affairs of state. But to a certain degree she has assumed charge of Christian morality and social conventions. She passes on the décolletage of ministers' wives, keeps track of the General's godchildren and distributes the layettes, but she mainly hits out at the obsession of so many good families, that ugly thing, divorce. Without pity she has removed all divorced persons from the entourage, has crossed off the intimate-dinner list those couples who were married only by civil law, and cold-shouldered anyone guilty of libertinage. Moreover, on various occasions, she has managed to rid the government of persons suspected of conjugal infidelity. People regarded by her as of dubious reputation, but who cross her threshold for reasons of state, are received with a polite, resigned mistrust—an erstwhile actress who has become a queen, a king in search of a queen to perpetuate his dynasty.

5. THE COUNTRY

Some of the General's close friends claim that he does not like his country home, the small park around which, he complains, he has walked "more than 15,000 times"; the somber, flat countryside with its rainy climate and gray skies. Friends have heard him say: "When I bought the Boisserie I was an officer stationed at Metz. Retirement was not far off. Where can a retired officer settle down except in the East, halfway between the Rhine and Paris? Besides, I didn't have much money and my choice was therefore limited. It was not what I really wanted but I was guided by practical considerations."

The "château" is indeed modest, devoid of any architectural style, poorly planned like so many old manor houses, and equipped with no modern comforts. Only one telephone connects the Chief of State with the outside world when he is at Colombey. His aide-de-camp answers it and the connection is poor. This is the way the most pressing problems are handled. Whenever he can, De Gaulle seeks the sun in the south of France. But Colombey is so much a part of the legend, of the myth, that he cannot give it up. With one church —that's all it boasts—the village has been chronicled in the *Journal Officiel,* in diplomacy, in history, ever since Chancellor Adenauer's visit.

And so, sighing, each Saturday the General gets into his black Citroën and drives to Colombey at 130 kilometers an hour. At every intersection the police are on the alert for crowds; the surgical sections of hospitals in Provins, Troyes, and Chaumont—the towns along his route—are held in readiness for an emergency; helicopters for civil defense stationed in the courtyards of police headquarters are alerted; and blood banks of the O type—RH positive—are watched over and checked. Meanwhile, seated in the back seat of the car next to Madame de Gaulle, impatient and on edge, the General knocks on the glass partition that separates him from the chauffeur, grumbling: "Let's not take forever, go faster, I'm in a hurry."

Kinship and Rank

1. THE KINGS, GOOD COUSINS ALL

EVERYBODY knows that all kings are cousins. Throughout the centuries their unions have woven a subtle network of kinship with the consequence that they have some connection with almost every throne. And if this is not always the case, their common fate is fully equivalent to a blood bond. No one is more closely related to a sovereign than another sovereign. a fact which does not prevent one from looking down upon another, or even from fighting amongst themselves.

De Gaulle has been compared to Charlemagne, to Louis XIV, to Louis Philippe, to the two Napoleons . . . It will suffice to say that long ago he emerged from the rabble of fortuitous rulers just as he stepped out of the military hierarchy, although a general. He is at ease among kings, both deferential—*noblesse oblige*—and self-confident. It is true that he never thought seriously of founding a dynasty. But he reigns, and what is more he governs, whereas many constitutional monarchs are nothing more than symbols. Thus his very real power compensates for what heredity has not bestowed upon him.

One might go even further: despite haughty denials,

shrugs of the shoulder, feigned indignation, General de Gaulle is, by temperament, a monarchist. There has been a good deal of talk about the possibility of his handing over power to the Count of Paris, the actual "pretender to the throne," "the descendant of forty kings who, for a thousand years, have created France." Some have maintained that the message, replete with respect, almost with promise, which De Gaulle delivered publicly to the royal pretender on the occasion of the marriage of his eldest son, Prince Henri de France, signified allegiance. And the Count of Paris has been received at the Élysée Palace several times. And is it not true that when he comes, the head of the Republican state, a man so concerned with protocol, so mindful of the slightest detail, has been seen to descend the steps of the Palace to greet His Highness at the door of his car, an honor reserved exclusively for the heads of states?

And so questions have been put to the General. He has reacted with irony: "I respect what the Prince represents and admire his very dignified attitude. But that's all. And I don't want to talk about it any more." There is a simple answer to this ill-advised question: If Charles de Gaulle could be the General Monck of a monarchist restoration, if, with his own hands, he could retie the thread that was broken in 1848, just as it was first broken in 1793 when Louis XVI was guillotined, he would surely do so.

But he is quite aware that of all the possible candidates to succeed him, of all those he could tempt or impose, if he so desired, the Count of Paris would have the least chance, would be the least acceptable, the most dubious. Any sounding of opinion would show most forcibly that public feeling remains secretly hostile to the monarchy, regarding it as an anachronism and as the most reactionary form of government possible. And so, being the realist, the pragmatist that he is, De Gaulle is resigned—a monarchical restoration is impossible. There is no point in even thinking about it. And it is in this sense alone that shrugs of the shoulder and denials should be interpreted. They signify, "I'm not thinking about it because unfortunately it is unacceptable and impossible," not, "I have never thought about it and would never do it."

For Elizabeth II—Versailles

To compensate for this frustration, special honors are reserved for all the emperors, kings, queens, and princes who in rapid succession, like April showers, have followed each other to Paris on official visits during the past five years. Oh, to be sure, there are categories and distinctions among sovereigns, just as there are first-class and third-class funerals. The welcome given a kingdom that counts for little in world affairs, especially if its dynasty is not ancient, is condescending, even haughty. It would not be fitting to give the King of Thailand the attention one would bestow on the Queen of England, nor to grant an African sovereign the honors one would confer on the ruler of an ancient European monarchy related to everyone in the Almanach de Gotha. But in any case the homage is paid to the principle and to the idea rather than to the man or woman who personifies it.

Her great dignity, her high sense of duty toward her subjects—in other words, the majesty of Queen Elizabeth II—account for the unforgettable welcome she received, as well as for an unprecedented occurrence. Paris was illuminated at night by fireworks so dazzling that all others pale in comparison, even the traditional ones on July fourteenth. For her the exquisite Little Theater of Versailles, built in 1770, closed for a century and subsequently made available to other royal guests, was magnificently restored and inaugurated. For her, English was spoken, to which she responded in French. The Duke of Edinburgh received more consideration and attention than any other visitor. Memories of the years the Free French spent in London hovered over her visit and, in a sense, a debt was being repaid.

Fabiola Arrives Late

The Belgian sovereigns—King Baudoin and Queen Fabiola—are less majestic, their dynasty is more bourgeois, their country smaller. Moreover, the Queen was in no condition to withstand the fatigue of ceremonies: she was expecting a child, and it was after a visit to Paris that a first miscarriage robbed the throne of its expected heir. General and Madame de Gaulle were waiting at the head of the stairs to the Opéra, in full view of thousands of passersby, while the center of Paris was completely cleared of traffic by security precautions as the guests of honor were awaited. It is said that the good manners of kings consist in being prompt. Whatever the reasons for the delay, it was severely criticized, greatly deplored, and even some acerbity was exhibited. Only Madame de Gaulle tried to justify and excuse a young queen whom she liked very much, in contrast to too many dashing and fashionable reigning ladies. The Belgian Queen's reserved manner, her religious turn of mind, and the relative modesty of her origins—Spanish petty nobility— brought her closer, made her more accessible than the heiresses of mighty imperial thrones.

Two Strong Women

Memories of war and exile join the former leader of Free France to the Grand Duchess Charlotte of Luxembourg and Queen Juliana of Holland—both of them strong women who assume supreme responsibility for their small countries. But Queen Juliana, who paid an official visit to Paris under the Fourth Republic, could not expect to be received a second time with pomp under the Fifth. She had to be satisfied with an "intimate" luncheon at the Élysée when she came to Paris on a "private" trip. The warmth of the reception given her more or less compensated for the absence of splendor. On the other hand, one day in October, Paris was decorated with the flag of the small Luxembourg principality, a flag bearing the same colors as the French, but in reverse order—red, white, and blue instead of blue, white, and red. For once the reception was an expression of homage to the woman far more than to the nation.

The three Scandinavian sovereigns, Frederick IX of Denmark, Gustavus VI of Sweden, and Olaf V of Norway, are gracious men who strike one as eminent citizens rather than as reigning monarchs. Simplicity and goodwill were the keynotes of their visits, with all the variations of the established ceremonies of a reception, official or otherwise.

Frederika of Greece and Farah Dibah

The late Paul I of Greece and Rainier III of Monaco were special cases. Did Queen Frederika, Paul's wife, seem too pretty, too elegant, and Princess Grace too Hollywoodish, too much the film star? The General did not appear to be put off by this; he even seemed responsive to the charms of both women. But Madame de Gaulle made no effort to conceal her coldness and disapproval. The effects of this were felt, especially by the couple from Monaco.

The King of Morocco profited from the prestige of his father, Sultan Mohammed V. Although the Sultan had been placed on the throne by the French, he had managed to establish himself in power by sheer strength of character, intelligence, and a natural gift for leadership. Hassan II, were he not a Moroccan prince, might appear to be the son of a noble family from the south of France who had mastered both the skills of the mind and worldly manners to perfection. It was in this manner that he was welcomed.

The Shah of Iran and the young student from Teheran, his third wife, who finally gave him the heir he had been hoping for, were popular in the streets of the capital, but among the guests at the Élysée Palace or at the Opéra they inspired curiosity rather than real liking. Reasons of state command conduct, but they cannot determine sentiments.

Nevertheless, ever since 1944, Mohammed Reza Pahlevi has been bound to De Gaulle by a debt of gratitude. When he stopped over at Teheran in October of that year, De Gaulle heartily encouraged the young Shah to stand up to the English, Americans, and Russians who occupied and controlled his country, to refuse to make concessions to them, and to patiently await better days. The Shah has never forgotten this. The splendid reception, worthy of the *Thousand and One Nights,* which he gave for De Gaulle in October 1963 spelled gratitude, admiration, and hope, because he expected France to help, just as she had done twenty years before, and to relieve him of the necessity of accepting American and British aid; but in this he was disappointed.

Kings Norodom Sihanouk of Cambodia and Savang Vatthana of Laos must be classified as representatives of France's moral and cultural influence in Asia; although the ties that bind them are not material, they are nonetheless cordial. And finally, there is the most gracious Queen of Thailand, who, far more than her husband, captivated not only the Parisians but even, it is said, their uncrowned sovereigns.

2. THE PEERS

Today General de Gaulle is the last of the great leaders of World War II still in power. His peers and real companions are Churchill, Roosevelt, Stalin, and (later) Eisenhower.

Pride? To be sure; the whole Free French adventure, which began in London in a B.B.C. studio on June 18, 1940, and ended in Paris four years later in a triumphant march to

the Arc de Triomphe, could not have occurred were it not
for the General's tremendous pride.

Churchill, What a Chap!

Each of these great men are allotted a full-length portrait
in General de Gaulle's war memoirs. But the name that appears over and over again, almost on every page, is obviously
that of Winston Churchill. Compared to the imposing Prime
Minister of His British Majesty, what sort of figure could the
mere colonel of a conquered army cut—a general with only
temporary rank, without soldiers and arms, condemned to
death in his own country and from the outset entirely dependent on the British government? Well, with calculated
coldness and lofty insolence, this general held out against the
old lion, claimed his right to receive help and in exchange
yielded only what he was willing to concede, refused to commit himself, bitterly criticized his protector and ally, and
constantly threatened to break with him . . . And this went
on for four years. The admiration these two proud giants
felt for one another even now cements their friendship. In
every line of their respective memoirs one can detect, whenever they refer to each other, the unexpressed feeling: "What
a pest, but what a chap he is!"

No to Roosevelt

Franklin D. Roosevelt was quite another matter. De
Gaulle the politician is responsive to established power: in
the game of domestic politics he pays a good deal of attention to the Communists (even when he opposes them), because they exist and are admittedly strong; by the same token,
he is respectful of the churches, of the important banks, of
leading intellectuals, whereas he holds outmoded political
parties and labor unions in contempt because they are weak.
De Gaulle the officer wrote some unforgettable passages

about military might and command. De Gaulle the diplomat has great respect for the important world leaders precisely because they are important, because they are influential in the game of politics—and this is true even, and above all, when he balks or opposes them, or when he criticizes them bitterly.

In 1942 Roosevelt obviously had great power, representing as he did the richest country in the world and commanding the largest army. De Gaulle therefore addressed him with a mixture of insistence and esteem, with the deferential but arrogant coldness which characterizes him; when, in the wake of his country's defeat, his influence was at its lowest, he displayed an even greater haughtiness. The few times he met Roosevelt in Washington or Casablanca during the war the atmosphere was chilly, glacial.

In February 1945, when the President of the United States, already on the brink of death, returned from the Yalta Conference (to which France was not invited), De Gaulle, to America's indignation and annoyance, and to the stupefaction of the entire world, refused to travel from Paris to Algiers to meet the President. To put it bluntly: Had Roosevelt been an infinitely less important chief of state, the president of a small nation traveling under a similar physical strain, De Gaulle would have gone to Algiers willingly. But since the invitation had come from the great American, a man so influential, the head of a country so wealthy and powerful, it constituted an order. Hence to go to Algiers, to meet Roosevelt on French soil, would have been to obey. De Gaulle does not obey. More than that, he cultivates a sacred disobedience, a necessary unruliness (which explains, let it be said in passing, why he has had to face so many rebel generals, so many insurrections and pronunciamentos). To say no savagely to a weakling is hardly difficult or courageous, but to collide head-on with a man of power, to provoke him, especially if he is an ally, raises the challenger almost to the same level; it's a calculated risk, a gamble. De Gaulle likes to gamble. His refusal to meet Roosevelt caused stupefaction, but in the end it increased his stature and signified that France, although scarcely liberated and still partially occupied, could say no to rich America. Such was his reasoning.

Tsar Stalin

Toward Stalin, the tactics were somewhat similar, but the atmosphere was quite different. For the first and perhaps the only time in his life, De Gaulle was fascinated. An Oriental potentate in a marshal's uniform, a court full of humble subjects who trembled constantly for their lives, whose very heads wobbled, the contrasts between the incredible abundance of banquets, the extraordinary amount of drinking each night, and the poverty of the people wandering among the ruins of a devastated country, the fabulous setting of the Kremlin, the intrigue and savage brutality—all this was truly another world. From then on a single concept must have haunted the man who signed the great Franco-Soviet Pact with Stalin at four o'clock in the morning, after a night replete with lightning, storms, great rage, and enormous laughter: the concept of eternal Russia. Stalin was the tsar with his moujiks, he was Alexander, Catherine the Great, the Pope, Rasputin, or Tamerlane. In one fell stroke this image blotted out Communism, the "Soviet," "Socialist," and "Republic" contained in the "U.S.S.R."

Even today, when he thinks of Khrushchev, De Gaulle cannot exorcise the ghost of a dictator in khaki, with a pepper-and-salt moustache. Because of Tsar Stalin, one of his peers, for De Gaulle the key to the U.S.S.R. lies and always will lie in the fathomless mystery of the Russian soul, not in doctrine or tactics.

A Wartime Crony

Although he became a chief of state much later, there is a fourth man in this world whom De Gaulle likewise regards as his peer: Eisenhower. Truman, Attlee, Eden were merely the successors of Roosevelt and Churchill, more or less brilliant, more or less transient latecomers. But Eisenhower was both a participant in and an eyewitness of the great adventure. In a way he is an old war crony with whom De Gaulle may have had quarrels or arguments but who shared his worries, understood his problems, and who, having endured much, also enjoyed a moment of glory. But De Gaulle is somewhat condescending toward him: after all, Eisenhower was merely an allied general who obeyed orders, not the personification of his country at a time when De Gaulle, in contrast, was alone responsible for the fate of France. But Eisenhower is a nice man, a good soldier, and well-liked. Whenever he comes to Paris he is invited to lunch so that the two men can reminisce about the war and plunge themselves into the atmosphere of those heroic days of twenty years ago. Since then, having doffed his uniform, Eisenhower apparently rose to a higher position in his country and had quite a career in politics. Good for him! But why did he gain power only to relinquish it, why didn't he stay in the White House until he breathed his last? What strange ways these Americans have—electing and re-electing presidents every four years, thinking of eight years as a maximum! Really! The country must be pretty unstable if it cannot see a great plan through to the end.

What? You say that for a half century or more France had governments that lasted only six months? Well, that's true of course, but it doesn't matter any more: De Gaulle has changed all that. He himself has personified French legitimacy without interruption for a quarter of a century. And he's not through yet.

3. THE PARTNERS

Take, for example, the late President Kennedy. When General de Gaulle was head of the French Republic's provisional government, the future President of the United States, then quite unknown, led the life of the son of an important and well-to-do family. When, ten years later, France was struggling in the grip of the Algerian war, Mr. Kennedy was known abroad merely as a young American senator who one day happened to make a speech on the subject of African affairs because he wanted to advise the French leaders; even if his advice were judicious it could not have been received with very good grace. Two years after the old General, weighed down with glory and prestige, returned to power, the young Senator took the center of the stage by becoming the head of the most powerful nation in the world. Very well. De Gaulle does not underestimate American power; he is a troublesome ally, of course, but a loyal one. He would be courteous to the man who represented the United States and gallant to his young and pretty wife. But no one could stop him from thinking to himself that he had been on stage long before Mr. Kennedy. For De Gaulle, Mr. Kennedy was just another among several partners, as is President Johnson now.

When President and Mrs. Kennedy paid an official visit to Paris, they were received with great pomp. Everything possible was done to make sure that the receptions were elegant, the entertainment perfect, the food of the finest, and the decorum impeccable—powerful America was being honored. De Gaulle had made some rather rude remarks about his guests during the 1960 election. He seemed pleasantly surprised by the lively intelligence and extensive knowledge of the young President. "He understands the ways of governments, he knows what he is talking about," De Gaulle commented. Direct contact had served its purpose, and although nothing essential had been discussed, no problem really solved in the course of their meeting—as was readily observed—a new custom was created at that time.

We know that during the difficult moments of the war, Churchill, Roosevelt, and Stalin, but mainly the first two, carried on an active and continuous correspondence, most of which has since been published. De Gaulle learned the advantages of this method; he confessed that several times he had wondered in vain about the secret motives of a decision reached suddenly in London or Washington, whereas the answer quite simply was to be found in an exchange of letters that had been kept confidential. Today, he follows this procedure with his partners. Letters, usually written informally in his own hand, which set forth his reasons, explain public opinion, supplement some official remark, or issue a warning, leave his small office at the Palace for the White House, 10 Downing Street, or the Chancellory at Bonn.

The confidential and private nature of this correspondence, which is more abundant and specific than the best-informed diplomats or even the foreign ministers sometimes realize, has generally been respected by the recipients as well as by the sender, save on one or two occasions. A personal bond is formed, a man-to-man exchange takes place between two chiefs of state, individuals who are unique in their own countries, and whose only equals are their foreign partners. Hence, one should not be surprised by the frequent disparities between the reaction of an American, British, or German minister or high official to some outburst on the part of De Gaulle, and the surprisingly moderate reaction of the President, the Prime Minister, or the Chancellor. The reason is that these people know something that their entourage, even their collaborators, do not know. Inversely, a phrase or an idea that arises in the course of one of the French Chief of State's speeches, or press conferences might merely be an echo of something said in confidential correspondence, immediately recognized by two or three men in this world, but only by them, and kept a close secret from everyone else in the know.

"Quelle Tragédie, Mr. Johnson!"

Before Lyndon B. Johnson acceded to the presidency of the United States, he had had but a single very brief meeting with the man who was to become one of his partners and also one of his worries. This first meeting between De Gaulle and the then Vice-President took place in Paris, where Johnson had stopped on his way to Berlin.

With his inimitable French accent and mannerism of just slightly Americanizing certain words of his own language, De Gaulle greeted his visitor from the steps of the Élysée (but from the top steps, the bottom ones being reserved for chiefs of state) with a resounding: "Do you make a good voyage?" The conversation lasted exactly thirty minutes, the compulsory allotment of time for such occasions.

When, following the Vice-President's departure, the General was asked what had been said and what his impression had been, his response was a succinct: "Ten minutes of civilities, twenty of banalities." Then, after a bit more reflection, and no doubt thinking of those who, in France, were putting pressure on him to accept the creation of a vice-presidency for the republic, he added: "A vice-president is, after all, a tenant who does nothing more important than wait for the death of the landlord." Several months later Fate was to impart a sinister, tragic significance to what had been but a lighthearted quip.

The second De Gaulle-Johnson meeting unfolded soon after President Kennedy's funeral. The new American president was in no way responsible for it. In fact, in the hours following the assasination, American embassies throughout the world received orders to discourage reigning sovereigns and chiefs of state from coming to Washington personally. There was fear of further developments in the wake of the Dallas tragedy, the difficulty of assuring the security of so many distinguished foreigners, and the desire to keep the period of national mourning free from any tinge of international politicking.

In Paris it was first rumored that De Gaulle would go to the funeral. This was soon belied by official sources. It was even announced quasi-officially that France would be represented by her Prime Minister and Minister of Foreign Affairs. The American Embassy answered all questions by saying that few chiefs of state would attend the funeral and, pressed by journalists and French diplomats, gave the list not of those who were preparing to leave for Washington, but of those who were definitely not going. Finally, several hours after all the others had made their decisions, De Gaulle surprised many by making it known that he would be in Washington the following day. On every television screen and in every newspaper his tall silhouette stood out above the shorter ones of the other foreign kings and presidents; he seemed, in fact, to be leading them, to be the chief of this disparate band representing America's principal allies.

The interview was even shorter this time. The President of the United States wanted to greet briefly all the attending personalities, and because he knew them anxious to start on the return trips to their own countries, could give only a few moments' time to each. When De Gaulle's turn came, the General opened the dialogue with a sonorous: "Quelle tragédie, Mr. Johnson!" The President asked if the plans for a meeting with De Gaulle set out by his predecessor (who was to have met with De Gaulle during three days of the next month in Miami) were still agreeable to the General and expressed his hopes that they were. De Gaulle answered that:

"keeping in mind the appropriate arrangements," he was
ready to meet with the President. The qualifying remark appeared insignificant and the acceptance complete. But for
De Gaulle every word, every shade of meaning is important.
In his mind the "appropriate arrangements" consisted of the
following: he had paid General Eisenhower an official visit, a
"visit of state," which had been reciprocated when General
Eisenhower came to Paris. Then President Kennedy had
journeyed to France for an official visit and it would have
been thoroughly correct and fitting for De Gaulle in turn to
travel across the Atlantic to see him. But with the new President, things were quite different: De Gaulle would have no
reason to return on a "state visit" since he had already been
received on this very occasion—in fact Mr. Johnson owed
France a visit. Conclusion: the "appropriate arrangements"
made it imperative that the new President come to Paris to
see De Gaulle and not De Gaulle to Miami to see Johnson.
This was never actually spelled out in black and white, but its
veracity is attested to by the fact that De Gaulle still awaits a
state visit from Johnson who in turn awaits one from De
Gaulle. It is also revealing that although, during his recent
trip to Mexico in March 1964, De Gaulle skirted Texas, he
took pains to avoid flying over American territory and thus
having to exchange the customary greetings of welcome and
bon voyage. He stayed five days in Mexico. He did not find
the time for a third meeting with President Johnson.

Weekends at Rambouillet

London and Bonn are nearer to Paris than Marseilles or
Nice. Therefore, letters to the British Prime Minister or
the German Chancellor are fewer and visits more frequent.
Weekends at Rambouillet, and Chequers, have repeatedly
been exchanged with Mr. Macmillan. In De Gaulle's eyes,
however, the Prime Minister was still the man who, as

Churchill's war cabinet minister, represented England in Algiers for the French Committee of National Liberation in 1943–44. A certain haughty respect emerged during those difficult times and facilitated personal relationships between the two men, despite the somewhat cold and stiff dignity De Gaulle displayed. But how could it have been otherwise between the most English of Englishmen and the coldest of Frenchmen?

They never really let themselves go when they chatted by the fire, while the rain splattered the windowpanes. After watching a carefully selected movie, usually the only diversion, the only interval of relaxation during those doleful evenings, the two men commented briefly. The most important discussions took place in the park, weather permitting. As they walked slowly, stopping to exchange a few remarks, followed at a respectful distance by their respective foreign ministers and chief aides (when they were invited), they confided to each other, at a safe distance from all eavesdroppers, their thoughts about the future. The French diplomatic service had to obtain the official reports of these conversations from the British Foreign Office because, although the British Prime Minister dictated an account of these meetings each night, General de Gaulle revealed little enough of the substance of the talks. This personalized concept of the relations of the supreme leaders was probably what led to some misunderstandings later on.

Lord Home has long awaited his turn to be invited to Rambouillet. He has been waiting since the very first instant when he kissed the hand of his Gracious Sovereign, thus signifying by this old, traditional gesture that he accepted Her designation of him as Prime Minister.

But that very day De Gaulle in effect let fall a definitive formula, sharp as the blade of the guillotine. He simply said: "He has a pleasant face . . . will stay awhile . . . as an interim man." Everything had been said. Before dealing with an interim man you wait for him to be well confirmed in his functions. And anyway it is far easier to converse with the person who will hold power tomorrow than with the interim man of today. You do not negotiate contracts or even enter the lists with a partner who is already on the way out. The interim man will wait.

Khrushchev Both Shocks and Disappoints De Gaulle

Of all De Gaulle's important partners, Nikita Khrushchev was the most disappointing. Long before he first made his acquaintance, the General had a very precise, probably over-precise, notion about the new head of the Soviet Union.

Leaning heavily on the classical writings of Tolstoy, Dostoevsky and Gorki, he imagined that the round little man typified the traditional Slav—impenetrable and sly, either affectionate or hostile, changing suddenly from affectionate friendliness to extremely violent anger, from exuberant gaiety to unfathomable melancholy. However, this correct but somewhat conventional notion of the eternal Russian was distorted by another memory, his own: the strong impression that Stalin had made upon him.

The new master of the Kremlin must surely be, like his predecessor, a nationalist patriot who more or less reconciled a touchy chauvinism with the official doctrine of the regime; in order to attain power, he undoubtedly had to wage a merciless struggle against rivals as ambitious and cruel as himself. He won only because he was the cleverest, the strongest, and the most persistent. One is always tempted to judge another by oneself, and this is especially true of De Gaulle. And so he thought that every gesture, every word, every step Khrushchev made was the result of careful planning, that he never left anything to chance or improvisation, that his rages were feigned and his outbursts deliberate, that Khrushchev too had a feeling for symbols and grandeur—in short, that behind his display of simplicity, even of brutality, he pursued with an implacable, iron will objectives carefully defined and determined by a powerful team of advisers and experts.

This being his frame of mind when he met Khrushchev, he was quickly taken aback, shocked and disappointed. First, he had to admit that Khrushchev's terrible tempers were not always feigned; the man was simply irascible and hot-tempered, and, although he sometimes deliberately played the part of a temperamental man, he often let himself go because he lacked self-control. Remarks made in conversation were not as clearcut, deliberate, and premeditated, nor documents as thoroughly examined, as one would have imagined. Believing that he was speaking to a man of iron who had complete self-control, to a clever tactician who was thoroughly well-informed, De Gaulle, without actually confiding in him, outlined his ideas of the future in a vague and suggestive way and assumed that Khrushchev would understand that all this was for his ears alone. In a sense De Gaulle spoke as one autocrat addressing another, as a French patriot speaking to a Russian patriot, as a responsible chief of state conversing with a colleague.

Alas! To his surprise, he quickly realized that he had not been understood. An unimportant phrase, a mere quip, was taken literally, whereas a rather transparent allusion that, on the contrary, had been made quite deliberately, went unnoticed. Surprise soon gave way to disappointment: Khrushchev was destroying the tacit contract which, in De Gaulle's opinion, more or less binds all the heads of great nations. Khrushchev publicly called attention to remarks that had been made merely to enlighten him, interpreted in his own way what had been said in confidence, and used these to argue that De Gaulle had contradicted himself, that the General was running with the hare and hunting with the hounds. As if all politicians didn't do likewise! This was a serious departure from the rules of the game, proof of Khrushchev's lack of understanding, almost of his disloyalty. It was quite plain that one couldn't count on people like that; they were not after all as clever or as strong as they wanted others to think they were.

The picture of a Europe that someday would extend "from the Atlantic to the Urals," so often evoked, was suddenly forgotten. The notion that the leaders of the U.S.S.R. were more Russian than Communist had to be revised. The Russo-Chinese quarrel, which had been predicted so often, ceased to be of interest. And it was plain that Mr. Khrushchev was not a gentleman. Thus, the Soviet leader's visit to France and the abortive four-power conference in Paris did more to reenforce the Western alliance, in spite of the jarring notes struck, than any other event.

Tito, Bourguiba, and a few other heads of state are also partners. Each in his own way pitches his camp on the international scene; each holds the reins of power firmly enough in his own country to be rated as a worthy and permanent partner. Such too was the case with Nehru. But India and Yugoslavia are of little interest, Tunisia is small, the three countries have their own problems and their own procedures which are not on the same planetary level. And so when they were received in Paris with great ceremony, it was for reasons of prestige, of honor.

4. KONRAD, THE FRIEND

Among all the past, present, and future heads of state, Konrad Adenauer is the only one who deserves a special place. Both peer and partner, he is above all a friend, something not to be taken lightly in the ritual of Gaullism.

When De Gaulle was with Adenauer he suddenly seemed

human, almost appealing. He displayed all his powers of
seduction, which can be great, enveloped his visitor in an atmosphere of constant warmth and attentiveness, played very
loud the sentimental note. Shrewd psychologist that he is,
De Gaulle understood, of course, that the octogenarian
reacted almost exclusively on the emotional level, like many
Germans and many old men. One real moment of true feeling, carefully elicited and cleverly exploited, was worth far
more than the most convincing, the most Cartesian proofs.

Konrad Adenauer is probably the only man in the world
who can boast that De Gaulle embraced him. This occurred
on the solemn occasion of the signing of the Franco-German
Treaty—an act mainly of symbolic significance, for if one
really studies the clauses, one sees that they verge on the absurd. The document had just been initialed, the ink was not
yet dry. And suddenly, as the two men stood facing each
other, De Gaulle was seen to step forward, extend his huge
arms, pull in his sizable stomach, and stoop to press the dry
little old man against himself and then to bestow two sonorous kisses on the wrinkled cheeks of the strange Mongol face.
The spectators were stunned; everyone held his breath as he
witnessed this unique scene. Tears, real ones, clouded the
eyes of the German Chancellor. His hand sought that of his
French friend. The picture that one hundred million European viewers saw on television, thanks to Eurovision, had a
much greater impact, a much clearer meaning, than any
speeches about reconciliation or treaties of cooperation. In
politics, appearances often count far more than reality; on
that day appearances were everything, the reality almost
nothing. The kiss of peace confirmed a sentiment, abolished
an entire past, offered a promise. It is plain that the most
spontaneous gesture, the most gratuitous act is, for De
Gaulle, the result of political calculation.

Adenauer fascinates De Gaulle for another reason. "He is

eighty-nine years old. Remember, he is eighty-nine!" The French President repeated after the so-called farewell meeting at Rambouillet, in October 1963, which preceded the retirement of the "old man." Should one deduce from this that at seventy-two, heartened by this illustrious example, De Gaulle sees seventeen good years of power still ahead of him, and that he is putting off until 1980 the moment when he, in turn, will think of retiring? Not really of retiring, for the General, having stated publicly the secrets and plans that had been confided to him in intimate talks, a thing which he does only rarely, expressed admiration for his friend, who in actuality was planning not to retire but to carry out fully his role as deputy, to control his successors closely, to speak up without hesitation whenever necessary. "In this way," De Gaulle said, "he is merely recovering his freedom of speech and will be able to use it as much as he wants, to grant interviews, to speak on television, to deliver speeches, without the care he would have to take as the responsible head of the government. While Adenauer was still chancellor and Erhard his designated successor, he suffered a kind of *diminutio capitis*. Today the situation is reversed: It is Erhard's power that is impaired, even diminished, by the existence and the acts of Adenauer. That's very clever!"

Fascinated as he is by Adenauer, De Gaulle has not yet shown himself responsive to the charm of his successor, Chancellor Erhard. The first quite important interview occurred in the period of mutual goodbyes between De Gaulle and Adenauer, when Mr. Erhard had already been chosen for the succession. The interview was frankly tart, not to say discourteous. The second, which took place in Paris in February 1964, was somewhat more relaxed, but not at all cordial.

As round as his interlocutor is long, as jovial and conciliatory—at least in appearance—as the other is somber and stubborn, the new German Chancellor is without doubt in all the world the man least suited to visit the inside of the singular historical monument known as General De Gaulle. The economist-politician who incarnates the new Germany, bourgeois, ventripotent and a bit strident, and the historical monument, this Joan of Arc become an old General, have just about nothing in common. We have all seen photographs of Erhard, half hidden beneath a huge Texas hat, as he visited the Johnson ranch and took part in the sundry country rites. It is difficult to imagine De Gaulle in such a setting and quite impossible to conceive of him sporting such headgear. De Gaulle himself, after examining the pictures with care, shrugged his shoulders and grumbled: "Voilà, he now takes himself for a cowboy!"

5. LIEGE LORDS, NOBLE SEIGNEURS, AND GENTLE LADIES

The twelve presidents of the black republics of Africa, having answered "yes" to De Gaulle and to France in October 1958, received complete and definitive independence two years later and were received in Paris with all the ceremony reserved for heads of state. The thirteenth, Sékou Touré, president of Guinea, alone asked for a vote of "no" and he is still waiting for an invitation.

The lovely Château de Champs, in the eastern suburbs of the capital, a part of the presidential domain, is the residence of African presidents. Some were vexed because they were not lodged either at Rambouillet or at the Quai d'Orsay, as has been done for other heads of state. It was even said in their faraway countries that their leaders had not been well received in Paris. Just think, instead of putting them up in "their homes" and treating them as friends, the French billeted them like strangers in "provisional huts," far from the tribe and outside the village!

The school for small children in the village of Champs was inspected by Léopold Cédar Senghor, professor of literature, Leon M'Ba, former customs clerk, Fulbert Youlou, former Catholic priest, and Modibo Keita, labor leader. The little boys and girls thought the imposing, black men were very nice indeed; the presidents of Senegal, Upper Volta, the Congo, Brazzaville, and Mali believed, as did their colleagues, that this visit was a special attention shown to each of them, whereas it was merely a way to kill time. These gentlemen also conscientiously toured the Renault automobile factories, the nuclear center at Saclay, the Eiffel Tower, and one hospital, while their wives were taken to a public nursery for children and to the great dressmaking houses. They laid wreaths on the Tomb of the Unknown Soldier, strolled down the Champs Élysées—beflagged with the colors of their young countries—at noon or six in the evening, during the rush hours, thus making sure of sizable crowds. They were given an official dinner, followed by a gala evening at the Élysée, attendance at the Comédie Française or the Opéra, a reception at the City Hall, followed by a boat ride on the Seine. They, in turn, "received" De Gaulle—at the Quai d'Orsay if their Paris embassies proved too small, which is often the case.

Finally, when the "official" visit was over, they could stroll about for a day or so as "private" visitors, with an evening at the Lido and eventually a weekend in the south of France. In their eyes, in wondrous, unforgettable improvised talks, De Gaulle had rebuilt the universe and magnified history— and this proved a very pleasant topic for the two or three hours set aside for political and diplomatic talks, talks that were entirely unnecessary since no one really had anything to say. Finally, there were personal gifts: Sèvres china, Gobelins tapestry, the latest model of a luxurious car, clothes from the great dressmakers, perfumes, to say nothing of toys for the children—all these plus a film strip recording the entire trip to take home as mementos and souvenirs.

Two of these "liege lords" of black Africa have been the

General's ministers, and they maintain direct and personal relations with him. They are Léopold Cédar Senghor—an *agrégé* in linguistics, the most difficult examination given at a French university, quite at the top of the hierarchy, and the physician Houphouet-Boigny, President of the Ivory Coast. Whenever they come to Paris, an informal luncheon is given in their honor. Political discussions with them are meaningful and have substance.

The two men are the General's advisers for African affairs and Africa's advisers on behalf of the General. At the U.N., in the midst of the Afro-Asian group, in African conferences, and occasionally but more discreetly in bilateral meetings, they intervene and arbitrate, aided by the twelve to fifteen votes they command in the international organization. Should the position of either one of them be threatened, should a revolt break out or a plot be uncovered, they can count on effective support from Paris. When they ask that their enemies, who have sought refuge in France, be rendered innocuous, such men are arrested and handed over to them, even though their countries have no treaty of extradition with France.

But year in, year out, the Palace has several hundred guests of note who are entitled to special consideration. First there are the Queen Mothers: Elizabeth of England, Elizabeth of Belgium, Wilhelmina of the Netherlands, have all been shown the courtesy of an informal luncheon. The late Mrs. Eleanor Roosevelt has been entertained. The same is true of Marshal Montgomery, Anthony Eden, Mr. Hammarskjöld, and of the innumerable premiers or foreign ministers of Canada, Finland, Italy, Turkey, Mexico, Brazil, Japan, etc., who visit the French capital . . . When Nixon, Rockefeller, or Stevenson pass through Paris they are readily given an interview. The "honorary Gaullists" of the American press are Walter Lippmann and Cyrus Sulzberger. Claire

Booth Luce is a special case: She proclaimed too loudly that her only interest in De Gaulle was his possible usefulness in getting rid of Kennedy. As for the Alsop brothers, they spoke ill of the General and his policies: they will no longer be received. Harold King of Reuters for the English press, Adjoubei, Khrushchev's son-in-law, of *Pravda*, Otto Frisch of the *Frankfurter Allgemeine* are all considered important witnesses.

The most Gaullist of the accredited ambassadors in Paris is certainly his Excellency, Serge Sergueivitch Vinogradov, ambassador of the Soviet Union. At the Rambouillet hunt, Vinogradov, who is an excellent shot, takes the honors each year. He apparently staked his reputation as a member of the Central Committee on the prediction that De Gaulle would quit the Atlantic Pact and that he would reverse France's alliances. There was a rumor that he would be recalled. But he is still there, still Gaullist, still worldly and wreathed in smiles.

General Gavin, too, unlike his predecessors and especially his successor, Charles Bohlen, must be included among the "honorary Gaullists." Never has there been an American ambassador so sympathetic toward the regime, so ready to be convinced that the General's position is well-founded, so wholly impressed by De Gaulle. He is missed.

But the greatest consideration has been shown to the English ambassadors—Duff Cooper, who was a friendly eyewitness during the historic days at Algiers, Gladwyn Jebb, and today Pierson Dixon. Perhaps an error of judgment is thus being rectified: many informed observers believe that De Gaulle was mistaken in seeking support from West Germany rather than from England in his policy of haughty independence toward America. But that's another story.

The Light Cavalry Party

In the Gaullist kingdom, the government party, called *Union pour la Nouvelle République,* or U.N.R., is sometimes ironically dubbed The Light Cavalry party. To understand the term, you must turn to the dictionary:

> Light Cavalry. During the Middle Ages it consisted of an inferior class of mounted soldiers. Seated on small horses of little value, the men were lightly armed. Under Henry IV, they were third in rank, below the bodyguard and the police; five years of service in the light cavalry conferred a title of nobility upon a commoner.

The U.N.R. is the holy battalion, ranking below the bodyguard and the police. And it is a small battalion—officially a hundred thousand, but actually about half that number. There would then be one militant Gaullist for every five hundred male electors and the same number of female voters —only one for about a thousand Frenchmen. This is very little, but it is enough.

For Gaullism has never really sought to be a "party of the masses," save perhaps for a short period around 1950; its very nature does not lend itself to this. On the eve of the war, and primarily during the period when De Gaulle launched against the Fourth Republic his first political party, the R.P.F., the numbers recruited were larger than today. But in any case, whether the party totals fifty thousand or a million, sympathizers come and go, depending upon the circumstances. Only the old cadres really count, those who took part in all the adventures of the Knighthood and who constitute the backbone, the hard core of the current U.N.R. They number twenty thousand at the most, probably a few less because of splits and expulsions. They are the true Gaullists, the faithful, the "unconditionals," as they are called. Of course, they are not all of the same breed, nor do they come from the same social milieu, and not all of them joined the family at the same time or in the same way. Cliques and groups have formed based on the moment and circumstances of their entry into the Knighthood; they compete with and envy one another, sometimes even tear each other apart. Thus, not one but many Gaullisms exist, as different in origin as they are in kind.

1. THE OLD-TIME GAULLIST

The ancestors are those who date from June 1940 in London, the first fighters of Free France. They are Caesar's legions, the Napoleonic veterans, Frederick II's grenadiers. As the antique dealers say about very old furniture, they belong to "a good period." They were Gaullists before De Gaulle.

The brief biographical sketches in this volume indicate the brilliant war service records of most of the Gaullists. If one were to multiply these portraits, to add a thousand or more names, the reader would realize that the members of the Guild are bound to one another because together they shared the fight "for honor and victory," as the sacred saying goes, for which every Companion of the Liberation was made a Knight of the Order.

Here were men who, at the age of twenty or thirty, found themselves launched on an incredible adventure. Some were officials, many were diplomats assigned to a post abroad. Others were army officers; a few, intellectuals. Many happened to be politically involved already: either they were active in extreme right-wing nationalist movements, perhaps Royalists or even had Fascist leanings, or they were left-wingers, very far to the left, members of Marxist and anti-Fascist political parties or organizations.

Just think for a minute: The Third Republic, which was beginning its seventieth year, a fairly advanced age for any political regime in France, had just collapsed under the blows of Hitler's armies. Half the population was traveling the roads of exodus, mixed in indescribable confusion with half of the army in rout. The other half of the army was already in captivity. Old Marshal Pétain, a relic of the preceding World War, was about to ask for an armistice and to seize power. And it was at this moment that an unknown general, but one with an aristocratic name, chose to call Frenchmen to London in order to continue the struggle—to London, when all the propaganda of the defeatist groups around Pétain was already accusing the English of having abandoned France and caused her downfall.

The words of the General sounded a nationalist note. Only a few people know that he once belonged to the Royalist extreme right, that he is by no means a revolutionary but rather an "enlightened conservative," just like Pétain, who wrote a preface to one of his books on the military profession, and like Paul Reynaud, who a few weeks before had made De Gaulle an Under-Secretary of State.

One would have expected that conservatives and middle-of-the-roaders would flock to him, patriots like himself, enlightened like himself, and therefore fully aware of the causes of the defeat and the need to turn one's back on despair. He personally had counted on the adherence of a few high-ranking generals, on some first-rate, distinguished political figures, on the leaders of the important traditional parties. But he was disappointed. Those who did respond to his appeal could obviously be labeled extreme leftist, leftist, and extreme right. Some had hoped by means of a revolution to establish a Marxist regime; others had dreamed of "strangling the bitch" (the Republic) and of using force to set up a strong, preferably Royalist government. They all had but one thing in common: a militant spirit. It was this that plunged them into the struggle afresh.

Thus, instead of welcoming his peers, the valiant knights, General de Gaulle witnessed the arrival of Jews excluded from the radical party because of their excessive left-wing tendencies, of the "Camelots du Roi," accustomed to smashing the windows of Communist headquarters and fighting the vendors of left-wing newspapers, of former "Cagoulards," participants in all the military conspiracies, bearded Socialists, left-wing Christians, Trotzkyites who had broken with Communism, and anti-Marxist fanatics. It was a strange conglomeration, in his opinion. Not a single general, no really important political figure, not one genuine leader. The generals didn't matter—he could get along with lieutenants and captains. As for the ministers, he would appoint them, too, but he would have to impose them on the country instead of imposing himself on them as he had hoped to do, and of receiving in return the support their prestige and authority would have lent him.

In a few months these first arrivals were joined by young officers motivated by patriotism, diplomats, and cadres who came to Free France for good and sufficient reason. Most of them joined the cause without reservation, many died in

combat on all the roads that led to liberation—Bir-Hakeim
in Lybia, Smolensk in the Soviet Union, Singapore, and Ta-
hiti. Others, veterans and heroes covered with decorations
and full of memories, were later to resume, with the elation
of having played a role in history, the thread of their lives
that had been momentarily interrupted. Still others, who
belonged to a political party, were destined to rejoin their
political family and assume their rightful place in the
ranks. The rest, finally, were to remain associated with the
struggle that marked them and with the great man who
swept them along and made them what they are. Gaullists of
1940 or '41, they will remain Gaullists forever.

The oldtime Gaullists feel a warm camaraderie for those
who shared their anguish, their enthusiasm and their hopes.
Like all veterans and former soldiers, they like to reminisce
about those dramatic days. Even though they may have
drawn apart politically, even though they have clashed and
fought, a sense of solidarity persists. Above all, the oldtime
Gaullists have a feeling of definitive admiration, almost of
adoration, a limitless, quasi-mystical affection for De Gaulle,
the chief, the leader. Make no mistake: they call him The
Big Man, or more familiarly The Old Man; they maintain
that "he has a terrible disposition," that "he doesn't know
what he wants," that sometimes "he really is impossible." It
would be foolish to take them seriously: they cannot bear to
hear anyone else lampoon or criticize their idol. Their cat-
echism is brief and can be summarized as follows: "The General was right in 1940, when everyone else was wrong; he is
always right and will always be right no matter what he says
or does. Even when he seems to be wrong, he isn't. He never
makes a mistake: he can see further ahead than we, than
anyone else, and so we must follow him, without hesitation,
our eyes closed."

Is this really servility, blindness, total lack of critical judgment? No. Émigrés, embarked on an incredible adventure, not without some misgivings and reservations, condemned to death in their own country, frequently repudiated by family and friends, subsidized by a foreign country, looked upon by neither the enemy nor their own allies as bonafide soldiers, they had staked everything—their past, their honor, their future, their very lives—on the word of an unknown but self-confident general; for four years these men lived an anguished existence. What if De Gaulle were to lose; what if they had bet on the wrong horse, the wrong card; what if they were wrong and he was wrong and had misled them? Then, one day, the survivors finally marched down the Champs Élysées behind their victorious hero, who had overcome all the pitfalls, and they were acclaimed by three million Parisians. They, with their general, were the liberators, the victors, they held the power—with the entire country behind them. At one stroke, on that day, they were repaid for all their fears, for their courage—their doubts were forever dissipated, and their wildest hopes realized. It was because of De Gaulle, that this was so . . . Henceforward, in their opinion, he would always be right.

All this aside, men are men, and there were, of course, oldtimers, a few, who fully expected to be reimbursed in both capital and interest—compound interest, if possible. A few others, after following De Gaulle for fifteen years or more, suddenly lost faith in him; they had come to Gaullism out of pure nationalism, for military considerations, because of their profound devotion to the army or their militant patriotism; or perhaps they were deeply wounded by the abandonment of France's colonial position in Africa, especially in Algeria, because they, too, had cherished a certain notion of France's educative and imperial role. Like lovers who have quarreled, their passion changed to burning hatred. They wanted to overthrow the man whom they had loved so much, to destroy his power, or at least to humble him. These Brutuses, few in number, to be sure, but determined, are the toughest and most violent enemies of Gaullism. And yet, whether they like it or not, their hostility is merely ihe counterpart of their earlier passion.

But most of the oldtimers willingly serve in the positions assigned to them, remain at the General's beck and call, never rebel at the many rebuffs they receive, even when occasionally they are shelved altogether, obey without argument, without even thinking, and kiss, if they must, the hand that smites them. For is it not true that the General always has good reasons for his acts, and that once again, as always, he is in the right?

2. THE SHOCK-TROOPER GAULLIST

He might be an oldtimer, but he is of a special breed whose origins matter less than his general comportment.

In 1939–40 he was a commando. Usually, and this is to his credit, a week after the armistice was signed he was already back in the fight on his own. If taken prisoner, he escaped. He might have had to cross through occupied France in order to reach Marseilles or a port in Brittany. Once there, he procured a fisherman's boat or he managed to slip onto a neutral cargo ship, or perhaps, clandestinely, he crossed the Pyrenees or the Swiss frontier. At any rate, he reached London and immediately enlisted—in the commandos, of course.

He took part in every battle: he was in Cyrenaica with the marching battalion of the Tchad, in Libya with Koenig, in Tunisia, Monte-Cassino, Corsica, or Normandy, Alsace and the Ardennes. He went of course to Berchtesgaden, where he sat in the armchairs of Hitler's "eagle's nest."

When peace came, he merely continued. What else was there to do? After hanging about in occupied Germany as best he could, he welcomed the creation of the R.P.F. in 1947 as the dawn of a new day that held the promise of a fresh fight. We find him in the party's security division, mounting guard on the Rue de Solférino, seeing that the General got an enthusiastic welcome at the *Vélodrome d'Hiver,* at rallies, at demonstrations in the Bois de Boulogne, and on election day, when he was not at all reluctant to exchange blows with any persistent opponent. He sold newspapers, helped re-build villages destroyed by forest fire in the Landes, stenciled slogans on walls and billboards; but for the most part he shouted himself hoarse, yelling, "Vive de Gaulle," or "De Gaulle to power!" This he did so often and so long that it was a wonder he had any voice left. Besides, he was a good fellow, always ready to click his heels and shout "present" when the roll was called, exuding that simple, brutal army camaraderie that smells of sweat, cheap tobacco, and red wine.

Then hard times came along. No more R.P.F., no more militant Gaullism, no more General, no more hope. He had to compensate, and it was not always easy. There were those who, approaching the world of business as they would a bat-tle, with drums beating and without bothering much with theoretical subtleties, were able to get ahead without making any concessions, and with a certain distinction. Others ex-perienced resounding failure; still others foundered in shabby, petty occupations or fell into debt. But from 1956 on, a light was once more seen to shine at the end of the long tunnel. The recruiting bureaus for plots and putsches worked overtime. Volunteers, groups, or substitutes were accepted and sent to Algeria. The smell of gunpowder, the noise of heavy boots—these were enough to revive everyone's spirits.

When a Minister of National Defense, in the spring of 1944, lost his glasses, his hat, and his dignity at the foot of the Unknown Soldier's grave beneath the Arc de Triomphe, it was a Gaullist, today an influential deputy, who slapped him hard in the face. When in the evening, mysterious men, their hats over their eyes, their coat collars raised, slipped in to see a state councillor—a moving spirit of many plots—they included, along with former ministers and future prime ministers, some specialists in violence, Gaullist shock troopers, one of whom boasted, not altogether idly, that he was the real "secretary-general" of the street. When young officers on the brink of rebellion organized "workshops" in Algeria to study the best way of overthrowing the regime, it was Gaullist shock troopers who encouraged them to influence the army in such a way as to make it lean toward De Gaulle when the right moment came.

Since the beginning of the Fifth Republic, the Gaullist shock trooper has been fully employed. Of course a member of the U.N.R. from the moment it was created, he quickly became a professional working for a cause. He is more easily recognizable for his strength and the size of his biceps than for his intelligence: he is the muscleman of the new order. If he shows some judiciousness, some competence in the art of political combat, he is justified in entertaining the highest ambitions. He will be counted among the responsible men of the party; he might become a mayor, a deputy, or who knows? Perhaps a minister. Unfortunately, on several occasions signals were crossed: a "muscleman" was chosen for an administrative position or entered Parliament, even became a member of the government. The results sometimes were surprising, either because the tough man, a former knight of the machine gun, was as successful in his high office as someone else might have been, or because his gait, as he walked through the hall of the ministries, flexing his muscles, did not differ from what it had been when he was walking through brushwood, scrambling over hedges in Normandy, jumping over wadis in Algeria, or taking an active part in electoral scuffles.

3. THE DRAWING-ROOM GAULLIST

Parisians have pushed the art of dining in town very far. Seated around a damask-covered table that is overloaded with precious crystal glassware and antique silver, pretty women in dazzling gowns, wearing expensive or gaudy jewelry, and their elegant escorts seem to be participating in a strange ceremony, almost a magical rite. As in a ballet, each gesture seems to follow the rules of a rigid yet discreet protocol; to conform to these complex customs with utter ease, to take them for granted, requires enormous skill.

Everything is either contrast or similarity: the lively colors of the gowns and the flowers, the freshness of the fruit and of lovely bared shoulders, the solemnity of the candlelight and the severity of the dinner jackets, the perfection of the food, first to the eye, then to the palate. Attentive and silent, almost invisible, the maîtres d'hôtel circulate. The wines are many, the conversation brilliant, interrupted by cascades of throaty laughter. Then suddenly a monologue emerges, extinguishing individual conversations until everyone is silent and a man's voice can be heard rising, with such excessively fastidious inflections of the voice, such affectation, that one is tempted to laugh.

"You see, my dear friend, Gaullism is a state of mind. A state of mind, I insist, almost a spiritual state, and not a passion. Passion is vulgar. Reasoning is for intellectual hairsplitters. A man of the world can't compete with legalistic minds or big brains, first, because he will certainly be bested, and second, because one should never stray from one's own fold. De Gaulle is one of us—even though he comes from petty provincial nobility, not ancient nobility at that. Even so, when you are with him you feel you are with a man of your own background. He's well-bred, he's an aristocrat.

"Obviously he isn't a man, he's a symbol. *The* symbol.

He sometimes reminds me of my Uncle Adhémar, who was also a symbol for us when we were children: full-blooded and arrogant, he personified the gentleman of the old school—a great hunter, a heavy eater and drinker—but I won't say more. Oh, what you almost made me give away!

"My Uncle Adhémar was of course a monarchist, a legitimist. De Gaulle is also a monarchist, in a way. Oh, I know you're going to say that, unlike Pétain, he didn't have the courage to destroy the Republic. But that was a matter of circumstances. The important thing, I'm sure you'll agree, is that he favors authority, a strong hand. You can't deny that he has style!

"In earlier times the symbol would have resorted to the sword to carve out a kingdom for himself. Today you have to be sly, to invent, to pretend. Oh, it's not at all easy or pleasant. When I think that sometimes he has to shake hands with Communists, that he had Thorez, their leader, as a minister, that he has to listen to Socialists, to Christian-Democrats—the name alone, what a joke!—to radicals, and to pretend to take such people seriously, I shudder! To be sure, people in our circles don't understand him, they criticize him, they even oppose him.

"As for me, I'm a Gaullist. I believe that men of our social class must take responsibility, and to do that you have to run some risks. After all, we can't always leave the administration of the State to unemployed lawyers or clerks. In 1940 the General executed a stroke of genius. It was perfectly natural that afterward he should believe that fate had designated him to rule. To tell the truth, many times I despaired of him. For example, in 1945, when he nationalized the mines, the Renault Company, banks and insurance companies. That was Socialism, plunder. But I quickly realized that he had no choice, that he had to save the situation. And then, in 1958, when he consorted with people like Mollet, Pflimlin, Pinay, and the rest of the rubbish of the Fourth

Republic, I was afraid that he would become their prisoner. Fortunately he gave them a rough time and they left.

"But what shocked me the most deeply was his abandonment of Algeria. For four years he struggled to save it; but the fruit was already wormeaten, and there was nothing he could do. I can hear you snickering. Believe me, if he of all people let it go, it only means that nobody could have saved it. And he himself was heartsick about it, it tore him apart. I was afraid he would resign at the time. You see, I have ways of ascertaining these things, I know what I'm talking about.

"You must realize that De Gaulle is a man who has sacrificed himself, that he's a martyr to duty. That's how I feel about him. And that's why I'm a Gaullist."

Individual conversations resumed and the volume of voices increased. Everyone at the table was commenting on this profession of faith. To be a Gaullist is rather shocking; one is not a Gaullist in high society. Every time the regime holds a referendum, a few dinners and a few gatherings are quite enough to create the impression that all of France will vote "no." This time, we've caught him. No doubt about it, it will be an overwhelming defeat. All the people one meets favor a negative vote. And then the day arrives, the ballots are counted, and 60 percent vote "yes," sometimes a good many more.

"But who on earth is voting yes?" a worldly man very much in the swim asked, not without naïveté. He added: "Except for a few drawing-room Gaullists and odd people here and there, everyone I know is voting 'no.'" One is tempted to reply: "That's because you don't know many people."

The drawing-room Gaullist is proud of his originality. He is a snob in his own way; the likes to shock his friends. Usually he is a right-winger, perhaps an extreme right-winger. Yet occasionally he adds another snobbish affectation to his Gaullism; he poses as a leftist, he talks about "the masses," dialectics, planning, "the winds of history," and justifies his Gaullism by his leftism and vice versa.

From time to time he utters one of his favorite aphorisms which goes something like this: "Actually, the General is an unconscious Marxist. In any case, historically, he belongs to the school of dialectical nationalism." Thereafter, when he looks a little insistently at the pretty women, they shiver deliciously; this revolutionary, by staring at them, lends weight and value to their jewels. But after a while he ceases to amuse, he becomes irritating; there is something excessive about his insistence, as if he had a need to reassure himself by endless repetition of his political opinions. And besides, everyone knows he wouldn't hurt a fly. He no longer frightens anyone.

4. THE PROFESSIONAL GAULLIST

His profession: Gaullist when the General is in power. His occupation: parliamentarian if he can make it, minister if he has any luck, leader of the Gaullist party if there is one, if not, he is unemployed.

In 1940, he was twenty or twenty-two years old. If he was a student, the war interrupted his studies. If he had just started to make a living, he was stopped short. Five years later, he found himself demobilized, more or less covered with decorations and glory, and he began to realize that he didn't know how to do anything except fight.

How did he happen to become involved in politics (he calls it action), in election battles (he calls it roughhousing), in ministerial cabinets (he calls them teams)? A war chum or a political leader who was friendly or loyal gave him his start. As for the rest, he had gotten into the habit of following De Gaulle about and this habit remained with him. Once he entered the political game, the professional Gaullist hung on.

One youthful veteran was asked to compete in the legislative elections in a distant province. He was told that the party had to be represented in this election, but that since there was not the slightest chance of winning, nobody else was willing to run. Our man accepted, thinking he might make some useful contacts and that, in any case, the country air would be good for him. To everyone's astonishment, to say nothing of his own, he was elected. During the last eighteen years he has been, successively, a member of three political parties, returning to Gaullism whenever the General seemed about to assume power. And he is still a deputy. Today, he is an old hand at the game. He has no other profession or trade, but he does have experience, contacts, and a name that is known.

The professional Gaullist is not loyal; he reminds one of the ancient mercenaries who could be relied upon only if they were well paid. Nevertheless, whenever he has the opportunity, he loudly proclaims his staunch convictions and his utter devotion to the General. Unlike the oldtime Gaullist, he has a need to trumpet his allegiance and to call attention to the services he has rendered. Moreover, he is an excellent barometer of public opinion: when he is critical, when he becomes unruly, the temperature is falling and a storm is brewing. When, on the contrary, he is obedient and steadfast, it is a sign of good weather ahead.

This type of Gaullist can never be counted on to work for the party. Under the Fourth Republic he was a parliamentarian, even a minister, but he used his authority and office to offer help discreetly to former friends who were in difficulty, to work against the regime he was serving. When the Fourth Republic fell, our man boasted about his subversive activities; to listen to him one would think that his sole purpose in getting ahead had been to destroy and overthrow the regime he had served. When De Gaulle returned to power, he played the same game in reverse. This time, our dignitary of the Fifth Republic maintained the most courteous, the friendliest relations with the opposition, in a more or less underhand way. He performed small favors for opposition leaders, his supposed enemies, and prided himself on being a moderating element in government councils or in the majority party. Perhaps tomorrow we will learn after the Sixth Republic has been created, the one after De Gaulle, that he was systematically betraying the present regime and preparing efficaciously for the future. Names come to mind, names well-known today but also well-known yesterday, names that will perhaps be well-known tomorrow. That's politics—a phenomenon we find throughout history in every country in the world.

5. THE TECHNOCRATIC GAULLIST

With the birth of the Fifth Republic a new breed of men entered French political life, a breed that until then had made itself felt only rarely, diffidently, and intermittently— the technocrat.

Gaullism claims to be first of all a technique of political leadership and administration. Under the Fourth Republic the important stewards of the State were faced with an extremely awkward dilemma, since they could never be sure that the same government they coped with one day would still be there the next. At the same time, precisely because of this political instability, their own positions were extraordinarily important, since they remained even though cabinets fell. All in all, however, the technicians were unhappy because they preferred to take orders.

Today they find themselves in a situation that suits them admirably. In contrast to the past, one power definitively resolves the problem of important national choices. Also, in contrast to the Fourth Republic, the government scarcely exists and therefore neither gets in their way nor hampers their plans. Better still, a goodly number of technocrats have

become ministers and thus exercise a twofold influence—
both political and technical—within the administration. It
is therefore understandable that, on the whole, the regime
should be accepted and supported by the technocrats in the
public service.

In the private domain, the change is equally radical.
Under preceding Republics, business lobbies tried to exert
pressure on governments and on parliamentary majorities,
and sometimes they were quite successful. They had their
own men, their own groups, who were well-known to everyone in politics. Often they had to operate openly, to ask for
a great deal in order to obtain enough. On days when important debates were scheduled, they flocked around the
corridors of Parliament or the antechambers of ministers like
swallows . . . Now the technocrats in the private sector have
a much easier task: they hold the fort. Installed in the ministerial cabinets, sometimes ministers themselves, they can cir-
cumscribe their requests because they are sure they will be
granted. No longer do they need to invade Parliament, because decisions are no longer made there. They are discreet,
more efficient than ever—in short, they are satisfied.

The technocrat is therefore quite often a Gaullist, or at
any rate has become one, because he can be more effective
that way. It is perhaps not the regime or even the party of
his choice, but unquestionably both come close to it. He
thinks the General is not always accommodating, that he is
too prone to act rashly about matters of great importance—
the European Common Market, for example, or the fixing of
tariffs. He is often irritated by the muddleheaded incompetence and restless ambition of pseudotechnicians who in actuality are professional Gaullists—defeated Parliamentarians,
self-seeking or distrustful leaders, unemployed dignitaries.
But he believes that they are useful pawns, easily maneuvered, and so he readily gives them their small place in the

sun, even granting them honorary titles and the semblance
of authority, whereas he carefully preserves his control over
the key positions.

Moreover, during moments of impatience, the Gaullist
technocrat entertains one hope—to succeed De Gaulle. For
he, too, objects not only to a rightist, conservative solution
("That would be to go against the current, to walk back-
wards," he says), but also to a leftist Socialist or quasi-Social-
ist solution, the breeder of more or less demagogic liberality
and hence of disorders. A technocrat as president would be
the man to insure the triumph of fresh cadres, of that "Republic of technocrats" which had suffered so much at the
hands of the "Republic of deputies."

6. WOMEN GAULLISTS

In the large city of Lyons, during a referendum in 1960, a
curious experiment in electoral sociology was attempted
with the consent of the authorities. Four large precincts were
carefully selected to represent respectively the bourgeoisie
and the well-to-do, the small businessmen and artisans, the
comfortable and educated working class and the lowest strata
of the proletariat. Both male and female voters were asked
to deposit their ballots in separate containers and everyone
complied most willingly. When the votes were counted two
surprising facts emerged.

First of all, in contrast to the men, everywhere and over-
whelmingly women voted "yes" for De Gaulle. Furthermore, contrary to all expectations, women of the most
modest circumstances, the wives of working-class men, were
apparently more Gaullist than middle-class or well-to-do
women. The lower the income the larger the pro-De Gaulle
vote.

The woman Gaullist who holds the center of the stage is a
kind of Amazon. During the war she was a nurse parachutist,

she drove an ambulance in the front lines, or she was an officer in one of the women's units. She has been decorated, she smokes like a chimney, speaks like a veteran campaigner, never blushes, and likes to reminisce about the war, the mess, the commandos. But although such women make a good deal of noise, and although the French fought uninterruptedly from 1939 to 1962, these women soldiers are not numerous.

The second category of Gaullists-in-skirts is less conspicuous, less noisy. These are the widows of officers of the Free French, daughters of old faithful Guild members, society women who, if they are quite young, see De Gaulle as the father they would have liked to have had, or if they are middle-aged, look upon him as the ideal, masterful male. Their Gaullism is visceral, occasionally passionate, rarely discreet. They speak of the General as a priest speaks of the Pope, as an English Royalist speaks of his Queen. Naïvely, they admit that they know nothing about politics, but they have confidence in De Gaulle. "Confidence" is the key word—the alpha and omega of their doctrine.

They do "social work," as they put it—during the war it was packages for soldiers, in time of peace it is layettes for mothers of large families, and at all times they address envelopes for tracts, meetings, and propaganda sheets. For them, Gaullism is a religion.

But this of course does not constitute an electoral body. There are others, however, the millions of women who vote for De Gaulle, who select the most Gaullist candidate on the ballot, and who sometimes make a mistake when there are two or three competing candidates, each claiming to be more Gaullist than the others. Why do these women react this way, what makes them vote for De Gaulle, often against the advice of their husbands, their priests, or their milieu? The simple answer is that they trust the General.

You know pretty well where you are with him. Naturally,

things could be better, wages could be higher, prices more stable, taxes lighter. But, after all, things aren't too bad. And there are two decisive arguments in favor of the General: First, he is there, has been there for five years, and will probably remain there for a long time; they are used to him and are afraid of what would happen were he to disappear and be replaced. Second, and this is most important, they know what risks they run with him and they also know what would happen with "others": the hellish race of wages against rising prices always speeding but never really catching up; strikes and inflation; unpaid bills for purchases made on the installment plan, maybe unemployment . . .

Whether they believe it not, the men of the Fourth Republic are closely linked in the minds of these women with hard times, instability, whereas Gaullism seems to represent a period of at least relative progress, stability in employment and in government, an era of economic equilibrium and health. And the lower the standard of living, the more haunting become the old ghosts of the past—unemployment, poverty, strikes, workers' struggles—and the more symbolic of security Gaullism becomes. Let the men grumble—they're never satisfied—the franchise for women, which De Gaulle himself initiated in 1944, restores the balance.

7. WOLVES HUNT IN PACKS

Everyone knows the old proverb: "Wolves do not devour each other." Well, it's not true. They certainly do; they tear each other apart; they fight ferociously. But they hunt together, in packs.

Gaullists who are not wolves—there are wolves among them, but there are also sheep, lots of them!—sometimes tear each other apart too. The cliques that sow dissension in the Knighthood are often closed ones, and often as relentless in their fratricidal struggles as wolves. There are several reasons for this.

First, the differences that exist in both recruitment and assignments. The shock-trooper Gaullist, the fighter who risked a thousand deaths in Free France, the old reliable who paid with his person in the fight against the activist terror in Algeria, and even in Paris, the "liege man," as he was called in the Middle Ages, who never spared himself in electoral scuffles have only contempt for behind-the-scenes strategy, for the professional politician, for the slacker who fought the war behind a microphone or desk. And the traditional parliamentarian, the serious, responsible or eminent citizen, in turn, cordially despises the tough guy who is all right in a fight, but is sometimes troublesome, often dangerous, and always unpredictable. The financier, the businessman who supports Gaullists with his contributions and tries to manipulate it to further his own interests, has only contempt for both groups of men, whom he regards as his hirelings. The technocrat who regulates and governs the future, not only of Gaullism but of both the regime and the country, feels vastly superior to the shortsighted businessman and considers himself to be in complete control of the situation. But the pedant who lives by theory and builds the regime's ideology thinks of himself as the brains of the entire machinery, the prime mover of the entire enterprise.

Seniority plays a role, at least for those who can exploit the fact that they were among the first to serve. The Gaullist of 1940 looks upon his war years as a period that earned him definite rights. The Gaullist who went to London regards the Resistance fighter who remained in France as a second-class Knighthood member who was neither lucky nor bold enough to shake the dust of his occupied country. And the Resistance fighter, in turn, mistrusts "all those reactionaries" who clustered around De Gaulle in Free France. They join forces, however, in regarding the 1944 adherent as a Johnny-come-lately, as a sort of opportunist. And this is true of every stage of the adventure—1947, 1951, 1958 . . . Every man believes that, after all, promotion should be based primarily on seniority, as in the army or in management.

Then there are the acquired titles. This one is a Companion of the Liberation, that one is in the General's cabinet, another is a deputy or senator . . . Rivalry is all the more keen since appointment to an important position will enable the incumbent to find jobs for others in his own clique. Thus, some important nationalized enterprise, some essential public service will be staffed from top to bottom by "left-wing Gaullist" directors, or former Free French fighters; or a certain ministry will choose for responsible offices only men of the Fourth Republic who saw the light during the dramatic days of May 1958 or immediately afterward.

But in the face of a threat from the outside, a surface solidarity ensues, the walls close in, an open season for hunting is declared. Today political observers can name at least four Dauphins: Pompidou, Chaban-Delmas, Debré, Fouchet . . . And yet, if De Gaulle were to die tomorrow, there might be as many as three or four candidates to succeed him. Yet one thing is certain, you would find only one true Gaullist among them. The danger of a threat would bring about an understanding. After having done a thorough job of tearing each other to pieces, after competing and fighting for high office, the Gaullist leaders would agree on a single name, and, like cardinals after a conclave, they would all pay homage to the new sovereign and publicly swear obedience and allegiance.

8. GAULLISTS ALSO DIE

Caesar saw Brutus standing among his assassins; Alexander the Great, Frederick II, Catherine II, Napoleon, were all betrayed by their generals. In the Knighthood De Gaulle has had loyal Gaullists, close associates, his own creatures turn their backs on him, stand up to him, make attempts on his power, even on his life. Like an army or political regime, Gaullism has not only had its heroes but also its traitors and renegades.

On the eve of World War II they were few and their rebellion had little impact, because then, after so much toil and danger, the moment had come to reap their just reward. It is also true that there were very few defections or dissidents from 1947 to 1952, when the Gaullist party battled for power. But no sooner had the hope of a restoration been disappointed than the crowd began to disperse. The most loyal followers joined the enemies of yesterday, contracted friendships with the men of the Fourth Republic, and sought either Judas' thirty pieces of silver, or at least, substantial compensation for the failure of their aspirations.

The General viewed these betrayals with sovereign contempt and a certain morbid enjoyment. Decidedly, his impression of politicians and their hangers-on was confirmed. He was not really angry; he merely took note of the defections and remembered that henceforward he would have to mistrust all those who had "lined up for soup," as he put it.

His return to power in 1958 did not take place in an atmosphere of euphoria. During De Gaulle's first visit to Algiers there were curious scenes. As the official parade went by, the crowd shouted "Vive Soustelle," which was a way of not shouting "Vive De Gaulle." At another place, a stern, old-time Gaullist, pointing to two former ministers of the Fourth Republic, party leaders who had become ministers of De Gaulle and who were accompanying him on his visit, publicly asked his chief to "sweep away the detritus of the System." At still another stage of the proceedings, these poor ministers were locked in an office whose key "couldn't be found" for about an hour, so that De Gaulle addressed the crowd without the presence of these two hostages.

It was a bad beginning and it continued badly. Instead of

the betrayals, expulsions, and revolts of the preceding years, the reaction was less that of men disappointed in their ambitions than of conflict over the policies of the regime. Perhaps only someone who was blind or naïve could have thought that De Gaulle, once in power, would yield to the generals, would spurn the idea of a negotiated peace in Algeria, impose an iron rule on both the army and the rebels, opt in favor of defending the colonial empire, outlaw Communism within the country, and insist that Algeria remain French. But millions of Frenchmen shared this blindness or naïveté regardless of whether or not they relished the intentions attributed to their leader.

General de Gaulle's utterances have always been enigmatic, preceded by vague allusions, euphemisms, soundings, and followed by disclaimers. What does he really think, what does he really want? Men like Jacques Soustelle (the General's close collaborator and minister since 1940) still misjudge him after eighteen years of service. How accurate then can less intimate associates be? And what about the generals, the youthful officers, or the simple Foreign Legionnaires and parachutists who easily lost their bearings in the tortuous maze of politics? Or the uncomplicated, straightforward men, unaccustomed to nuances and subtleties, who are used to giving and receiving orders, not to interpreting and dissecting every remark, or to guessing the meaning of every gesture?

Then, in 1961–62, came the great wave of betrayals, which ended when peace was declared and Algeria became independent. Men filled with rage lay in ambush in order to kill De Gaulle. The most intransigent anathematized him and then sought refuge, if they had not already done so, in foreign parts. With all the hatred of deceived lovers, disappointed doctrinaires turned furiously against the man they had adored and took it out on his regime and its policies, on those who remained faithful to him. And finally there were the sneaks who kept their mouths closed but secretly helped the rebellious generals—which was quite consistent with their past records and their patterns of behavior.

One had to sanction, exclude, track down, condemn, imprison. But let us not exaggerate: the referendums showed that those in favor of keeping Algeria French represented at the most 2 to 3 percent of the electorate. As for Gaullists rejected by the Knighthood, or those who had rebelled, they numbered only a few hundred, including about thirty deputies and perhaps three or four first-rate personalities. But they made enough noise for thousands.

Having broken with Gaullism, these men found they had no place to go. A few who translated words and speeches into action and armed revolt are in prison. Others sometimes followed or preceded them; but at any rate they approved and thus chose exile. They now wander from continent to continent without any hope save that of one day being able to return unnoticed to their own country; but neither their former associates nor their former enemies will ever again give them positions of power lest they thereby set the stage for another round of betrayals. The best of these unfortunates left public life of their own volition, without waiting for expulsion, yet also without indulging in immoderate acts. One of them, a former associate, General Larminat, had been named President of the High Court of Justice and was thus called upon to pass sentence on erstwhile comrades, the generals and colonels of the 1961 putsch. He chose another form of escape, shooting himself in the head after writing a long letter to De Gaulle affirming his respect, his loyalty, and his refusal both to obey and to disobey. There is no crueler way for a Gaullist to tender his resignation. Gestures of this kind also make one realize how unconventional a political party Gaullism is and the extent to which the bonds that link its members to each other and their chief transcend the ordinary rules and customs. To the myth, to the symbol, the mystique replies, *perinde ac cadaver,* for Gaullists also die.

9. CHAMBER MUSIC

Restored to power by the Algerian putsch, De Gaulle invoked legality to appeal for high office as head of the government. This was on June 1, 1958. Confronting the deputies, he showed himself to be amiable, conciliatory, insistent but courteous, firm but smooth. This was "operation-seduction." An extremely experienced politician who has gone wrong since, Georges Bidault, witnessed not without some irony the spectacle of a stiff general addressing with considerateness and cordiality the parliamentarians he despised. And he made the following remark, an excellent forecast of the more martial spirit that was to imbue the high office, the regime, and its chief: "Today chamber music, tomorrow military music."

Since then Gaullists have replaced many elected members of Parliament. At first they thought their numbers and presence would change everything. Little by little, they became living illustrations of that eternal law of Parliaments in every country and in every period: Parliamentarians tend to devour every power that does not emanate from them until they succeed in finally establishing that "Republic of deputies" of which they dream. Very soon the office becomes more important than ideas.

For the Gaullists in Parliament, the office plus professional solidarity soon overcame principles and doctrines and so greatly blurred the line of demarcation between ideologies that they were practically obliterated. However, these men, unlike others, became neither 100 percent parliamentarians nor a conventional political party, and they never will. First of all because their leader is Charles de Gaulle. He alone makes decisions, confides his plans to no one, never pays attention to objections, and exacts from all his men, total, immediate, and definitive consent. This tends in a curious way to limit the possibilities of maneuvers on the part of the elected, who were designated by the General and are therefore wholly indebted to him for their positions (so much so in fact that some of them set foot for the first time in the districts they are to represent only three weeks before the election), who have sworn loyalty to him but know not where or how he will lead them.

Their freedom of choice is likewise limited by very rigid and severely enforced rules. They can neither overthrow the government nor refuse to pass the budget. They cannot initiate legislation, save in specific and very rare instances, nor can they make decisions about referendums, resolve to hold special sessions, or reject laws that are submitted to them in a certain form.

They have tried all that. For example, in 1960, faced with an agricultural crisis, they decided they would have to hold a special session. More than half of the deputies had petitioned the President on the required forms. In a contemptuous and haughty letter, De Gaulle replied "no." And so Parliament remained on vacation. The deputies did overthrow one government, the Pompidou Ministry, in October 1962. But it was not Pompidou or his ministers who left, but the deputies. The government stayed where it was and the National Assembly was dissolved by De Gaulle. If the deputies refuse to vote the budget, a decree takes care of that. If they want to discuss plans for legislation to be initiated by themselves rather than by the government, the bills will not be included in the agenda; the government will decide at its own discretion. It's not very much fun to be a member of Parliament under the Fifth Republic. But it's relaxing; with very rare exceptions, attendance at meetings keeps declining.

Some deputies have not entered the Palais Bourbon three times in the space of five years, even though they are formally obligated to assemble two hundred days a year.

Some seek consolation for this relative inactivity by playing a dirty trick on the government—thumbing their noses, making faces—whenever De Gaulle's back is turned. A law is torn to pieces, an entire section of the budget is rejected, the key feature of a plan is altered . . . But the Prime Minister looks annoyed, the General threatens or grumbles, and immediately, with heads lowered, our elected Gaullists fall back into line and vote as one man.

Trips are a nice diversion, a good antidote for boredom. And so French parliamentarians travel a great deal: missions, visits, inspection tours, investigations . . . They go preferably to the Mediterranean countries in the spring, to Africa in the winter, to Scandinavia and Eastern Europe in the summer, and to the United States, South America or Asia all year round. You take your wife along and pass her off as your secretary, or perhaps you take your secretary and promote her for the duration to the status of wife. You send postcards to friends and bring souvenirs for the children. It helps pass the time. Those who said that the regime would be moderately parliamentarian were right. However, they were wrong about the Gaullists, who learned to play chamber music and, once elected, did become parliamentarians—but not in moderation.

10. MILITARY MUSIC

All Frenchmen who were forty in 1960 have had the priceless luck, since reaching their majority, of witnessing or participating in the birth of three regimes, to say nothing of two provisional ones. In 1940, they saw the Third Republic collapse under the blows of the German army; in 1958 they saw the Fourth Republic disappear under the threat of the

French army—which, all things considered, clearly represented a step in the right direction. Connoisseurs by now,
they could assess the three attempts to organize the country's
institutions. To these must be added the thirteen constitutions, drafted with éclat in absolute and final terms, that
France formulated successively within the space of a century
and a half. Under their very eyes a presumably strong—because it was military—power was twice established, first under
Pétain, then under De Gaulle. In addition, they witnessed
the entire career, from beginning to end, from birth to demise, of a political regime based on government by assembly.

One has to go back a hundred and fifty years to find a
generation that had the opportunity to acquire a comparable
political experience. And we certainly haven't seen the end
of it yet.

To such a blasé spectator, to such a tired and skeptical participant, Gaullism seems a transition, and a rather curious
one at that, because it rests on the almost absolute power of
one man who can be a dictator if he chooses but who refrains
from taking advantage of his authority. Actually, because the
regime rests upon one man, it can only be transitory.

A strange nation, France, yet one that disposes of its political system now in one way, now in another. When she
runs up against an obstacle that she cannot surmount by ordinary methods, a problem that cannot be handled in the
traditional way, she secretes and then proceeds to establish
an unusual kind of government, a supreme and provisional
magistracy, with orders to circumvent the difficulty. The
reign of General de Gaulle, born of the Algerian war, began
with a very explicit but arduous mission: to insure decolonization. It continues at present with another mission no less
difficult but equally mandatory: to usher France into the
nuclear age. Everything else, even the construction of a
United Europe, is a matter of mere administration.

Within the space of five years France has withdrawn from a colonial empire that took a century and a half to build and subjected 120 million men to her laws. Simultaneously, she has become a young and dynamic country developing at one of the highest rates ever recorded among the most civilized nations. In 1965–70 she will have twice as many twenty-year-olds as she had in 1950–55.

More Frenchmen are being born every day in a country that is in the throes of great change. Regardless of their social milieu, these people will have one thing in common: the absence of traumatic memories. They are easily irritated by the theoretical aspect of doctrines, the muddleheaded incompetence of Parliaments and political parties. They like order, of course—concrete, thoroughly explored plans, with the mechanics of government operating smoothly and harmoniously. To put it in rather extreme fashion, it doesn't matter a bit to them that Russia is Communist and America capitalist. In their opinion, the state should be run like a huge, complex enterprise, by specialists who do not change jobs every week.

Unlike their fathers, the workers do not feel quite so isolated and oppressed by the collectivity. They are gradually becoming integrated into a nation from which, for perhaps 150 years, they had felt excluded, from a state that had seemed alien. The peasants, for their part, seem inclined to think that the ownership of land no longer is important: what counts is to have modern equipment and markets for what they produce. Youthful businessmen are no longer ashamed of being "bosses," believing as they do that competence provides them with a far better justification for leadership than inheritance. Finally, the cadres, the experts and technicians, are pragmatic, oriented toward progress.

These groups, whose numbers increase daily, naturally include the many who trail behind as well as a small vanguard.

The stragglers struggle desperately to preserve a France that, though temperamentally home-loving and chauvinistic, had once gone off to faraway places to found colonies, a France rich but Malthusian and autarkic, a France of poetry and cathedrals, of great dress designers, perfumes, and red wines that still bears the marks of religious and class strife.

What has all this to do with Gaullism and the Gaullists? All or nothing. All, because Gaullism is a form of government that was rather well-suited to a country in the midst of a great transformation, and it was accepted despite the loss of habits that are dear, despite the inevitable or necessary change. All, because Gaullists constitute the new cadres that are replacing the former elite, because they play upon the lyricism of the turboprop jet, the cult of efficiency, the respect for facts, the penchant for concrete achievements that characterize the French of today.

But, at the same time, this new France has really no relationship to Gaullism: Gaullism did not create her, it merely was satisfied not to prevent her from being born or developing. It does not really control or orient her; it merely administers her as best it can. It does not even have the assurance that it will continue to assume this responsibility to the very end of its course, until 1970–75. Perhaps the Gaullists will be able to establish themselves permanently in the center of the national political scene; the essential precondition, of course, is that their leader will stay where he is for five more years, that during this time he will retain the confidence of the majority of Frenchmen, and that God will grant him life and the people votes. Perhaps the Gaullists will not succeed. But in any event, once the page has been turned, after De Gaulle, new Frenchmen will begin to write the history of a new France.

Part II
The Directory

How To Use the Directory

(✠) Free French Movement

(🏛) Civil Cabinet or General's Special Staff, London-Algiers (1940–44)

(★) Companion of the Liberation

(🦊) Special Services

(🔫) French Resistance

(🏛) Cabinet or Special Staff in Provisional Government, Paris (1944–46)

(💣) Membership in Gaullist party, the R.P.F.—Rassemblement du Peuple Français—(1947–53)

(⚘) Visits to Colombey (1953–58)

(📖) Interviews in Paris (1953—58)

(𝔇) Consultations in Paris (1953–58)

(🐫) Faithful to De Gaulle during "the crossing of the desert" (1953–58)

(🛡) Fall of the Fourth Republic (May 1958)

(🪑) Minister of the Fifth Republic (June 1958–)

(○) Former Minister

(♟) Deputy in the National Assembly

(◎) Former Deputy

(⊠) Senator

(⊘) Former Senator

(📦) Gaullist who held high post under Fourth Republic

(🗝) Membership in official Gaullist party, the U.N.R.—Union pour la Nouvelle Republique—(1958–)

(👢) Latecomer to the U.N.R.

(Ⅰ) Not in U.N.R. but member of other Gaullist movements

(🏠) Cabinet or Special Staff under Fifth Republic

(⊓) Dignitary of the Fifth Republic

(Ⅹ) Specialty

To Understand
the Symbols Fully

THE CROSS OF LORRAINE (✝) is the emblem of the Free French Movement begun by General de Gaulle on June 18, 1940, with a broadcast over the B.B.C., asking Frenchmen to continue the struggle alongside the Allies. It became the symbol of Gaullism.

THE OUTHOUSE* (⌂) is the insignia of someone belonging to the civil cabinet or to the General's special staff, an envied but formidable honor. Indeed, although intimate collaborators can claim public respect and, on a family and personal level, special consideration, in work situations they are often humiliated by a demanding and sometimes rude taskmaster. Furthermore, they are never allowed to forget that they are there to obey, not to have ideas of their own; to serve, not to seek promotion. Often, after they have been thoroughly worn out by their jobs, they are shelved and replaced by others.

The letter L in the outhouse refers to the period of Free France in London (1940–43) and of the French Committee of National Liberation, as well as to the era of the Provisional

* In French, *cabinets*.

government first established in Algiers (1944), and then in liberated Paris (end of August 1944).

THE STAR (★) that adorns the title of Companions of the Liberation is the symbol of high rank in the Gaullist Knighthood. This Order, founded by De Gaulle, never had more than 2000 members and today it has less than 1000 survivors, the last awards having been made in 1948. The Companions were chosen one by one by the General himself from among the bravest or the most representative of the Free French fighters, and also, but in a lesser degree, from among the Resistance fighters within France.

THE WOLF (🐺) is an insignia of those who belong to the special services, and might have been distributed more generously, since Gaullism has always had a predilection for the secrecy, the confidential and clandestine qualities that so strongly marked its origins. But the principal characteristic of a secret agent is precisely secrecy, and it was thought best not to expose too many people to the necessity of having to make denials.

THE MACHINE GUN (🔫) like the plastic bomb was the weapon of the Resistance in France. Possession of a "watering can" was a sign of some importance in the clandestine movement. The machine guns captured from German soldiers were supposedly better weapons than the English or American ones parachuted to fighters; besides, they conferred a special prestige upon their owners.

THE OUTHOUSE (🏠) marked with the letter P for Paris designates the successive cabinets and headquarters of the Provisional government (August 1944–January 1946) and is much more widespread than the machine gun. Actually, almost all the dignitaries of the Fifth Republic, beginning with Michel Debré and Georges Pompidou, were members of De Gaulle's post-Liberation cabinets.

THE GRENADE (🜚) is the weapon that the R.P.F. (Rassemblement du Peuple Français), founded by De Gaulle in 1947 after he resigned from office, would have liked to use to blow up the Fourth Republic. But the General intended to overthrow the "bad regime" exclusively by legal means. Failing in this, he announced the dissolution of the R.P.F. in 1953 and retired to Colombey-les-Deux-Églises to write his *Memoirs*.

THE MOTORCYCLIST (🜚) only rarely preceded the private cars of visitors who came to see the solitary man at Colombey, perhaps because they were often high officials, very anxious to go unnoticed. But each year the visitors dwindled in number until finally they were restricted to the faithful alone.

THE DOOR AJAR (🜚) was opened a little wider than in Colombey for interviews in Paris, where the General came once a week, on Tuesdays, to see people. He stopped at the Hotel La Pérouse, near the Arc de Triomphe at the Etoile— *noblesse oblige!*—and worked in the drab little office, with its tiny entrance hall and its two small rooms, which he maintained on the Rue de Solférino, fifty yards from the Ministry of Defense; there he set up his Parisian secretariat. In actual fact, this secretariat was reduced to Olivier Guichard, the only permanent worker, Colonel de Bonneval, who represented the entire military cabinet, and Jacques Foccart, the attaché in charge of external relations.

THE EAR (🜚) which the General lends to the remarks of visitors, an ear especially attentive to someone he has summoned and whom he wants to consult about some current topic, trend, or situation. Actually, such consultations were rarely requested of Gaullists but rather of politicians, men in the financial or economic world, jurists, high officials, all fairly far removed from the Knighthood. Since they were not bound to De Gaulle and expected nothing from him, they could speak more frankly than his close collaborators or loyal followers. To a goodly number of them a summons from De Gaulle came as a surprise, but nobody had ever been heard to refuse an interview. To be sure, they were addressing a historic personage who, for the occasion, was amiable, charming and tolerant, not a leader of the opposition.

THE CAMEL (🐫) seemed a fitting symbol reserved for the rare Gaullists—and each year their number decreases— who had remained faithful to their chief during that period (1953–58) when he turned his back on political action and seemed definitely to have renounced all hope of acquiring power. Among themselves, the Gaullists speak of this period as "the crossing of the desert."

THE TANK (🛡) appeared on the streets of Algiers during the dramatic night of May 13, 1958, when the French of Algeria (the *"pieds noirs,"* or "black feet," as they were called) revolted against the Fourth Republic and the army joined them. On the following day, tanks also appeared in the streets of Paris and even on the Champs Elysées. This was a decision made by the last government of the Fourth Republic, which announced it was prepared to maintain order and to combat the rebels in Algiers as well as their accomplices in the metropolis. To tell the truth, nobody knew what the troops would do in the event of a clash. While awaiting it—fortunately it never occurred—soldiers camped in the heart of Paris, quietly stressing each syllable of the phrase *Al-gé-rie Fran-çai-se* (three long ones, two short); then toward the end of the month, they changed their chant to *"Vive De Gaulle,"* which, at the very least, indicated a certain lack of enthusiasm for the defense of the Republic against the rebels and against the successor. A very civilized revolution, those May days resulted in no victims other than the regime itself.

THE MINISTER'S ARMCHAIR (🪑) is not as steady as one might think. De Gaulle has been in power since June 1, 1958; he has had two prime ministers in five years; the key words of his regime are stability and continuity. Ah! No more of that terrible cabinet instability that France had experienced for almost a century, with governments, ministers, and policies changing every three months.

No, that's not quite true. Under the preceding Republics governments changed but the same ministers often remained. During the period between the two world wars, power in actuality was divided between three, or at the most, four leaders. Under the Gaullist Republic, the Prime Minister admittedly changes more rarely. But after five years there are more than forty men sporting the title of Former Minister—a turnover that is at least comparable to the consuming waste and instability of yesterday's French Republics.

THE MACAROON (◌) of the former minister is thus widely distributed. A few examples will suffice: From 1958 to 1963, in De Gaulle's Debré and Pompidou cabinets, there were eight successive ministers of National Education, seven ministers of Information, four ministers of Justice, and four of the Interior and Communications, three ministers of Finance, Agriculture, Industry, Public Works . . . During these five years, one man alone remained where he was: Couve de Murville; and his post, the Ministry of Foreign Affairs, is unquestionably an important one. Confronted with such a merry-go-round, the French public knows its political leaders no better than it did before, perhaps even less so, since those of yesterday either returned or remained longer on the cabinet lists. And, of course, foreigners know them even less.

THE SEAT (🪑) of the deputy is only symbolical; actually deputies sit on benches. The numerical, to say nothing of the political, evolution of Gaullism in Parliament is curious. The regime held its first election in November 1958; at one fell swoop more than two hundred deputies of the U.N.R. (Union pour la Nouvelle République), the Gaullist party, entered the Palais Bourbon, seat of the National Assembly. This was the largest contingent belonging to any one group to force to open the doors of Parliament in a single election since the Second Empire and Napoleon III. But splits, quarrels, expulsions gradually reduced the number to 160 Gaullists out of about 500 deputies. Although the constitution that he managed to get adopted was conceived in such a way as to assure him adequate control over Parliament, De Gaulle witnessed with amazement and chagrin the overthrow of the government by the deputies, who thus behaved just as they had always done. And so he dismissed Parliament, decreed its dissolution, and kept the government in his own hands.

The Gaullists came back stronger than before after new elections in November 1962; this time they numbered 233, to be exact. But unfortunately there are 482 deputies in all. The U.N.R. just barely lacked a clear majority.

THE COCKADE (●) of a former deputy is not at all common among the Gaullists. Almost all those who had already served in Parliament at the time of the first Gaullist party, the R.P.F., returned to it wearing the colors of the U.N.R. However, in the elections of 1962, a number of Gaullist deputies were not re-elected; for, strangely enough, a certain number of regions that had voted for De Gaulle in 1958 retired their U.N.R. deputies, while some provinces that had stayed with the opposition in 1958 now rallied to De Gaulle, thus justifying the saying, "Everyone in France has been, is, or will be Gaullist," but not at the same time.

As for former parliamentarians of the opposition, they

are legion. In 1958, about 400 deputies (384, to be exact), who were trying to keep their seats, were swept away by the Gaullist wave.

THE FOOTSTOOL (⚲) of the senator is vastly inferior in dignity to the simple chair that denotes a deputy. The reason for this is simple: In spite of several partial or total renewals of the Senate, this second chamber of Parliament has never contained more than forty Gaullists out of about 300 senators. And the president of the Senate, who is third in the formal order of succession to the throne—oh, pardon me, to the presidency of the Republic—appears as the leader of the opposition.

THE INSIGNIA (⊘) of former senators, therefore, belong only seldom to Gaullists, save for a few who decided to become deputies after having been senators. There is, however, one exception that applies to all parliamentarians. A new stipulation unknown to all the previous constitutions of France—and there have been fifteen in a century and a half —forces parliamentarians to resign from the Chamber or the Senate when they become ministers. But since they change about so often, many who had to leave Parliament to sit in the armchair found themselves very quickly—after a few months—falling between two stools; no longer ministers, they could not return to Parliament where their places had been taken.

THE MESS TIN (⬒) was chosen to designate those Gaullists who had sought or accepted ministerial, high bureaucratic, or prebendal posts and promotion under the Fourth Republic between the dates of the General's departure in 1946 and his return in 1958. De Gaulle himself described them with the contemptuous remark: "They lined up for soup." To eat soup you need a mess tin.

THE SOLDIERS' BOOTS (👢) signify membership in the U.N.R. for similar reasons. This time it was not De Gaulle, but one of the successive secretary-generals of the Gaullist party who declared one day at a congress: "People say we are the General's boots. Well, we are, and we are proud of it." The phrase has remained.

A SOLDIER'S SINGLE BOOT (👢) is the sign for those who, although now absorbed into a single party that is actually called the U.N.R.-U.D.T., come from the small group of "leftist Gaullists" whose official designation was Union Démocratique du Travail. They defended their leftist positions until 1962 when, spurred by the elections, they gave up and joined the Gaullist family. But they are still anxious to preserve the semblance of a particular point of view, so when the real U.N.R. members click their heels like soldiers standing at attention (for that you need two boots), they are content to drag their feet, grumbling a little (like Napoleon's retreating veterans who had only one boot left).

THE ORDINARY BOOT (𝗝) designates the Gaullists who are not members of the U.N.R.-U.D.T., but belong or have belonged to other movements, such as the National Association to Support the Action of General de Gaulle (which, for a time, especially in Algeria, played a certain role). Are they not, as we say, "at the mercy of the general's boot"?

THE OUTHOUSE (🏠) marked with V for the Fifth Republic, is reserved for the members of the civil or military Household. It adorns the names of men who in some cases were similarly honored twice before—in the London and the Liberation cabinets. It also adorns the names of men who today are in prison for treason.

THE LITTLE BENCH (🪑) of the dignitary of the Fifth Republic reminds one of the benches of the hereditary dukes who alone had the right to sit in the presence of the King and were not obliged to doff their hats.

THE KNIFE AND FORK (χ) are the symbols chosen in France by a famous hotel and restaurant guidebook, the *Guide Michelin,* to indicate where the food is good. This guide also uses a good many other symbols and it goes without saying that, in order to establish this directory, the author was inspired by the *Guide*'s ingenious system.

Biographies

ARON, RAYMOND, writer, 58 years old

χ *Intelligence*

✝ 🎖 🎚 🎵

Editor-in-chief of the monthly published in London, *La France Libre,* member of the National Council of the R.P.F. —one of its few thinkers—Raymond Aron gradually separated himself from Gaullism as it lost its doctrinal content and drew closer to power. He has become a firm and, at times, regretful adversary of the regime; he is one of those who are more at ease in opposition than in unconditional devotion.

A lecturer at Cologne and Berlin, a professor at Havre and Toulouse before the war, this *agrégé* of philosophy of the École Normale taught at the Institut d'Études Politiques and at the École Nationale d'Administration before receiving a professorship of sociology at the Faculté des Lettres de Paris. He is one of the most fascinating and reliable of teachers.

A member of the great group that included Camus,

Bourdet, and Ollivier, he too wrote editorials for *Combat* right after the war and subsequently contributed to *Le Figaro;* his rare articles on Algeria appeared on page fourteen, but his economic analyses were always printed on the front page. He is one of the best French newspapermen, with a style as incisive as his ideas are penetrating and, more often than not, daring. He was a Gaullist long enough to warrant inclusion in this dictionary.

BARBEROT, ROGER, colonel and diplomat, 48 years old
✘ *Friendship*

In combat he is an ideal comrade, volunteering for the most difficult assignments, never losing his head, a good pal, always jesting. One is amazed to learn that this infantryman is a graduate of the École Navale, but not at all surprised that his *Croix de Guerre* is adorned with eleven army citations. He is no different in peacetime. For him, any electoral contest is a real battle. Baylot, the former Paris police prefect, learned this to his sorrow.

Roger Barberot represented the leftist Gaullists in the XIV *arrondissement*—a working-class neighborhood—against the former prefect who was a candidate of the conservatives. A tract and an election sheet signed by Baylot reproduced a letter by Jacques Soustelle in which, among other things, he said: "Colonel Barberot is known to be a crypto-Communist orator who specializes in slander against the Algerian army." Incidents and fights ensued, climaxed by a court trial. Barberot did not go alone to the witness box: he was accompanied by twenty Companions of the Order of the Liberation, all ready to intervene. The court decided in his favor. When, late in 1960, he assumed his post at Bangui as French ambassador to the Central African Republic, Colonel Barberot found in the files a telegram sent a few months prior to his arrival; dispatched by a member of Debré's ministry, it cautioned all the African governors against him.

BARRÈS, PHILIPPE, journalist and writer, 67 years old
X   *Illusions*

After twenty years of loyalty, elected as a Gaullist deputy in 1951, a Gaullist candidate in Paris in 1958, in April 1962, on the eve of the Algerian peace, Barrès suddenly had pangs of conscience. Matters became dramatic, he broke with the party, an action doubtless precipitated by the death of his son in Algeria. He deluded himself into believing, as many others had done, that his rebellion would lead to widespread changes, upheavals, perhaps even a split.

His father, the great nationalist writer Maurice Barrès, would have been a true Gaullist. But would he have remained one for long? Would he have broken with the party after so many years? The critic Taine voiced the following opinion of the father, an opinion which the years have belied: "That young Monsieur Barrès will never get any place because he is swayed by two irreconcilable tendencies: a penchant for meditation and a desire for action." The son, a darling of the ladies, prefers the art of conversation to meditation, seduction to action.

BAUMEL, JACQUES, senator, 45 years old
X   *Propaganda*

"Rossini" was the name he assumed during the period of clandestinity when he was an unusually intrepid fighter in the Resistance. The war had interrupted his medical studies, and after a vain attempt to reach England in the wake of the Armistice, he joined the *Combat* movement. In 1943, when *Combat, Franc Tireur,* and *Libération* merged, he became the first secretary-general of the M.U.R. (United Resistance Movement).

When peace came he began an active and brilliant political career as deputy in 1945–46. But twelve years went by before he returned to Parliament as senator for the Seine.

Entirely immersed in Gaullism, he became an expert propagandist, first for the R.P.F., then for the Gaullist U.N.R. (Union of the New Republic). Commissioned in 1949 to stimulate political action within the R.P.F., he was subsequently assigned to the Paris area; then, from 1958 to 1962, he assisted the four general-secretaries of the U.N.R. (Albin Chalandon, Jacques Richard, Roger Dusseaulx, and Louis Terrenoire), and traveled to the United States with Jacques Marette to study Kennedy's electoral campaign. He imitated American methods when he organized the electoral campaign of November 1962 in France and was so successful that he was rewarded with the key position of secretary-general of the U.N.R.—the Gaullist party.

Baumel concentrated on the difficult problem of creating a synthesis between the various conceptions of militant Gaullism. Michel Debré envisaged a great conservative party like Great Britain's, with its study groups, its staff conferences, its careful compilation of dossiers, and its intensive preparations. Jacques Chaban-Delmas, who conceived of a modernized neo-radicalism without well-defined frontiers and whose axis would coincide with the watershed between the right and the left, supplied this notion of an "open" party, a reservoir of cadres rather than a mass organization. From the technocrats, typified by Albin Chalandon, came much of the vocabulary.

To this "cocktail" of so-called "functional" elements,

Jacques Baumel was to contribute the kind of careful effort —today called "efficiency"—that would give life to the heavy party machinery. He thus hoped to see Gaullism survive De Gaulle. For the presidential election, the first in France, since 1848 to take place on the basis of universal suffrage, he made preparations that were influenced by American methods, including a special train for the General.

BENOUVILLE, PIERRE GUILLAIN DE, general, former deputy
✗ *Secret trips*

☦ ★ 🦊 ✈ 🎖 ♟ 🎖 🐪 🚜 ✪

The strangest thing about him is his voice, which is barely audible, high-pitched, and sometimes goes out of control, ending in a squeak. It is scarcely the voice one would associate with a general accustomed to issuing orders. And the man himself can hardly be described as swashbuckling. He is short, pale, with a high balding forehead and very soft blue eyes.

Yet his military past is filled with high deeds and his political career has been quite dynamic; moreover, as a writer he is far from unimportant. In 1940 he ceased fighting eight days after the Armistice; his unit, locked in fierce combat until the very last moment, had pursued the enemy into the Vosges Mountains. His first attempt to escape dates from that period. Taken prisoner twice, once near Düsseldorf, the second time near Gérardmer, he got away and wandered in uniform through occupied France. Covering 850 kilometers on foot, he hid in the woods whenever he felt tracked or threatened. He failed in his third attempt to escape. He had left for North Africa, hoping to reach Gibraltar and from there to get to London, but he was denounced and arrested. Released provisionally, he headed toward Central Africa but was recaptured, repatriated, and interned in France; after spending eighteen months in jail he was tried by a council of war and acquitted on the strength of his 1939–40 war record.

He joined the Free French, enrolled in the secret service, and became a specialist in escape techniques and in the establishment of foreign contacts. Fifty-four times he crossed the frontier clandestinely, directed the M.U.R. (United Resistance Movement), and was then given control of military operations in the southern sector. After participating in the Italian campaign, he returned to prepare for the landings. In 1944 he exchanged his second-lieutenant stripes, received in 1939, for the two stars of a brigadier-general, and a *de* made its appearance before his name.

At the age of nineteen he wrote an essay on Baudelaire and some articles on Chateaubriand, Stendhal, and André Chénier. The author of an excellent book, *Le Sacrifice du Matin* (*Sacrifice in the Morning*), that appeared in 1946—as clear, powerful, and vigorous as its title—he well deserved the success it enjoyed. It was one of the first accounts of the Resistance movement to be published immediately after the Occupation. A political career awaited him. He played an active role in Gaullism and was elected deputy in 1951.

Closely associated with Soustelle, he became a collaborator of Marcel Dassault, the airplane manufacturer (Mystères and Mirages) who gave him managerial positions in his business enterprises and made him editor of his magazine, *Jours de France*. Pierre de Benouville definitely tends to lean toward the right, a militant, powerful right, not a lukewarm conservatism. Temperamentally he remains a man given to clandestine, underground activities, to undercover contacts.

It was altogether natural that he should have become the intermediary between the Gaullist staff and activist groups. When he is thought to be in Paris he is actually in Algiers; he is seen in the streets of Madrid and immediately leaves for Lausanne. Spotted in Ghent, he pops up in London. It was he who organized Jacques Soustelle's escape during the May days; he chartered a plane in Switzerland and, just as it was about to land at the Algiers airport Maison Blanche, he sent the brief cable that was to sow unrest in Algiers and cause an upheaval in the entire political life of France: "General de Benouville to General Massu. I'm landing. Request cars and escort. Governor-general Soustelle aboard with me. Best wishes." A few hours later he returned to France, carrying with him documents, messages, and a long letter addressed to General de Gaulle. He is the traveling salesman of the coup d'état.

A deputy of the Gaullist party in 1958, for four years he submitted to discipline, or seemed to do so at any rate. But in June 1962 he broke dramatically with Gaullism and his earlier loyalty. At Salan's trial he testified: "The accused has kept his sworn oath." Banned by his erstwhile friends, he is now free to revel once again in some new underground activity whose nature and implications will doubtless become clear only when accounts are written of the next revolution.

BIAGGI, JEAN-BAPTISTE, former deputy, 45 years old
ᚷ *Tommy gun, Lewis gun, machine gun, bazooka, etc.*

It is surprising to find this right-wing anarchist intermittently (1944, 1951, 1958) in the Gaullist ranks. He had been a member of the royalist party of the extreme right, the Action Française, and it is said that he never joined the Resistance right after the "phony war," in which he fought as leader of a unit and was seriously wounded. On the contrary, his first loyalty under the occupation was to the Legion of Vichy Veterans, and his first political post was that of delegate in charge of propaganda for the Vichy Veterans' group at Bastia. After the North African landings he went to Paris and executed a turnabout. We next find him in the O.C.M., a civil and military organization, and subsequently with the commandos. During the years following the war he spent his time building up a clientele as a lawyer while playing a short-lived but active role in the Gaullist movement and in the most lively veterans' organizations. In the 1951 and 1956 elections he was a Gaullist candidate but was unsuccessful.

The real legend of Biaggi begins with the Algerian war. A friend of Soustelle's, he accompanied him to Algiers when the governor-general was preparing to leave. He was in the front ranks of the demonstrators on February 6, 1956, haranguing the army veterans who greeted Guy Mollet, then the head of the government, with insults and tomatoes. These tomatoes were to change the Algerian policy of the Fourth Republic which, at that point, abandoned all efforts to seek a peaceful solution and tended more and more toward war.

From then on, Biaggi took the stage and, with obvious delight, gave a fine imitation of a veritable fire-eater. He became an instructor in the use of tommy guns, a revolutionary nationalist, the terror of good people, and a typical Fascist. Everything he did served to advertise his person and his activities.

Having participated actively in and helped to bring about the explosion of May 13, he finally was admitted to the Palais Bourbon during the 1958 Gaullist upswing—something he had been determined to achieve for a long time, even if he had to break down the doors. He had become a Gaullist once again, along with Blocq-Mascart, Debré, and Soustelle, quite opportunely, since this was the moment when De Gaulle climbed back into the saddle. No sooner did he make a few judicial proposals, whose purpose was to safeguard the army from public attack by imposing strict censorship regulations on the press, than he quit the U.N.R. Thereupon he founded the Rassemblement pour l'Algérie Française (known as the R.A.F., a party devoted to keeping Algerian French), and proceeded to play an increasingly active role in all matters concerning Algeria. In 1962 he failed to get himself re-elected.

His friends and his Corsican compatriots allude to "Bat" as a kindhearted man, perhaps somewhat excessive and quick-tempered at times, but a person of amazing courage and wild generosity. His enemies think him either mad or an out-and-out Fascist, ready to make any compromise or commit any act of violence in order to "throttle that bitch" (independent Algeria)—at best an impostor and agitator. His clients consider him an excellent lawyer. The Franciscan monks of the Bastia monastery say he is a good Latinist and a good Christian. To the Gaullists, who have banned him, he is a "hatchet man." He remains nonetheless a member of the Gaullist family.

BILLOTTE, PIERRE, general and deputy, 57 years old

X   *Promoted from lieutenant to three-star general in ten years*

† ▯ ★ ▮ ♣ ▯ ♪ ♣ ☉ + ◈ 👢 ⌐

A lucky soldier with a brilliant career, he rose from the rank of lieutenant to that of divisional general within the space of ten years. His political career was less startling since it took him twelve years to change from a Gaullist of the right to one of the left—such is the public image of General Pierre Billotte. Deputy, minister, and straight party man, his impetuous temperament, occasional arrogance, almost brutal inflexibility, as well as his authority, daring, and courage, are holdovers from his life as an officer. Perhaps all these traits account for the great success of his military career as

well as for certain parliamentary and electoral disappointments.

A soldier he certainly was, and how could it be otherwise
since his is one of the great military families? His father—
General Billotte, military governor of Paris—commanded,
among other units, Lord Gort's British expeditionary force
in 1940. Graduated from Saint-Cyr at the age of twenty, the
recipient of a Staff College certificate, and with a record of
service in the Far East, the Middle East, and Africa, Captain
Pierre Billotte was already a specialist in the use of armor.
Employing heavy tanks, he succeeded in holding up the German advance toward the Ardennes Canal for several weeks,
thus arousing the curiosity of Heinz Guderian, the father of
the Panzer divisions, who paid a visit to this able and tough
adversary in the hospital where he lay wounded.

Once recovered from his wounds and taken to a prisoner of
war camp in Pomerania, Pierre Billotte became the hero of
one of the most spectacular escapes of the entire war. With
a small group of friends he succeeded in reaching the Soviet
Union where all were interned, transferred from a camp to
prison, and detained there until the morning of June 22,
1941. On that day the German invasion suddenly converted
the Russians into allies, and Billotte became first the informal, then the official military representative of Free
France in Moscow. Having left the Oflag in small groups,
their numbers had swelled to two hundred by the time they
arrived in London, where Billotte was appointed General de
Gaulle's chief of staff.

From then on he was to assume, in turn, politico-military
responsibilities and command posts, ascending the rungs of
the hierarchy with record speed. In less than four years he
had exchanged his three stripes for the two stars of a brigadier-general, as head of a "tactical unit" of Leclerc's division
during the interim between the Normandy landings and the

liberation of Paris. In 1948 he celebrated simultaneously his departure for New York to direct the French delegation to the United Nations' Committee of the chiefs of staff, his third general's star, and his fortieth birthday. Four years later, opposing the government's Atlantic policies, he resigned both from his position and from the army, which is rare. He quit "the system" and once again joined the R.P.F. and its leader.

In this way he began the second phase of his career. It started auspiciously when, after a strenuous battle, he triumphed as a candidate for deputy in the elections of June 1951. But he soon left the R.P.F. after voting for Pinay.

The role he played in the discussion between Free France and the Allies, as well as in the preliminary debates over the Atlantic Pact, led him to take a particular interest in the strategy of the West's foreign policy. Thus, in November 1954 he presented the London and Paris agreements to the National Assembly, agreements which replaced the plan for a European Defense Community to which he had been firmly opposed. Eleven months later Edgar Faure, reshuffling his government, put Billotte in charge of national defense. But a few weeks later, when a cabinet crisis ensued, his ministerial activities were interrupted and he was unseated as a deputy.

Once again, in March 1958, he was a candidate in a Paris by-election. He became president of the France-Occident Association, was the animating spirit of various Atlantic movements and committees, and often took a lively and public part in political affairs and in issues involving military honor. In October 1957, at a time when he was neither prominent nor readily tolerated by his peers, Billotte dared as an officer and former general to denounce the use of torture in Algeria. He protested to General Massu in an open letter: "One does not obey orders that are contrary to the rules of war . . . Torture, regardless of the form, must be condemned."

He rejoined the Gaullists of the left upon the advent of the Fifth Republic and helped to found and direct their Union Démocratique du Travail (Democratic Labor Union), whose incisive and persistent spokesman he was. To allay his impatience, he streaked across France, going from meeting to meeting, delivering speech after speech, and writing many articles. He was obviously supremely bored with his thankless role of loyal opponent and peevish Companion of the Order, and the small separate branch of the Gaullist family tree seemed a little like a poor relative in contrast to the wealthy, all-powerful U.N.R.

But in March 1962, on the morrow of the Évian agreements, he was again offered both action and combat. De Gaulle summoned him. He was to be the last "proconsul" of France on African soil. Fully aware that he would be accused, criticized, and attacked by men of every political persuasion, he also knew he would be perhaps suspected or misunderstood by some in his own camp. The blows would exceed the honors by far.

His strategy was to take the offensive. Feverishly, he made preparations for his mission, including a number of startling announcements: since he was to carry the flag he would do so not only with honor but with éclat. It was learned that he would make his entry into Algiers on board a ship of war, as was done during the period of colonization, visit the monuments to the dead, and take up residence at the summer palace, which for months had been abandoned in favor of an entrenched camp at Rocher Noir. These ideas were too fancy, there were too many arrogant pronouncements and altogether too much fanfare to suit De Gaulle, who has never liked his people to be so conspicuous or to attract so much attention. Billotte's appointment was tossed into the wastepaper basket, and the more diplomatic Christian Fouchet was chosen instead. In the November elections, Billotte won a seat in the Assembly—a slight compensation. But he was denied the presidency of an important parliamentary commission and was merely given, and not with the best of grace, the management of a committee whose sole task was to elaborate a doctrine for the Gaullist movement, and whose total effectiveness was precisely nil.*

BLOCQ-MASCART, MAXIME, 69 years old
X   *Nocturnal conspiracies*

Always anticipating a revolution, Blocq-Mascart cannot be taxed with opportunism: he invariably arrives too late for a reign or a regime. Immediately after World War I, in which he participated courageously as an aviator, he published a small book entitled *L'Illusion Capitaliste* (*The Capitalist Illusion*) that predicted a bit prematurely the disappearance of current world leaders. In a second book, *Les Biens de ce Monde* (*Property in Our World*), he philosophized on the subject. Then he was made a manager of several industrial firms.

Not until his forty-sixth year was he able, at long last, to give free rein in the Resistance to his penchant for clandestine activities, to his talent as a born conspirator, but also to his calm, even lofty courage. Blocq-Mascart was involved in every foray, in every undertaking no matter how wild, in every group that, in a feverish, naïvely Machiavellian, and somewhat confused atmosphere, laid plans for the ideal democracy of the future. He became vice-president of the movement he founded, the O.C.M. (Civil and Military Organization), whose initials were used to deride him gently.

---

* Billotte's wife is American-born and he himself is well known at the Pentagon. He has often sought to bridge the gap between French and American military leaders.

(It was called "Où Caser Maxime?"—which literally means, "Where can we find a job for Maxime?")

For he was one of the few underground leaders who was not a Companion of the Order of Liberation. Although he founded and briefly directed an important daily, the *Parisien Libéré*, others, not he, reaped the rewards; and although he presided over the Alliance Française, it was merely an honorary and temporary position. With all the arrogance of a blueblood, but also with a penchant for irritability, he defended the rights of the Resistance fighters against De Gaulle—a blank look in his eyes, invective on his lips. But when De Gaulle left politics, he drew closer to him although he often quarreled with the leaders of the R.P.F.

The thirteenth of May gave him his second wind. He was made a special duty councillor of state and, according to his own favorite phrase, he protected the law during the day and undermined it at night. It was at his home that the leaders of the conspiracy met with General Cogny and his friend Griotteray, with Michel Debré and J. B. Biaggi. But no sooner had the conspirators brought De Gaulle back to power than Maxime Blocq-Mascart once again went his own way. We find him working on the committee to draft a new constitution, yet shortly thereafter his name appeared on the list of declared enemies of the regime; always enamored of plots and putsches, he flirted with the activists and got into difficulty with every opposition group. He quoted Teilhard de Chardin and Lanza del Vasto in turn, invoked *Antigone* as well as the deputy Baudin, all the while preparing for the advent of the Sixth Republic which, in all likelihood, he will found only to become in the end its sworn enemy.

BOEGNER, JEAN-MARC, ambassador, 50 years old
X *Discreet and delicate missions*

✝ 𝕡 ⚑ ▥ 𝔇 🐫 Ⓜ ⌐

His Quai d'Orsay manner, his extreme courtesy, a certain cold solemnity—all this may lead one to think of him as a diplomat of the old school. But this would be a serious mistake. His somewhat conventional façade conceals an enthusiastic Gaullist, a convinced liberal whose freedom of mind and expression is altogether surprising. A confirmed Gaullist he certainly is, from the time of his commitment to the F.F.L. (Free French Forces) in 1941, which led to his recall as embassy attaché and—*horresco referens*—even to the loss of his French nationality. Only a loyal supporter would have been assigned to the posts he held, none of them easy. He was General de Gaulle's diplomatic adviser in 1958–59, ambassador to Tunis the following year when tension between that city and Paris was at its height, and representative to the European Community when the clash with Brussels occurred and when the policy of grandeur reached its peak.

BOISLAMBERT, CLAUDE HETTIER DE, 57 years old,
Great Chancellor of the Order of Liberation
X *A round trip in 1940*

✝ 𝕡 ★ ✪ ⚑ ▥ 🐫 ✪ ⌐

In 1940 he was the hero of a strange adventure which, among all the exploits of the Free French, deserves special attention. After having fought in Lorraine, Belgium, and the Somme, he reached London in 1940. Thereupon De Gaulle appointed him to his staff, then made him associate director of his cabinet.

In August, in this capacity, he was sent to Africa with the

future General Leclerc and Pléven, future president of the Council. All three men laid the plans for the A.E.F. and the Cameroons to join Free France. Then he returned to Dakar to organize the Resistance. And it was there, while Admiral Cunningham's British fleet was cruising around with De Gaulle on board, that he was taken prisoner. Transferred to France, judged, condemned to hard labor for life, he was interned at Gannat. Thus he was one of the first Gaullists, and one of the most prominent, to fall into Vichy's hands. What makes his story rather special is that he escaped from Gannat and managed to get back to London, which he had left only a few months before in order to arouse Africa.

After the Liberation, he went from Parliament to various proconsulates. A deputy in 1944, he served as governor of the Rhenish Palatinate from 1946 to 1951; during the next five years, he was again a deputy; in 1960 he became France's ambassador to Mali, then to Senegal, after the Federation of Mali blew up. Finally, during the worst moment of 1962, he was given one of the supreme responsibilities of the Court: the post of Chancellor of the Order of Liberation, the Gaullist Knighthood, which made him a field marshal of sorts in the unwritten hierarchy of the Companions of the Order of Liberation.

BOISSIEU DE LUIGNE, ALAIN DE, colonel, 49 years old
X   *Son-in-law*

✝ ⬛ ★ ⬛ ⬛ ⬛ ⬛ 🐪 🛡 ⬛ ⬛

On January 3, 1946, Commander Alain de Boissieu married the daughter of his general, a very standard procedure except for the fact that the general was De Gaulle, who for another two weeks presided over the Republic's Provisional government.

A brilliant debut was in store for this young officer who

graduated from Saint-Cyr in 1938, was taken prisoner in 1940, escaped the following year from Oflag II D in Pomerania and, via the U.S.S.R., rejoined Free France and received quick promotion. He had fought in all the campaigns, was a Companion of the Order of Liberation and a member of his future father-in-law's military cabinet.

Yet seventeen years went by and he still had only two additional stripes. Did the Fourth Republic intend to make him pay for his overly brilliant marriage? Salan, a "Republican" general at this time, appointed him director of his military cabinet in Algiers.

The Fifth Republic did little to hasten his promotion. Yet he had never departed from strict Gaullist orthodoxy. How could it be otherwise since he spends his weekends at Colombey, is the only person outside the government privileged to invite the Chief of State, whom he calls "father," to his family dinner table or to his apartment on the Rue Daru, near the Étoile?

BOLLARDIÈRE, JACQUES DE, general, 56 years old
X̄ *The tough fight*

十 ★ ◨

"Bolo" had one of the most brilliant service records in an army which comprised a goodly number of crack soldiers. He fought in all the campaigns: Morocco with the Foreign Legion; Norway in 1940; Dakar, Gabon, Eritrea, Egypt, Palestine, Syria, Libya; and Tunisia with the twenty-third Armored Division. He was parachuted into France in 1944, into Holland in 1945, into Angkor to fight for five years in Indochina. After that he served in Algeria.

In 1957, he finally said no. He broke the silence imposed by discipline and wrote in *l'Express,* Mendès-France's paper, denouncing "the dramatic aspects of the revolutionary war we are facing and the terrible danger entailed in losing sight, for reasons of urgency or expediency, of those moral values which until now have been solely responsible for the greatness of our civilization and our army." Then he asked to be relieved of his command.

Bourgès-Maunoury, his comrade in 1940 during the days of Free France, and later Minister of National Defense, began to spread the rumor that the General had quit his command to visit his ailing sister; then he claimed that so many years of combat had made Bollardière extremely nervous. Finally, he sentenced him to sixty days of detention in a fortress. "Bolo's" career was ruined. In Germany and in the A.E.F. he found friendship; but there were no more command posts for him. Triumphant Gaullism, which had awarded so many stars to factious, rightist generals, did not dare to impose upon them the presence of a man who had broken the law of their clan. It did not even dare to send him back to Algeria, something which De Gaulle had promised. And so, regretfully, he left the army. He now lives in Quimperlé in Brittany with his five daughters and his memories, resigned and forgotten.

BONNEVAL, GASTON DE, colonel, count, 52 years old
✗ *Loyalty*

His life is divided into two parts, before and after. Before —until 1945—he was a very conventional graduate of Saint-Cyr who served in the Foreign Legion, fought courageously in the Resistance, and then, seized by the Gestapo, was deported to Germany. After—since his return from deportation in 1945—he has lived in De Gaulle's shadow and, depending upon the circumstances, carries his briefcase, his hat, or his army cap, opens and closes doors for him, ushers in his visitors, refills his drinking glass, breathes when De Gaulle breathes, and weathers his tempers. When the General has a cold, Bonneval sneezes; he laughs when the great man is gay, and looks funereal when the wind blows the other way.

He followed the head of the Provisional government wherever he went, accompanied the President of the R.P.F. on all his trips, during all official ceremonies stood at his side, and shared exile with the General when he retired to Colombey. He alone was the entire "military household." He came back to the Élysée Palace as orderly, aide-de-camp, messenger, errand boy, scout, even as telephonist or secretary when necessary—in short, he is the general factotum. He rose from captain to lieutenant-colonel without ever assuming new duties and, except for the Republican Guard, has not seen a private soldier for twenty-three years.

But he is a member of the family. As she knits in the company of Madame de Gaulle, his wife discusses the marriages that take place among the petty provincial nobility to which both women and their husbands belong. The Bonnevals' seven children spend their vacations at the family estate of Thaumiers, part of which burned down during the latter half of 1962. Life unfolds calmly and monotonously behind the curtains of History.

BOULIN, ROBERT, Secretary of State, 43 years old
X *An acceptable representative*

Twelve years of militant activity in the Gaullist movement fully deserved such rewards as membership in the National Assembly, the mayoralty of Libourne, and half of a portfolio. Boulin was appointed to the Ministry of Repatriation, then to that of the Budget. But secretaries of state are few and his assignments made him competent in many areas.

Also, since the Senate has no ministers (this is how its speaker is punished), Robert Boulin has the heavy responsibility of sitting alone on the government bench in the hemicycle of the Luxembourg throughout all parliamentary sessions. He is the government representative with whom De Gaulle would like to saddle the Senate.

What is more, he discharges this task creditably, but in so doing he has established an impressive precedent. Is it not true that the example he sets his colleagues in the government leads them to entrust the task of representing them to secretaries of state and to abstain from appearing in the National Assembly? In this they are imitating many deputies and senators, who rarely venture beyond the library or restaurant.

BROUILLET, RENÉ, ambassador, 54 years old
Χ   *Barometer*

It was Georges Bidault, with whom he collaborated intimately during the Resistance (Bidault was then head of the National Council of the Resistance), who introduced this well-bred graduate of the École Normale to General de Gaulle. Brouillet began his career at the Treasury. As assistant chief of the presidential cabinet of the Provisional government that was set up on the eve of Liberation, René Brouillet subsequently embarked on a diplomatic career.

Early in June 1958, De Gaulle summoned him to an important and sensitive post: secretary-general for Algerian affairs. When the Household was transferred to the Élysée, he became chief of the presidential cabinet.

To find out whether the atmosphere is favorable, whether the General is in good form and things are going well, one has only to look at René Brouillet. If he is beaming, gay, if he talks about poetry, historic old houses, the province of

Auvergne, then all is well. But if, on the contrary, things are going badly, he is pale, tired, ailing. He is the barometer of the Household: faithful, devoted, sentimental. He accepted his appointment to Vienna, but, although it took him away from the Élysée and gave promise of calmer days than those he had known, he acquiesced with a mixture of pleasure and pain. Alas! For a while Austria became the privileged refuge of the French activists. The French ambassador had to remonstrate repeatedly with the Austrian government. On occasion his complaints concerned Georges Bidault, who had the good taste to choose Germany as his domicile but then found himself obliged to emigrate overseas. Now René Brouillet can smile again.

BUIS, GEORGES, colonel, 51 years old
X   *A book in his haversack*

† ★ ◰ 🐫

He is a soldier who rendered exceptional service to his country but whose biography defies accurate description: Saint-Cyr, the Levant, the Free French Forces, the Second Armored Division of Normandy, Berchtesgaden, Indochina, Morocco, Iran, Algeria, the military staff, five superb citations, the Cross of the Knighthood, five full stripes . . .

For this warrior, as indeed for his ancestors during the period of the Fronde, literature constantly served as an accompaniment to the military profession. In the *Histoire de Vasco* by Georges Schéhadé, General Mirador says to Lieutenant Septembre: "I respect you, lieutenant, because in secret you think . . ." Septembre, in actuality Buis himself, is used as a model by Georges Schéhadé, his best friend ever since they served under Catroux at Bayreuth.

In secret? Not really. In 1961, George Buis, returning from Algeria where he had just assumed an important command, published a book, *La Grotte* (*The Grotto*), a romanticized version of the Algerian war that reconstructs better than anything else the very special psychological climate of this absurd and, in certain respects, baroque conflict in which he had participated as an officer responsible for one sector.

The jury that awards the Renaudot literary prize reportedly considered his name seriously, but in the end decided to give it to someone else. This was during the good old days of the O.A.S., when it was rather risky to honor a Gaullist.

BURIN DES ROZIERS, ÉTIENNE, ambassador, 50 years old.

X   *The Dignitary of the Household*

† 🏠 📰 ⚱ 🏛 ⚖ 🐫 🏺 🚪

Everyone knows that the General does not like new faces. For almost a quarter of a century a few men, who were among the handful of Free French in June 1940, have taken turns serving at his side. One of the oldest and closest, besides Geoffroy de Courcel, Gaston de Bonneval, and Gaston Palewski, is Étienne Burin des Roziers.

In London, where he was a junior embassy attaché, he served as an orderly. In Paris in 1945, he was on De Gaulle's staff. Today he is the secretary-general of the Élysée. He had been France's envoy in Warsaw and was recalled to occupy the post. But make no mistake: in the unwritten hierarchy, the dignitaries of the Household are more important than many ministers. Georges Pompidou, chief of De Gaulle's cabinet in 1958, was one day made Prime Minister even though he had never held any government post. When he arrived at the Élysée, Étienne Burin des Roziers was tempted to make a few changes, to open the windows and doors wider in order to let a little fresh air into the close atmosphere of the Court. But he soon encountered so-called traditional habits, a certain penchant for solitude, and the rigidity of protocol. A few provincial notables, however, were invited to official receptions, and the supposedly representative delegations that were received annually at the Palace were slightly broadened to include leaders of high finance and private enterprise, as well as intellectuals and artists. Thanks to Étienne Burin des Roziers, a smile, a certain affability, have come to attenuate the stiffness and to lessen the solemnity somewhat. Things being what they are, this is no small accomplishment.

CABANIER, GEORGES, admiral, 57 years old
✗ *The "Ruby"*

✝ ★ ◫ ♪ 🐪 ◍ ⊢

As early as June 1940, he brought to Free France its first submarine, the *Rubis*. Such a feat was not likely to be soon forgotten, nor was it. In 1945 De Gaulle appointed him to the French delegation at the San Francisco Conference, then to the finest command in the navy: the École Navale. Under the Fourth Republic his career continued in only average fashion. But De Gaulle, after his return to power, gave him the strategic post of Chief of Staff of National Defense on June 1, 1958, then appointed him squadron commander in December of the same year, and finally Chief of the Naval General Staff in 1960.

Paradoxically, neo-Gaullism was to find its most reliable support in the navy rather than in the army or even the air force, although sailors were rare in Free France, the overwhelming majority of them having chosen Vichy, together with Darlan, out of sheer hatred for the English. During the difficult period of the sixties, when the work of equipping the fleet at Toulon might have alerted the generals in

Algeria, when discipline was trampled underfoot and Parisians scrutinized the sky in hourly expectation of parachutists, Admiral Cabanier stood by with his ships ready to defend the government against the rebels.

This was not forgotten nor will it ever be: Cabanier was given an intimate luncheon for forty guests at the Élysée when he retired, and probably will have won a flattering allusion in the fourth volume of the *Memoirs*.

CAPITANT, RENÉ, deputy, 62 years old
X *More Gaullist than De Gaulle*

All the Gaullists know him—for a long time and very early he was more Gaullist than De Gaulle himself. Every law student also knows his name; he is the son of the famous jurist Henri Capitant, author of those civil law manuals over which an entire generation has slaved.

During the "phony war" he became acquainted with Colonel de Gaulle at Fifth Army Headquarters. This professor of the law faculty of Strasbourg, president of the vigilance committee of Alsatian intellectuals, flaming anti-Fascist orator —enthusiastic, courageous, but given to utopianism—and the officer of traditional outlook, prophetic and icy, already destined for an incomparable fate, took to each other at once. While one, speaking from London, appealed to Frenchmen to pursue the struggle, the other, at Clermont-Ferrand, founded one of the first Resistance groups from which the clandestine *Combat* movement was to be created.

He was appointed to Algiers in 1941; his students still recall that they were asked to stand up and observe a minute of silence in honor of the Yugoslav Resistance or in commemoration of some Allied victory. His animosity against Giraud, after the North African landings was no less fierce than was his earlier hostility toward the Vichy regime. It was Giraud who dismissed him in April 1943 for "anti-national activity."

Six months later he became Commissioner of National Education and remained a member of the Provisional government until the end of 1945. He founded the first Gaullist nucleus in the Palais Bourbon, the Democratic and Social Action group, and of course he joined the R.P.F. as soon as it was created. He became a leader of the *Rassemblement,* and De Gaulle made him president of his National Council. Relentlessly, Capitant proceeded to develop a theory of Gaullism that was both doctrine and mystique, and which he regarded as democratic, anti-Fascist, and revolutionary. He availed himself of every opportunity, when making a speech, to reiterate feverishly his dearest theses: hail to 1789 whose principles had never been applied; a curse on 1793 whose evil still endures; vive Rousseau, a true prophet; a curse on Abbé Sieyès, the wretched imitator; hurrah for total democracy which is above all total liberty for the citizen and is therefore incompatible with capitalism.

We can hear him at congresses proclaiming that "juridical analysis confirms almost entirely the Marxist analysis, or at any rate its critical part." Bankers, prominent citizens, wealthy bourgeois, and officers who constitute the nucleus of the Gaullist clientele, or at all events people its staff, shivered deliciously at the thought of spearheading a revolution. This inflamed orator was the only one who did not seem to realize that he was preaching in the wilderness and that he would soon become a source of embarrassment.

Was it his determination to refute the absolute, his stubborn search for a doctrine, that cost him his seat as deputy in 1951? He returned to the university and, after a few capricious excursions, again sounded off. When Al Boumendjel, a lawyer from Algiers who had been his student, "committed suicide" between interrogations in March 1957, he interrupted his lectures for two months. In a letter that was made public, this gesture was made to appear as a protest against "the atrocities of repression." Penalized, dismissed, and exiled to Tokyo as the director of the Franco-Japanese Institute, he missed the "revolution" of May 13, which doubtless would have filled him with both hope for the future and disappointment in the present.

Back in France in 1960, he gave a fresh demonstration of his independence of mind, his determination to swing the Gaullists leftward; to the horror of all good people, he became for a few months the legal adviser of Farès, who presided over the provisional Algerian executive from the Evian accords to independence. Finally, in November 1962, he entered Parliament, having earned a seat as deputy, and what a seat it was! His constituency was the Latin Quarter. Once again his faith was put to a hard test; he presided over the Legal Commission of the National Assembly, whose primary function was to confirm the special tribune which had been set up to fix sentence against rebels, initiate constitutional reforms, and supervise the general administration of the Republic—hardly an easy task even for a revolutionary jurist.

CATROUX, DIOMÈDE, deputy, 47 years old
ɣ *To dispose of Jean Médecin*

A nephew of the General, he was active in the Resistance and joined the Free French in 1943. He belonged to several ministerial cabinets—those of his uncle, of Christian Pineau, and of André Malraux—before embarking on a brief diplomatic career that was interrupted when he joined the R.P.F., where he assumed responsibility for its press and propaganda services. Later, he became a deputy for the Maine-et-Loire.

In the Palais Bourbon, he joined the "young Turks" who supported Mendès-France, despite obstacles and party disapproval, and was named his Secretary of State for Aviation, then for Rearmament. Temporarily distracted by business concerns, he returned to the National Assembly in 1962.

His great ambition was to end Jean Médecin's electoral dictatorship, which was already gravely impaired by Gaullist successes, and to wrest from him the mayoralty of Nice.*

CATROUX, GEORGES, general, 86 years old
✗ *Difficult assignments*

✝ ◻ ★ ▣ ▦ ◖ ⊘ 🐪 ☉ 𝙹 ⌐

The following is an excerpt from the first volume (*The Appeal*) of General de Gaulle's war *Memoirs*:

On my return I was to discover a noteworthy source of encouragement. It was caused by the arrival of General Catroux. When he came to London after I left for Africa, the professional pessimists suspected the British of trying to use this army general, accustomed to important assignments, as a means of bargaining, while the punctilious conformists wondered if he really would be willing to take orders from a mere brigadier. He had been to see Churchill several times and there was a good deal of gossip about these interviews, in which it appeared that the Prime Minister did indeed suggest that Catroux take my place, not in order to let him try his hand, but rather to pursue the traditional policy of divide and rule . . .

Thereupon Catroux arrived at Cairo. At dinner I raised my glass in honor of this great chief for whom I had always

---

* Catroux is the Director of United Aircraft in France and has been active in establishing close contacts between the French and American aircraft industry. He worked especially hard at developing the French helicopter industry after studying American methods and, in exchange, acquainted the United States with French means of troop transport.

felt a deferential friendship. Very generously and simply he answered that he would place himself under my command. Eboué and all the others present understood that in Catroux's eyes De Gaulle now stood above considerations of rank, that he was invested with a power that could no longer be subordinated to any hierarchical system. No one could mistake the weight of his example. When, after discussing his mission with him, I parted from General Catroux near the plane that was to take him back to Cairo, I felt that he was leaving a greater man than when he came.

His career as a soldier, administrator, and diplomat, from Morocco to the Middle East and Indochina, followed the imperial road. Nothing was to be spared him under De Gaulle. He commanded the Free French in the Middle East during the Syrian affair; he was the Gaullist spokesman who negotiated with Giraud in 1943; and Jacques Soustelle, who mistrusted him and occasionally opposed him in secret, described him at that time as "a brilliant negotiator whose character and every quality make him lean heavily toward negotiation." When disturbances erupted in Lebanon, off he went, endowed with full powers. Instability returned after the Liberation, and disorders broke out in Algeria, in Tunisia; General Catroux was appointed Minister for North Africa. The Cold War loomed—he left for Moscow as ambassador. Upon his return in 1948, would he at last find peace in the seemingly uneventful post of governmental adviser? A speech on Indochinese affairs, but primarily the ties that bound him to De Gaulle sufficed to make him lose it.

Did this mean retirement? Not at all. The Fourth Republic, which named him Grand Chancellor of the Legion of Honor, appealed to him whenever difficulties arose, and the Fifth Republic was to do likewise. A determined believer in a liberal solution for the Maghreb, he left the Gaullist party in 1952 because he was not in agreement with its atti-

tude toward Tunisian and Moroccan problems; the following year he was declared *persona non grata* and practically
forbidden by General Guillaume to visit Casablanca. In
1955 the government sent him to Antsirabe to negotiate with
the Sultan Mohammed Ben Youssef for his re-enthronement
and Moroccan independence. In 1956 Guy Mollet appointed
him Minister for Algeria, but he never assumed the post
because, on February 6 at Algiers, the Premier was attacked
with those famous tomatoes that transformed the entire
policy of France. After Dien-Bien-Phu, he was president of
a commission empowered to fix responsibility for the fiasco
in the Indochinese affair. In 1961, at the age of eighty-four,
he agreed after the April putsch to sit on the high military
court that condemned the rebellious generals—Challe, Zeller, Bigot, Petit, Nicot, Gouraud, and, *in absentia,* Salan,
Jouhaud, and many others. He probably isn't through yet.

CECCALDI, ROGER, colonel, 50 years old
✗ *The gunner of Koufra*

✝ ★ ▥

The invitation read: "General de Gaulle requests his
Companion Roger Ceccaldi to do him the honor of attending
the reception given on the occasion of the anniversary of the
18th of June . . ." On the envelope was written: "Please
forward"; and so the address was crossed off and replaced
by another, the Fort de l'Est of Saint-Denis. Despite his arrest, and although he was waiting to appear before the high
military court that was to sentence him to five years in prison
with reprieve for his participation in the Algiers putsch,
Colonel Roger Ceccaldi nonetheless remained, in June 1961,
a Companion of General de Gaulle.

This title, like the green and black ribbon that denotes
it, was acquired toward the end of 1961 when Ceccaldi, with

four hundred men and a single cannon, took the post of Koufra, in the desert of Libya, that was being defended by five thousand Italians. And he earned both title and ribbon again at Bir-Hakeim where, as one of those who fought the last stand, he was seriously wounded and taken prisoner, only to escape two days later and join the Allied forces. He was in Paris with those who attacked the Hotel Meurice, in Berchtesgaden to capture Hitler's eyrie, in Indochina, Madagascar, Algeria, Suez . . .

The following are excerpts from his trial.

The Accused: General Zeller came to my command post. I had never seen him before. He gave the impression of a chief visiting people who were on his side . . .

The President: Did you ask him for news of General Saint-Hillier?

The Accused: Yes. I said to him: "This affair that began with the arrest of General Saint-Hillier is a monstrous stupidity." He answered evasively: "I will do what is necessary . . ." Then I saw General Sauvagnac, who exclaimed: "What! Are you arresting me?" I answered: "This is no time for jokes." He suggested taking me in his Peugeot to see General Gouraud. I accepted. When we passed in front of the tanks, he said: "They are symbolic." I answered, "I certainly hope so."

The President: And did you see General Gouraud?

The Accused: Yes. He received me graciously. I asked him for orders. He merely inquired about my intentions. I replied: "I intend to carry out your orders."

The President: Did he seem to hesitate?

The Accused: It's hard to tell what General Gouraud is thinking.

The whole story of the army and especially of the brave officers whose names are mentioned in this book is summed up in these few answers.

CHABAN-DELMAS, JACQUES, president of the National
Assembly, 48 years old
X   *Charmer*

☩ ❑ ★ ⚐ ⬟ ⚱ ▯ ♪ ⛟ ☉ + ⬡ ⌘ ⬥ ⊓

In his own way, each of the great dukes of Gaullism brings
his historic personage to the center of the stage. Debré is
Saint-Just, burning with passion, aggressive and uncompromising. Pompidou evokes a Father Joseph whom the king
would have made into a Richelieu; he is reassuring in his
simplicity, his flexibility, but behind his apparent self-efface-
ment he goes his own way, always making ever more sure
of his influence. He has already assumed the air of executor
of the General's last will and testament; tomorrow he will
be the disciple and spiritual son, and soon perhaps the privileged heir. Soustelle thinks of himself as Cinq-Mars and may
incur a similar fate. Fouchet resembles Berthier telling the
marshals: "Nobody knows HIS thoughts and our duty is to
obey." Fouccart is the Fouché of the regime . . .

Well then, how does Chaban-Delmas see himself? As Ney,
some say, thinking of the twenty-nine-year-old general who
rose up out of the clandestine or revolutionary struggle.
Those who knew Chaban-Delmas when he was successively
or simultaneously a radical deputy and leader of the Gaullist
party, a minister under Mendès-France, Mollet, or Gaillard,
and working to undermine the Fourth Republic, a May 1958
conspirator attempting to destroy parliamentary traditions,
or a trustee and guardian of those same traditions, liken him
to Talleyrand. The gossips say he is a Deschanel or Felix
Faure, adding that one day he will succeed them. But this is
merely a game.

The truth is that he is a happy man. To be happy, you
have to be lucky, and he is. You have to know how to use
your luck, and he does. But luck alone does not explain

how, after several dangerous missions, performed for the Resistance, he could have passed the examinations for inspectors of finance six months later in Paris (March 1943); nor how he could have received an appointment to the military delegation of Free France in London (October 1943); or how it happened that eight months later a decree issued by the Algiers Committee (May 15, 1944) made him a brigadier-general; nor how, less than half a year later, he could have become Chief of General Inspection for the army (November 1944). Luck alone does not account for the fact that for seventeen uninterrupted years he was a deputy for the Gironde and for sixteen mayor of Bordeaux, always re-elected to both positions. And it was not luck that enabled him, after presiding over the Gaullist parliamentary group in the Palais Bourbon, to become a minister of the Fourth Republic the following year, and to continue in this capacity for thirty months, only to receive the second highest position in the Gaullist regime.

To succeed in all these things one has to have a steady hand, a cool head and a good deal of know-how. He has all that. It is surprising to hear him speak most conventionally, at times, proclaiming obvious truisms, uttering vacuous statements, confining himself to official phrases. He lacks neither imagination, style, nor a sense of reality—quite the contrary. But he has learned that you will never be reproached for a speech that fits the circumstances, for the kind of eloquence appropriate for the end of a banquet, but you will be slapped down for a phrase such as "from now on Hitler no longer has even the hope of acquiring power" (Léon Blum, the Socialist leader in 1932), or "the iron ore road is cut off" (Paul Reynaud, head of the government in 1940), or finally, "no more enemies on the left." Far better to be elliptical, at the risk of seeming conformist or even insipid, than to be overly precise and brilliant. He also knows that in politics only a strong position counts and that all the rest—clear-sightedness, dependability, intransigence —are of no avail. Influence depends on the extent to which the controls are in your hands, on the favors you can do and the trouble you can cause. It is a good thing to be discreet about such things, to have your way unobtrusively. You can then be sure of a gratitude or respect all the more impressive because all the people involved are in the same boat, and you have obeyed the unwritten laws of your milieu.

Jacques Chaban-Delmas has never drawn public attention to the quiet and effective support he gave to many of the Fourth Republic's premiers. He is silent about his frequent interviews with General de Gaulle. He has never boasted that it was he who organized the "workshops" for youthful colonels that were designed to undermine the regime of which he was the Minister of Defense. He is very careful to say nothing about the closed luncheon meetings that the principal Gaullist leaders, the princes of the regime, hold once a week, usually on Mondays, at the Hotel de Lassay, headquarters of the speaker of the National Assembly. He has never flaunted his hesitation—it didn't last long, to be sure —on the evening of May 13, 1958 at Bordeaux when, in a hurry to reach Algiers, he decided to head for Paris and to play the revolution legally. He has never revealed that during a day of very tense argument he managed to dissuade Jacques Soustelle from going to Algiers, nor does he mention his own refusal to accept an official mission to Algeria despite the insistence of Gaillard and Pflimlin. You don't have to worry about him; he is the soul of discretion and, whether fighting or supporting them, he never betrays his peers, his leaders.

And so when he opposed Paul Reynaud openly—he couldn't do otherwise since there was a public vote—in order to obtain the presidency of the Assembly, the wink of an eye was enough for all men of good will, whether Gaullists or not, to reach a common accord (against the wishes of the General himself, who wanted him only for a minister like the others, just a minister among others) and insure his triumph.

His election methods are quite simple and conventional, but not as easy to apply as they might seem. They consist in always talking loudly in favor of union, in quietly disrupting traditional center and rightist parties, and in reaching an agreement with eventual leftist competitors. All the cork and lumber aristocracy, all the commercial world of Bordeaux are represented in cleverly chosen proportion at the Municipal Council and in the Center of Regional Expansion. A solid team of dynamic and determined propagandists and agents, sometimes a little alarming, play up the candidate's well-known personal charm for the benefit of women voters, young and old, his bold policy of systematic borrowing, a promise that Bordeaux will obtain credits and subsidies thanks to the influence of a man of national stature, regardless of the kind of regime—all this insures his sway and explains his continuance in office. Of course you need luck, but how persistent, how shrewd he is!

If we have expatiated at length on the local aspects of his career we have done so because the key to his success lies there and nowhere else. In losing a mayoralty or a parliamentary election a politician loses everything—take Mendès-France some time ago and Paul Reynaud more recently. But we have also done so because electioneering methods are inevitably the same at the national level. The run-of-the-mill deputy can be two-faced—a Dr. Jekyll in Paris and a Mr. Hyde in his own constituency; he can pose as a moderate leftist in one place and as a man of the right in another. A real leader cannot oppose the secretary-general of an important political party and at the same time reach an understanding with his local counterpart; he cannot join forces with ministers of a rival party and then crush their local candidates and cadres. He has to choose. A formal or tacit agreement at the top signifies at the bottom either the kind of discreet support that will not compromise him or at least a well-intentioned neutrality. Inversely, local support helps to insure national support. This is not only the rule but the custom: the elevator goes up or down when the button is pushed. Jacques Chaban-Delmas always sends the elevator down.

His desire to please, to which the voters of Bordeaux react favorably, is apparently ineffective when he is competing with leading politicians, and it could, paradoxically, be a handicap in a national election. The mayor's charm certainly affects the voting of the elderly in the Cheverus home for old people; his prestige as a former international rugby player impresses the spectators at the municipal stadium whenever important games are being played; because of his rank in the reserves, he can speak to veterans in their own language; his prestige as an Inspector of Finance recommends him to the attention of the Gironde industrialists when he discusses economic matters; finally and above all, many women of Bordeaux have a weakness for him because of his slim elegance, even though the first woman candidate on his municipal list was placed thirty-third when only twenty were to be elected.

But the rub is that the important political leaders are not very sensitive to this kind of charm, nor are they easily impressed. And the strange thing is that the ten million Frenchmen who watch television when something special is on the screen do not seem to react like the voters, both male and female, of Bordeaux. Is Chaban-Delmas too obviously striving for effect, is his gallantry excessive, his reputation exaggerated, or is the lukewarm response due to a lack of skill and experience on television? In any case, his charm does not work, the women are not swayed by his eloquence and the men are not convinced by his arguments. This is a serious handicap. But his clear-headed, practical common sense will doubtless lead the Gaullist charmer, Jacques Chaban-Delmas, to take note and rectify all this in the near future.

CHALANDON, ALBIN, banker, 43 years old
X   *"Planned" economy*

Attractive, distinguished, very British in appearance, he gives the impression of being the perfect Inspector of Finance who has given up a poorly paid public life for a well paid private one. His biography is impressive. In 1943 when he was twenty-three, he commanded five hundred *maquis* near Orléans; he served in the army that liberated Paris and received the ribbon of the Legion of Honor.

In 1945, after taking a degree in philosophy, he became an Inspector of Finance. For a few weeks he was a member of Léon Blum's cabinet (Socialist), then of René Mayer's (Liberal), and finally joined the Gaullist party, which soon named him delegate-at-large to the workers' action committee, believe it or not. Author of the comprehensive "Chalandon Report" on the nationalized aviation industry, he became, in 1949, the administrator of the African branch of an important bank in Algiers. Three years later, when he was thirty-two, he was made general director of the Banque Commerciale de Paris. In five years it increased its business tenfold, becoming the bank of the Dassault group. Simultaneously, he administered other enterprises and became president and general director of a powerful Franco-Belgium chain of supermarkets.

In 1958 the newly created U.N.R. entrusted its exchequer to this financier, and in the following year it gave him the key position of secretary-general. Both open and clandestine criticism was leveled at him, actually, he defended and per-sonified the concept of the U.N.R. as "the party of cadres," clashing with those who thought of it as a "party of the masses." Caught in a crossfire, he withdrew after ten months and resumed his career in industry. He continued, however, to play a certain behind-the-scenes role and to cut a figure as a theoretical expounder of "planned economy." At the party congress late in 1960, he could be heard vaunting "the moralization of capital" and asserting with a straight face: "Yes, capital must be domesticated."

CHALLE, MAURICE, ex-general, 58 years old
X   *Misled*

🦊 🐾 ◫ 📖

Yes indeed, the "boss" of the April 1961 putsch was a Gaullist, and even, in his own fashion, a leftist Gaullist with unconcealed sympathy for Socialism. In occupied France as early as 1942, he had organized and directed on behalf of Free France one of the most effective intelligence networks. In May 1958, the Fourth Republic's last Minister of National Defense considered him dangerously Gaullist and suspect enough to warrant house arrest. Escorted by the police, he was taken to the maritime prefecture of Brest. De Gaulle gave him back his rank as major-general of the armed forces and showered him with honors. In September 1958 he was made a general of the army; on the first of October he suc-ceeded Jouhaud as Salan's interarmy adjutant in Algeria; finally, on the twelfth of December, he became commander-in-chief of the army. He was reportedly slated to succeed General Ely in the highest post of the military hierarchy. During the days of the barricades, he proved to be both "loyalist" and disciplined; but obviously incapable of commanding obedience, he was recalled and shunted onto the command of the central European zone of NATO.

There, tormented and bitter, he champed at the bit, quit the army, and considered affiliating himself with an important industrial company. But friendships, temptations, and events decided otherwise; he was so misled by the putsch the colonels were organizing that, on April 12—nine days before the explosion—he agreed to head it along with Jouhaud and Zeller. Then came surrender on April 25, imprisonment in La Santé, the trial, two weeks of detention; and finally imprisonment at Tulle in Corrèze where he plays volleyball while waiting for the wheel of fate to turn.*

CLOSTERMANN, PIERRE, deputy, 42 years old
X *Thirty-three victories and one defeat*

An ace in the 1939–45 war, he flew 420 missions, won thirty-three certified victories and twelve probable ones in aerial combat, destroyed on the ground seven airplanes, seventy-two locomotives, 225 trucks and five tanks, sank two torpedo boats and one submarine. He is a high-ranking officer of the Legion of Honor, his *croix de guerre* is adorned with twenty palms, and he commanded a squadron in the R.A.F. His book, *Le Grand Cirque* (*The Great Circus*), a story about the life of a pilot in the Free French Forces, sold over two million copies and was translated into thirty different languages. He's proud as punch of himself—and justifiably, to be sure. In 1945, on V-E day, he was twenty-four. His political career had more ups and downs than his dazzling war

* Because of his American military friends and the high posts he held in the SHAPE and NATO commands, he was suspected by some people of having enlisted United States' support for his *coup.* Zealous Gaullists willingly spread this rumor throughout Paris during his trial. He vehemently denied these allegations which, as a matter of fact, were unfounded.

record. He is probably the only deputy who, between 1946 and 1962, changed his constituency four times and his political label almost as often. He still found time to go off to Algeria, just to keep his hand in and reap a few extra medals —the military cross and others. In 1958, he made a mistake that led to his only election defeat: he failed to change his constituency and his party label and lost to his U.N.R. rival. Having learned his lesson he joined the U.N.R. in 1962; with its support, he is now back in the Palais Bourbon.

COLONEL RÉMY, pseudonym of Gilbert Renault, 59 years old, writer

✗   *Free France's No. 1 secret agent*

✝ ◻ ★ 🦊 🔫 📰 💣 ◻ 🐪

Boarding a small trawler for England on June 18, 1940, he returned to France on a secret mission shortly afterward, in the month of August. By November he had already organized the first secret information network, the "Notre-Dame Brotherhood." It was to extend its activities from Brittany to the entire occupied zone, then to Belgium, only to be ravaged by betrayals, but managing to survive until the Liberation.

Identified by the Gestapo, he succeeded in escaping from its clutches. It took its revenge by arresting his mother and three sisters and killing four other members of his family. Colonel Roulier—another of his aliases—was Free France's number one secret agent. Later he recounted his adventures and those of his network in books that were received with enthusiasm.

By temperament he is precisely what the English call "provocative." He was noisy, very noisy, and when peace came he was not resigned to keeping quiet. To begin with, he attacked the Communists violently, polemicized their leaders and their newspapers. His major contention was that they were Communists first and then Frenchmen—nothing less. The Pétainist bourgeoisie, frightened by their knife-in-teeth liberators, once again heard the reassuring and familiar collaborationist formula—*Kommunist nicht französisch.* Their courage renewed, they loudly applauded. Here was a man of the Resistance—and what a man!—who himself was demanding that the Resistance be purged. Well then, if they tear each other apart the wall must have some cracks in it. Rémy's second theme was amnesty, especially for Pétain. Untiringly, from every platform, in every newspaper column, he demanded the release of "the oldest prisoner in the world," a review of his trial, an end to the purges, and a pardon for everyone. Thereupon the entire Right overwhelmed him with praise. But one day he maintained that De Gaulle told him in 1940 that France must have "two strings to her bow." The chairman of the R.P.F. expelled him, the General repudiated him, and the Free French Association struck him off its list. He claims nonetheless that he has remained faithful to De Gaulle.

A little later, he dropped another bombshell: the champion of amnesty now demanded an arrest and trial. This time, to be sure, he was after an unappetizing individual, a crook by the name of Joinvici whom Rémy accused of having been a Gestapo agent. He was obviously distributing his blows fairly, some here, some there.

With the passage of time he apparently calmed down. As the *enfant terrible* of Gaullism who has been rejected by the Knighthood, he is a twofold hostage—prisoner of a glorious past yet the captive of his new friends.

COURCEL, GEOFFROY CHODRON DE, ambassador, 51 years old

ꭗ *The only witness of the June 18 appeal*

☥ ⬚ ★ ⬤ ⚷ ⬚ ♪ 🐪 🛡 ⬚ 🎹

He is not merely discreet, he is secrecy itself in human form. This tall and courteous diplomat knows better than anyone else what De Gaulle is thinking. And he tells less than any other member of the General's entourage.

Yet at decisive moments he constitutes the entire entourage; he unquestionably ranks first among Gaullists. On June 17, 1940, when De Gaulle was an Undersecretary of State in the Paul Reynaud government, Courcel was in General Spears' plane that flew the General from Bordeaux to London. He was De Gaulle's only companion the following day when the fateful words of the appeal were broadcast over the B.B.C. He was chief of De Gaulle's personal staff until September 1941, and, after two years of fighting, in 1943–44 he became assistant director of his cabinet in Algiers.

He now resumed a career begun as a youthful embassy attaché in Warsaw and Athens before 1939. At the San Francisco Conference, in the Council of Four, at the Rome embassy, then at the Quai d'Orsay, where he is affectionately called "Godefroy de Bouillon," he has patterned his brief utterances as well as his silences on those of the General. In 1954, at the time of decolonization, the Fourth Republic named him Director-General for Moroccan and Tunisian Affairs, then permanent Secretary-General of National Defense, where his silence was greatly admired. Of course, he owed both these positions to Christian Fouchet and Gaston Palewski, two other faithful Gaullists.

After May 13, De Gaulle first put him on ice by appointing him ambassador to NATO, then recalled him to serve at his side as secretary-general of the Élysée. For three active years he held this difficult post, finally receiving as his reward the ambassadorship to London. This, people say, was his dearest wish, not only for family reasons—his grandfather had held the same post in 1885—but also because of a yearning to return as France's representative to the scene of his 1940 adventure—an adventure that had left its imprint on his entire life.

CREPIN, JEAN, general, 55 years old
X *An about-face*

He arrived in Algiers in January 1960, the era of the barricades and great agitation, to assume the difficult and responsible post of replacing General Massu as head of the army. The ardent Gaullism of this former associate of Leclerc, who later became Valluy's adjutant in Indochina, had earned him this dangerous and confidential mission. He discharged his task by issuing rather orthodox statements, which turned out to be totally ineffective, but reaffirmed his loyalty. There is only one dark spot in the picture. For several weeks a certain Colonel Argoud, who was later to lead the extremists in the putsch of 1961, gave him a hard time; regretfully Crepin quit his predecessor's chief of staff. Well, no matter, two months later he was asked to replace Challe himself as commander-in-chief in Algeria. But during the following autumn, like a trail of powder, the rumor spread from mess hall to mess hall and from one army headquarters to another that "Dudule" had turned in favor of French Algeria. Like so many others, he was swayed by the arguments of those who opposed the regime and wanted to keep Algeria French.

Transferred to Germany to head the French forces there, he was soon joined by other activist leaders. According to his reports everything was going well, no officers under his command had the slightest contact with the colonels who had kicked over the traces. At the time of the 1961 putsch he sent countless reassuring messages. Simultaneously he protested against the suspicious activities of the military police, claiming: "If Vichy had had such a military police, there never would have been a Resistance!" *

DASSAULT, MARCEL, deputy, 71 years old
X   *Money*

He is a rather extraordinary man—small, delicate, with a sallow complexion, and a look in his eyes that is at once vague, rather sad and cold, but that suddenly becomes animated and stern. His lips are twisted in what might seem to be a smile but which really expresses arrogance and disdain. His bald head is forever covered with a small, black felt hat and his neck is wrapped in a thick scarf, regardless of the season. He takes short, hurried steps, rarely shakes hands, never nods to people, and his voice is nasal and high-pitched. It is plain that, save for his arrogance, he is quite the opposite of the conventional picture caricaturists paint of full-blooded, dynamic, and important captains of industry.

He alone controls all his business affairs, which are extremely complicated; he has never shared authority or ownership with anyone. His wide-ranging enterprises include a bank, electronics and airplane plants, real estate companies, food industries, supermarkets, newspapers, moving picture companies, and bowling equipment. He is the King Midas of industry. His entire enterprise is based on the simple theory that the state, France's greatest purchaser, is the best customer.

* He has recently been appointed to a key NATO command.

When Parliament voted 442 billion old francs for the 1960–65 program of aeronautical construction, its first step in creating a deterrent force, Marcel Dassault's General Aeronautics Company received orders worth 350 billion. The nationalized companies—airplane construction was nationalized in 1946—became mere initials devoid of any substance. "Mr. France-Aviation" definitively supplanted them one by one, either taking over their administration or subjecting them to insuperable competition.

To succeed in carving out such a place for himself in the state, he obviously required, in addition to experience, great political influence. Dassault's experience is long and extensive. Too often people forget that it was not at the end of World War II that he began to build planes, but after World War I. Although his four-motor transport plane, *Languedoc 161,* which was not mass-produced until after the Liberation, was a huge success, the *Bloch 200,* which a critical public familiarly dubbed "the flying coffin," was built well before 1939. For his name was Bloch and two of his brothers have kept it. One brother voluntarily added a hyphen and the pseudonym Dassault; the other retained the original name without change and was content to quietly pursue his occupation as bailiff in Nice.

Dassault has political influence as well as experience. Employing several well-tried methods, he surrounds himself with a network of collaborators and friends, people who owe him favors. Actually, the system is no more complex or intricate than the companies he directs. The list of his staff members is imposing. It includes or has included a good many generals: Pierre-Marie Gallois, one of the few officers who campaigned for the European Defense Community and subsequently favored the creation of a nuclear striking force; Edward Corniglion-Molinier, who had administered many of the Group's enterprises between his two parliamentary candidatures and his two ministerial posts; Guillain de Bénouville, the director of *Jours de France,* a weekly owned by Dassault; Auguste Le Reverend; Admiral Ruyssen, who commanded the naval aeronautics; Colonel Dugit-Gros, former assistant director of the flight test center, and Commander René Bigand, who was a pilot at the same center; Maurice Roy, initially general director of the National Bureau of Study and Research in Aeronautics, and thereafter the representative of the Dassault group in Eurospace; Albin Chalandon, erstwhile secretary-general of the U.N.R. and now a director of the Banque Commerciale de Paris, the financial foundation of the group. General Dassault, former grand chancellor of the Legion of Honor, brother of the industrialist, is the administrator of the group . . . When the question of aerial construction came up during an important parliamentary debate under the Fourth Republic, emissaries and advisers swooped down on the Palais Bourbon like a swarm of swallows. Under the Fifth Republic it is no longer necessary to lobby so openly.

But Dassault wanted to enter Parliament and have a chance to plead his own case. For a long time he also cherished the ambition—perhaps he still does—which is neither incongruous nor excessive, and it is surprising that he has not achieved it: to become Minister of Construction. Playing the Gaullist cards his own way, he gave financial support to the movement. He was rewarded with a seat in the National Assembly in 1951, and during the election campaign, it is said, he rained a manna of subsidies and favors upon the little communes on the southern coast of France where the voting took place. But in spite of his generosity the industrialist lost the election in 1956. A year later, a Social Republican senator from the Oise, Sené, sold him a local newspaper, *L'Oise Libérée,* and decided not to seek re-election. Dassault entered the Senate. But he remained there only eighteen months, exchanging his senatorship in November 1958 for a seat, which he retained in 1962, as one of the Gaullist deputies from the Oise. In a brilliant account of the 1958 *coup d'état,* two journalists, Merry and Serge Bromberger, authors of *Treize Complots du 13 Mai (Thirteen Plots on May 13),* describe as follows Soustelle's flight to Algeria: "All the preparations were made that afternoon in the offices of *Jours de France.* The owner of the weekly, Marcel Dassault, manufacturer of the *Mystère* and the *Mirage,* furnished unlimited credit."

Some say that although he thus played a part in the birth of the regime and supported the U.N.R. when it was first organized, Dassault today is on bad terms with General de Gaulle. On the other hand, one can be sure that the industrialist remains on the best of terms with practically everyone else of importance in the state.*

DEBRÉ, MICHEL, deputy, former Prime Minister, 51 years old

X *Sacrifice*

✦ 🗐 🎐 ⚱ 🗐 🌙 🐫 🚂 ○ ∅ 🪑 🗼 🛏

"We are nothing as individuals, and even our institutions have meaning only insofar as they serve the State." These words were uttered on January 15, 1959, by the head of the first cabinet of the Fifth Republic before Parliament and deputies who listened to him more than to anyone else. This gesture of humility inaugurated a tenure of three years and

---

* Dassault has been haunted all his life by fear of blindness. He keeps no records, has not a single file, and even memorizes the telephone numbers of his principal assistants. All his business affairs are likewise filed in his head; he can open one drawer at a time, then attend to his bank for a while, employ his fabulous memory to trip up his assistants on the most insignificant facts, and finally turn in succession to each of his other enterprises. He distrusts Americans, even though he likes to say that he is the typical American success story in France.

three months, which broke all records for longevity in Republican France.

In the same speech, Michel Debré also said: "The nation needs security, prosperity, social harmony, and in addition a sense of pride." And yet one would have thought that what France needed most at that time, far more than security, which is factitious, or social harmony, which is fragile, was peace. The Algerian war, then beginning its fifth year, was the last link in a chain that included Indochina and world conflict and that had bound the country for the last twenty years to rear-action combat, to battles it had lost in advance and settlements that tore it apart. But the Prime Minister's statement carried no promise of peace; to tell the truth, he had to struggle with himself to put at the bottom of the list the one thing that mattered most to him: national pride.

Nine months to the day before his acceptance speech, on April 15, 1958, this same man spoke before another tribune and a different assembly. Debré was then a member of the Fourth Republic's last traditional cabinet, the Gaillard ministry, whose overthrow that same night by the National Assembly precipitated the crisis that led to May 13. Here are a few passages from Debré's philippic, which had as its theme the "fine services" of England and America which the President of the Council had mentioned so favorably.

> How can one refrain from shouting to all Frenchmen: You are being misled and your candor is being abused; emulate your ancestors of 1789, 1830, 1848, and revolt . . . No, it is not true that you have no choice between abdication and reconquest. Tell me, without political authority like Clemenceau's, would you establish peace in Algeria . . . reform the regime? Fashion a government devoted to the public welfare, restore the power of France. If you do these things, all the forces now working against you might very well become your allies.

Passion, violence, exhortation, diatribe, denunciation, arraignment . . . Placid on their benches, the senators smiled, some embarrassed by an outburst so inappropriate to such a select group, others resigned or ironic, even amused. They were used to it: for ten years this had been going on. In the debates on the European Coal and Steel Community, in the European Defense Community, Euratom—"that plot against France"—and on countless other, less dramatic issues—the installation of American launching sites, the sale of the steamship *Pasteur* to Germany, etc.—one could be sure to find the senator from Indre-et-Loire in the vanguard of the opposition. He fought every government and every policy indiscriminately because, through them, he sought to get at the regime.

For ten years he attacked this regime of "shame, resignation and impotence" (these were the least violent of his expressions) with a vigilant and tenacious hatred that plainly resembled a great but thwarted love, a passionate affair in which he had been betrayed.

He really believed that there had been treachery against the ideal Republic as sketched by the General Study Committee of the Resistance to which he had belonged; against the principles laid down by General de Gaulle, whose adviser he had been on constitutional and administrative questions. Even De Gaulle had been dismissed by "those princes who govern us," the targets in 1957 of Michel Debré's resounding pamphlet. Dark, thin, sharp-featured, given to highblown phrases, ear-splitting voice, sharp as a razor blade, always active, ready to leap, to lash out, to strike, he reminded one of a Goya painting.

He spared no one, no one was blameless. Diplomacy: "Has the Quai d'Orsay lost its sense of national honor? What is being done to counter the tremendous blackmail exacted by Germany and America?" His colleagues in Parliament:

"Tomorrow, you might as well know it, the road to the guillotine will be cleared." The government: "Our princes, those traitors and defeatists, promise happiness to all Frenchmen and peace for tomorrow, always tomorrow, yet each today is more somber than the last."

The amazing fact that under the Fourth Republic this Fouquier-Tinville of the anti-regime was found to be implicated in only one plot—the affair of the "bazooka"— hardly speaks well for the perspicacity of his enemies. He not only took part in all the plots, all the secret meetings, all the preparations, he was their very soul, their instigator, their mastermind. His aim was well known—to bring De Gaulle back to power. And his methods were in nowise mysterious: in Parliament, opposition that paralleled Jacques Soustelle's efforts at the Palais Bourbon; outside Parliament, creation of a nucleus comprising men and mechanisms superior to those of the administration, mobilization and utilization *ad usum delphini* of all the malcontents, emasculation of the regime's authority, promotion of a psychosis of insecurity, instability, failure . . . In 1952 the Fourth Republic had absorbed as best it could the wave of the R.P.F.; it had neutralized without effort the current of Mendèsism in 1954; it had easily eradicated the Poujade trend in 1956 and resisted in its own way the mounting military agitation. When it finally did crumble, its demise was due far more to Michel Debré, Jacques Soustelle, and their friends than to the circumstances which they had tried so hard to exploit. Debré was, in a sense, the Monck of the new Restoration and if he denies this, however feebly, the tactical reasons for his sudden modesty are self-evident.

Finally he achieved power. As Keeper of the Seals he was the principal author of the new constitution. He now had to work with men whom yesterday he had attacked. They, surprisingly enough, were at the council table, seated around the restored monarch. As for the constitution, it was not altogether without merit, but it failed to bring into being the hoped-for ideal Republic. It was necessary to make concessions, pretend, procrastinate. Yet what mattered most was its application. And it was the application, the actual implementation of the new constitution, the construction of the new state, that was Debré's mission. His task was clear: to endow the regime with its most unpopular, its harshest features. But beside the fact that De Gaulle made all the major decisions on important questions, Debré had to countenance being contradicted and allowing the General to yield what he had refused; he had to grant the General the advantage of showing leniency and even the power to disown him. Thus, his mission was one of self-sacrifice, and this he fully realized.

In the beginning Michel Debré brought to the exercise of power the same traits of character and almost the same spirit that he had displayed for ten years as a member of the opposition. He did not guide Parliament toward internal regulations, attitudes, or ways of operation that would insure harmony between institutions: he lashed at it, struck out at it, hauled it over the coals, or expressed contempt for it. To the deputies he spoke in the cutting tones of a schoolmaster: "You can be quite sure of this: It is imperative that all Republicans should avoid generating disputes by disguising problems under the shimmering but misleading mantle of political verbiage, which usually is just another expression of partisanship. In view of France's present situation, there is no more important way to serve your country honestly than to shun considerations of clan, class or party interests."

To his ministerial colleagues, even and primarily to the most loyal Gaullists, he sent imperiously cold, almost insulting notes. They would begin with "My dear" but end with "I must request that you act accordingly, otherwise I shall be

obliged within a week to ask that you be replaced by someone more responsible, less incompetent, less muddleheaded
and less unqualified." As leader of the U.N.R., he pursued a
difficult and, to be honest, impractical course; he favored a
great conservative party like England's, one that would be
bound unconditionally to the will of a single person. He
wanted it to be dynamic, efficacious, active, yet extremely
disciplined and docile. How could it be bubbling over with
ideas if it had no right to show initiative; how could it re-
flect life in all its diversity if freedom of discussion and the
right to criticize were abolished?

Curiously enough, faced with an army that had such a
great need to be commanded, faced with activist Gaullists, or
Gaullists with Fascist leanings who during one decisive thrust
had been his allies, but who now had to be made to toe the
line, Michel Debré seemed to hesitate, to weaken, to vacillate.
One cannot reproach him for changes in policy that reflected
someone else's decisions, for uncertainties that did not stem
from him. Also, it is admittedly painful to break with old
friendships, with a camaraderie that began during the war,
with a long chain of involvements. Yet it is impossible to
forget that his uncompromising nationalism made him a
champion of "French Algeria," a determined foe of the peace
that entailed defeat, the peace that would bring independence and put an end to "disentanglement."

So long as plots once again abounded, so long as barricades
rose and were pulled down, and pronunciamentos and
putsches succeeded one another, he denied what had long
become evident. He pleaded the sincerity of his motives, the
honesty of his intentions; but later, haggard and drawn, he
appeared on television to urge Parisians to go to the airports
in advance of the parachutists and dissuade them. It was only
after two years of this astonishing life, in which violence
replaced the ministerial crises of yore, that his eyes were

finally opened. Suddenly he realized that De Gaulle was going to sell the Algerian problem short, that the accusations of civil and military activists were entirely well-founded, that he, Michel Debré, would have to carry out this policy as well as the repression that it entailed.

This was too much. He wrote a twenty-five page letter of resignation to the General, who shrugged his shoulders, filed it, and went on to more pressing matters. Debré continued his thankless task, tracking down rebellious generals, setting the military police against the peasants, supervising and intervening in the negotiations with the Algerian nationalists, ordering employers not to yield to the demands of their employees, and forever ruling ministers, deputies, and high officials with an iron fist. But his heart was no longer in it. Like a cardinal whose faith is gone, he had to feign, out of loyalty and fidelity, a mystical ardor he no longer felt. It could not last.

And indeed it did not. Hardly had the peace been signed at Évian than Michel Debré was relieved of his post. He did everything to bring this on, willingly exposing himself to the blows that felled him. In his haste to discard a responsibility that now weighed so heavily, he urged dissolution and immediate elections. He could not lose: if he were heeded, he would be freed from his burden as soon as the balloting began; if his advice were spurned, he would be repudiated, someone else would take his place, and a new period in the life of the regime would begin. And that is precisely what happened.

Imperiously, he was advised to travel, which was a way of making him realize that he had become a source of embarrassment. Perhaps he was secretly pleased by his failure in the elections; it meant that he would no longer have to attend council meetings. Defeat he accepted with good grace; it was too much in accord with his tendency to resist, with his destiny as a lone wolf, to take him by surprise. He would have to start all over again by going to the other end of the world and representing in Parliament one of the last remote possessions of France, the Isle of Réunion. Although he became majority leader, he remained at heart the leader of His Majesty's opposition. This was to become plain, for now he aims higher and farther. When the day comes, he will, if he can swing it, be the faithful candidate to succeed General de Gaulle.*

DEJEAN, MAURICE, French ambassador, 64 years old
ᚷ *Gaullist of the Paul Reynaud tinge*

╈ ⏻ ⏻ ⏻ ┰

He made the acquaintance of Colonel de Gaulle in 1934 through Paul Reynaud whose chief of staff he was at that time. In 1940 he followed General de Gaulle to Free France and became first his diplomatic adviser, then his representative in London after De Gaulle was installed in Algiers. In 1944, after the Liberation, he served President de Gaulle as General Director of Political Affairs at the Quai d'Orsay.

He had been ambassador to Czechoslovakia and Japan before his former boss, Paul Reynaud, appointed him High Commissioner in Indochina. He remained there for a year, until Dien-Bien-Phu and the Geneva armistice. Since 1955 he has been France's ambassador in Moscow. Thus he is again serving De Gaulle despite the shifts and about-faces of the General's Soviet policy, but he remains divided between genuine Gaullism and an older political loyalty. Fortunately he is nearing retirement, which will resolve his dilemma.

---

* However cool his official attitude may have been toward the United States, Debré has many American friends and is a great admirer of the United States. He sent his son to America to complete his education.

DELBECQUE, LÉON, former deputy, 44 years old
X   *The balcony of the Forum*

Everything began for him one day in December 1957. Until then he had been a very young member of the Resistance, a model employee of an important textile mill in the north, a rather obscure but militant Gaullist who failed in two attempts to get elected at a time when the Gaullist party represented about 3 percent of the electorate.

His adventure began the day his "boss," who supported and financed the Gaullist party, called him into his office, saying as soon as he reached the door: "Delbecque, stand at attention. I want to read you a letter from the Minister of National Defense." The minister in question was Chaban-Delmas. The letter requested the head of this textile mill to release Léon Delbecque so that he would be free to serve on his personal staff.

Flanked by a short, bronzed, and moustached man by the name of Guy Ribaud, who in 1962 was to become Georges Bidault's companion in exile in South America, Delbecque was to represent Chaban-Delmas in Algiers as head of the "Antenna" of the Ministry of National Defense. Feverishly he maneuvered and organized, seeking to create an opposition party and all the while maintaining contacts with Soustelle, the politicians, the press, the activist colonels, the clandestine workers, and agitators. He naturally found himself behind Salan on the balcony of the Forum at Algiers on the crucial May 15, 1958. The putsch that he had minutely prepared and openly encouraged was a success. Algeria seceded, and the army joined the insurrection. The victory would now have to be made decisive.

Facing the overexcited crowd that had just granted its initial acclaim, Salan relinquished the microphone, walked away, then suddenly returned and shouted the "Vive De Gaulle" that changed the mutiny into a pronunciamento and clinched the victory. Later, the sound track used on the occasion of this major event was carefully examined in an attempt to determine the voice of the man in the background who had given the signal, who had seized the arm of the commander-in-chief, forced him to turn back, whispered to him the three words that Salan repeated—voluntarily or because he was coerced, it does not matter—into the mike, words that were shouted to the crowd, to France, to the world. The master of the game was the vice-president of the Committee of Public Safety, Léon Delbecque.

On the following June 3, De Gaulle embraced him in Paris; but on the fourth of June he forbade him to organize committees for public safety in the metropolis. After twenty months of being an activist, Léon Delbecque, a deputy of fifteen years standing, ceased to be a Gaullist. He soon left the U.N.R., joined the activists, and lost his seat in 1962. Ever since the scene on the balcony of the Forum, which was the symbol and culmination of a protracted enterprise, the prodigal son has remained nevertheless a member of the Gaullist family.

DEWAVRIN, ANDRÉ, consulting engineer, 52 years old
X   *Administrator of a department store chain*

☦ ◖ ★ 🦊 ◧ 🐫 ⌡

M. Dewavrin? A peaceful bourgeois, a successful business-man who lives in the wealthy suburb of Neuilly, he shuns political conflicts and detests adventure. Just think of it! A consulting engineer for the Worms bank, an administrator of powerful business firms, among them the Bon Marché department store, all safe and quiet occupations. And yet this is the same man who, having begun an apparently conventional military career before the war, was the mysterious, formidable, and ominous Colonel Passy. Head of the secret service (Deuxième Bureau) of the small General Staff of London in 1940, he continued to head it when it became the Central Information and Action Bureau. This was during the time when "Information" spelled danger because thousands of patriots were involved in it in occupied France; and "Action" meant the Resistance . . . Parachute jumps, clandestine missions in the metropolis, grave conflicts between Free France and the Resistance inside of France, between the "civilians" and the military, between professionals and amateurs, between the spirit of the "Cagoulards" and that of the Resistance—all these were part of the picture. It was fashionable to use the names of *métro* stations as aliases: Barbès, Corvisart, Dupleix. Passy deliberately chose the name of one of the most beautiful sections of Paris.

After the Liberation he went back to the secret service. From time to time a "Passy Affair," more or less explosive, burst into the open, and the Free French tore each other apart to the astonishment of the liberated French citizens. There were rumors of plots, scandals, strange deaths; one guessed at the presence in the background, in the kitchens of heroism and adventure, of a whole swarm of informers, false policemen, real spies, and musclemen. The leaders took turns arresting each other. The word had not yet been invented, but Passy was both the symbol and the boss of the "barbouzes." * One day, after a particularly complicated "affair," one that was very serious for him, he decided he had had enough and he gave it all up. The colonel disappeared, the businessman took over. He remained a Gaullist but turned his back forever on the Secret Service—at least that is what he vehemently claims. And yet, can one be absolutely sure?

* "Barbouze" is a slang term meaning someone who has a beard. During the Algerian war it was used to denote special police units who often resorted to illegal means.

DRONNE, RAYMOND, former deputy, 55 years old

χ   *Slammer of doors*

✝ ★ 🍶 ▥ 🐪 🛡 ⊛ ∅-🗝

Those who watched Captain Dronne, first officer of Leclerc's division in the Allied vanguard that liberated Paris,
get out of his tank on August 24, 1944, would certainly not
recognize him today. He hasn't just grown heavier; he is
five times his former size. This enormous Falstaff, his face
framed by a round beard, has nonetheless retained the rigorously summary officer's judgment. After fourteen years in
Parliament he has also preserved the marked accent of his
region, the Sarthe, plus a solid peasant common sense.

But this picturesque and truculent individual has made
his common sense serve his intransigence. He went to Algeria in May 1958. In the U.N.R. he agitated for a long time
in favor of keeping Algeria French. Deliberately slamming
doors, just as he had done throughout his career, at the end
of 1961 he was finally ejected from the Gaullist family.
Thereupon he founded a movement that proposed "to resolve the Algerian problem within a French framework" and
that hoped to accomplish this by regrouping those militant
Gaullists "who refuse to be either unmitigated robots or
activists." But the movement was unsuccessful; it had no
sequel and cost him his seat in the National Assembly.

DUMONT, CLAUDE, former senator, 38 years old

χ   *"Lux" of the O.A.S.*

The following is an excerpt from a petition addressed to
the president of the Senate, on December 8, by Mr. Aydalot,
general prosecutor of the Court of Appeals of Paris, requesting authorization to prosecute:

Considering that:

On the basis of our information it is clear that sometime after October 25, 1961, a certain *Lux* received the sum of 400,000 francs from a certain *Saponite*, which he was supposed to give to *Palmolive*; that he appropriated 100,000 francs of this sum before giving the rest to the addressee; that on November 7, Claude Dumont gave Dirler, his secretary and personal friend, the sum of 300,000 francs in the form of a check made out to him . . . ; that charges of the gravest nature lead one to believe that *Lux* is Claude Dumont . . . ; that the facts herein stated therefore represent serious and circumstantial evidence of a plot against the authority of the State . . .

The following is an excerpt from the interrogation of Daniel Dirler, thirty-three years old, parliamentary secretary, at the session of the military tribunal of the Fort de l'Est, on December 11, 1962:

The President: What was your role?

The Accused: A very simple one. I received messages in sealed envelopes from persons unknown to me whom I met in cafés by appointment. I gave these letters to Dumont who returned them to me with instructions to take them to other people likewise unknown to me, whom I met in other cafés.

The President: This is what you did on October 12, 1961, in the Place du Trocadéro. What were the names of your two interlocutors?

The Accused: I was told that their names were Martinet and Jean-Luc. Since my arrest I learned that they were Lieutenant Godot and Captain Sergent.* But at the time I did not know this.

Verdict: Claude Dumont, escapee, twenty years of criminal detention in absentia; Dirler, two years of imprisonment.

Until this episode Gaullism had been Dumont's career.

* Two of the most formidable leaders of the terrorist organization, the O.A.S.

DUPÉRIER, BERNARD, deputy, 56 years old
χ *Perilous missions and parachute jumps*

╪ ★ ◙ ♦ ▣ ♪ ᙏ ♘ ⏌

Engineer, former test pilot, a builder of planes, he shared the finest commands of the Free French Air Forces—the Ile-de-France and Alsace groups, then a French pursuit squadron stationed in Great Britain. Finally, and this was a very high honor, he was put in charge of a British air squadron. He thus bagged the greatest reward ever given to a French aviator. After the Normandy landings Colonel Dupérier, along with Passy and Eon, parachuted behind the German lines; his mission was to coordinate the work of the Allied Secret Service with the activities of the Resistance inside France. On August 5, 1944, he and two of his comrades "liberated" Saint-Brieuc. The following day, gravely wounded, he was put in a hospital where he began a year-long convalescence.

This specialist in daring adventures and parachute jumps owed it to himself to participate in the R.P.F.'s sallies against the Fourth Republic. He was in the front row of Gaullists in May 1958. At that time his parachute jumps behind enemy lines took the form of the "National Association to Support the Action of General de Gaulle," which he founded and of which he was co-president. Its assignment was to attack the regime from the rear, to widen the breach, to give all declared or potential Gaullists a chance to regroup and act without feeling that they were enrolled in a political party. In this respect Dupérier's work was highly successful. The Association, having proved its usefulness, repeatedly engaged in more or less clandestine activity. This went on until the elections of November 1962, when its three presidents, having "parachuted" once again and been elected deputies, merged with the U.N.R.

DUTOURD, JEAN, writer, 43 years old
X *The revenge of the dairymen*

Taken prisoner in 1940, he escaped and joined the Re-sistance. He was arrested in 1944 by the militia, but escaped to join the fight for the liberation of France. A Jacobin of the N.R.F. and one of its successful authors and literary advisers, he flirted with the idea of a political career. But the dairymen of the seventeenth *arrondissement* in Paris must have a good memory. They had not forgotten the ferocious satire in one of his first books, *Au Bon Beurre (At the Buttery)* which lampooned the "B.O.F." (abbreviation for butter, eggs, and cheese)—*(Beurre, oeufs et fromages)* during a period of famine. The leftist Gaullist Jean Dutourd accepted defeat philosophically.

And so, with equal ease, he continued to write sparkling prose, excelling in treating serious matters lightly and, on occasion, light matters seriously.

FOCCART, JACQUES, Secretary-General for African Affairs, 50 years old
X

Where does he get the reputation of being a specialist in Intelligence, a Secret Service expert, a mysterious figure, an *Éminence Grise?*

At first glance his biography seems quite ordinary, devoid of mystery. Born in Mayenne, launched in business at an early age, he fought the war of 1939–40 as a sergeant, joined the Resistance, fought bravely and, demobilized with the rank of lieutenant-colonel, went back to exporting. A Gaullist, he joined the R.P.F., which made him its secretary-general in December 1954. In June 1958, General de Gaulle's confidence won him an appointment on the Premier's staff; in January 1959 he was named Secretary-General in the office of the President of the Republic; finally, in the following year, he was given the same post at the Élysée and placed in charge of African and Madagascan Affairs. Obviously Jacques Foccart's career as a public official in nowise justifies his reputation as a man of mystery.

And yet there are curious lacunae in this simple biography. The real name of this exporter and reserve officer is Koch-Foccart; but the fact that he discarded the first part in order to shorten his name is scarcely extraordinary. Nor is there anything odd about his having been for a while in the Secret Service of the Free French and later a member of the Provisional government, unless he tried to conceal these facts. It is altogether possible that Safiex was the real name of his exporting firm. That he had many friends in the various security services, that because of this he was the center of a veritable network of . . . friendships, that this network was active during the weeks preceding May 1958, that it was responsible for coordinating, on behalf of the Chief of State, the operations of security, intelligence and information—all this might merely signify that he was utilizing his talents to the best of his ability and nothing more.

On a few occasions, however, Jacques Foccart was "exposed"; this happened on May 13, in April 1961 at the time of the putsch, and during the fight against the O.A.S. One of these incidents even brought him to the witness box of the Court of Assizes in the Aube during the trial of the men who engineered the Pont-sur-Seine attempt on the life of De Gaulle. A certain Simon wrote a letter accusing Foccart of having been the real instigator of the affair, which was intended to fail but at the same time to impress De Gaulle, "who did not fully appreciate the danger of the terrorist threat." These fantastic charges the peaceful Secretary-General could only deny indignantly and note the nonappearance of the man who accused him. Nonetheless, mention of his name in this connection was in itself surprising. Besides —one might as well admit it—among loyal Gaullists Jacques Foccart is one of those who did the most to steep the Knighthood in a secret-society atmosphere, to give it its detective-story quality, its penchant for clandestine activity. Too many honest and sincere men, warped by the epic of the Resistance, and spurred by a contempt for the kind of politics that had become dogma, tended to believe that secret funds, police files, moral pressure, and material interest were a government's best weapons. They thus ended up with the notion that politics was merely a camouflage for people conspiring behind the scenes, their hands forever reaching for money or guns, it was hard to say which. Of all the forms of Gaullist deviation, this was the most vulnerable, the most reprehensible. But unfortunately, this kind of warped mentality was an integral, indissoluble part of the legacy.

FOUCHET, CHRISTIAN, minister, 52 years old

✗ *Answers all summons*

      ✝ 🏠 🌐 ♰ 📦 🐪 🪑 ⊕ + 📦 🥾 🛷

Three times in the course of his career De Gaulle summoned him. On each occasion he responded immediately and left the post he was holding.

The first time, to be precise, was on the evening of June 18, 1940, in London; Fouchet arrived the day before, having fled from Bordeaux concealed in a British plane. For four years, either as a war correspondent, a fighter, or on an official mission, he was to roam over all the combat areas, from Tchad, where he served under Leclerc, to Fezzan in Libya, from Italy to the Soviet Union. After the Liberation he resumed a diplomatic career begun when he graduated from law school and the École des Sciences Politiques.

His return to embassy life lasted scarcely more than two years. In 1947, the same voice that had appealed to Frenchmen on June 18, 1940, again summoned them to unite. Christian Fouchet promptly took leave from the Quai d'Orsay and, a short distance away, on the Rue de Solférino, enrolled in the Gaullist party, the R.P.F. In 1940 enlistment had made a soldier of him and, whenever necessary, a journalist beneath his uniform. Now he became a politician.

This apprenticeship, in which he was to win his stripes as a propagandist and agitator, was different in nature. The Parisian region was his stamping ground. After the "stamp campaign" (two million letters brought more than three million stamps to Colombey) in 1948, the dual purpose of which was to replenish the movement's coffers and create a favorable climate of opinion for elections, he was given, as general delegate, responsibility for organizing all important public demonstrations.

Naturally, Fouchet became a candidate in Paris when the Gaullists, who had already been successful in breaking down the doors of the Senate, tried to force their way into the Palais Bourbon on June 17, 1951. He was elected and, a very courteous deputy, presided over the Gaullist faction in 1953. At the court he struck a liberal note, often presenting the views of his friends on Indochina and North Africa. During his career in Parliament he was to receive another summons on June 18, and to make another clandestine trip. In 1954, Pierre Mendès-France, who was forming a government, asked Fouchet to take the portfolio for Moroccan and Tunisian Affairs. Before accepting, as a well-disciplined Gaullist, Fouchet went to Colombey to ask for approval. Doubtless he received it, because he moved back to the Quai d'Orsay, which he had quit for seven years. The Gaullist sanction, granted to the Premier in view of the impending battle over the European Defense Community, was to play a part, *volens nolens,* in another affair. On July 31, when Mendès-France, who had left Paris secretly, landed at the Tunis airport to announce Tunisia's autonomy to Carthage, two men accompanied him: Marshal Juin and Christian Fouchet.

During the next six months it fell to Fouchet to negotiate the accords that confirmed the promise of the preceding summer, but in the meanwhile the cabinet had begun to founder. There were endless disconcerting discussions which were interrupted a dozen times and resumed. When the cabinet finally fell, no conclusions had been reached. Christian Fouchet, returning to the Palais Bourbon, was to watch his successor terminate the mission he had undertaken, which he approved; just as a little later he was to support the dissolution of the National Assembly, even though it cost him his seat as deputy.

When General de Gaulle resumed the reins, the future High Commissioner for Algeria seemed to hesitate: Would he be a diplomat this time or a politician? He finally decided to pursue his first profession to which he had devoted in all only thirty months out of the last eighteen years. But the post he was given, that of ambassador to Denmark, did not prove absorbing. He devoted his leisure to the blueprinting of a European political community in accordance with the views held at the Élysée.

Once again he became involved in thankless negotiations, in plan and counterplan that made little progress; but they led him to the presidency of a Study Commission of Six whose task it was to explore the possibilities of a compromise between a Europe of sovereign states and a supranational community. This work at last enabled him to spend more time in Paris than in Copenhagen. Several times when the presidential Household was reshuffled, his name was suggested for a key post at the Élysée. He was also high on the list of deputies likely to be offered cabinet positions.

On the eve of the Évian accords which established peace in Algeria, and after General Billotte's short-lived assignment, he was again summoned by his former chief. His appointment as High Commissioner in Algiers, which he accepted on the spot, invested him with a delicate, thankless, and dangerous mission. The last French proconsul on African soil, his task was to establish a semblance of authority until July 1st, when the time would come to hand the keys to the new rulers of an independent Algeria and to haul down the French colors.

When he made his first appearance on television, everyone immediately realized that he would handle himself well and with dignity. He struck the right note, the initial impression he conveyed being one of energy and well-grounded authority. His powerful physique, his square face with its firm jaw, his vigorous air and thumping voice—all this was a revelation to thousands of viewers. Quite naturally, upon his return and after a brief moment of uncertainty, he was promoted to Minister of Information. Although he would be less persuasive in this post, at least he would be once again in line for promotion. And indeed he was given the Ministry of National Education, a most difficult department, but essential in the eyes of the Élysée. One thing is clear: This taciturn man who speaks so well when he does speak, who doubtless ranks with Debré, Pompidou, and Chaban-Delmas, is one of the Grand Dukes of the reign, of the kingdom.

FOURCADE, MARIE-MADELEINE, 54 years old
X　*The post office*

She joined the Resistance in 1940 and has never left it. A co-founder of the Allied intelligence network, Alliance, for a while she even directed it. Arrested, tortured, deported, since her return she has dedicated all her energies, which are considerable, and her dynamism, which can be fantastic, to the mission of destroying not only the enemies of Gaullism but even those who do not adhere rigorously to the General's every position. She is the *Pasionaria* of the Knighthood. Her favorite weapon is the post office; she was a persistent propagandist for the "stamp campaign" of 1948 which for months flooded the little post office of Colombey-les-Deux-Églises. She intervened in the battles over the European Defense Community by sending charming little coffins to the "Europeans." May 13 gave her a chance to make good use of her experience. While others wasted time in vain discussion, she and a few faithful instigated a tidal wave of letters and postcards addressed to the President of the Fourth Republic, Coty, urging him to summon De Gaulle. Trucks loaded with huge sacks of mail arrived at the Élysée where people literally trampled on letters.

FOYER, JEAN, minister, 42 years old
Ӿ *Canon law*

🔔 📖 🐪 🪑 ✡ 🔩

Grandson and son of notaries in the village of Contigné in Anjou, he owes his political career to a mistake in spelling. It was almost by chance that he left behind his wooden shoes —called *pillons* in Anjou—put on his jacket and gave up singing Gregorian chants with the monks of Solesmes in order to become the Minister of Justice.

Well, let's not exaggerate; he had already experimented a little with public life in September 1944, when he was twenty-three. Like many others, he had studied law and become a member of the bar. It took him a while to complete his doctoral thesis, but once he finished it, nothing could stop him. He passed his exams easily enough, published an authoritative manual on civil law, and gave free rein to his immoderate love for canon law. He was a professor of law at Lille when, in June 1958, his friend Michel Debré asked him to help prepare the new constitution, or, to be more exact, the section relating to the Community. To simplify matters, he was named technical adviser in the office of Houphouet-Boigny. (At that time Houphouet-Boigny was a French minister; only later did he become President of the Ivory Coast).

All this was well and good but not in the least sensational.

As a faithful Gaullist and the choice of the Prime Minister, he had been named as alternate to an old "worthy" of the movement, Victor Chatenay, mayor of Angers, who, in November 1958, had won an easy victory in the elections to the National Assembly. Six weeks later, Michel Debré formed his cabinet. The ink on the announcement of the list of ministers was barely dry when the radio and press trumpeted the name of Chatenay as one of the Premier's secretaries of state. This was without doubt a reward for the loyalty of the mayor of Anger; he was seventy-three and ever since 1948 had been a Gaullist member of Parliament. Alas! The next day he was singing another tune; the new Secretary of State turned out to be Pierre Chatenet, whose name had been misspelled on the first published list. Victor Chatenay was furious, whereupon he was compensated with an appointment to the highest court of the regime, the Constitutional Council. And his alternate, Jean Foyer, entered the Palais Bourbon in his place.

The following year, Foyer became a secretary of state, and in 1961 Minister of Foreign Aid. When Michel Debré left the government, he persuaded his successor, Georges Pompidou, to give his friend Foyer the post of Minister of Justice. This was the only clause in the "last will and testament" of the departing Premier.

When he arrived at the Place Vendôme, the new Keeper of the Seals found on his desk a request that Jouhaud be granted clemency. Seeking to avoid execution, he urged compliance with the plea for clemency; it took months. No sooner was he installed than Salan's trial began. From then on he was deluged with trials—court cases which constitute the most imposing if not the most worthy monument erected by the Fifth Republic—with all its special courts, its legal ups and downs, and also its blunders. More than once, while brandishing the whip of repression, the young Minister sighed when he thought of canon law, of the law faculty at Lille, of Contigné and his wooden shoes. In 1962 he won for Gaullism the only seat the movement lacked in Anjou. Then he returned to his ministry, a little balder, as sly as ever, not too pleased, apparently, to play the thankless role of the regime's magistrate.

FREY, ROGER, minister, 50 years old
X *Politics*

He is a real politician, one of the few in the Gaullist movement, and one of the cleverest. Yet everything suggests that not until he was about thirty-five did he enter public life as a member of the Gaullist party.

We know little about him before then either, because his official biographies have deliberately and prudently been kept secret or because there simply is not much to tell. Official documents show that he was born in Nouméa in 1913 and married in 1936. Newspaper articles about him say that he fought in the Pacific Battalion in 1940, that his war record was brilliant, and that he is an industrialist. No mention is made of his life before the war, of what he studied and what university degrees he received, of his army rank at the time of demobilization. Occasionally you read that he was a member of De Gaulle's staff in London or of his cabinet in Paris; that during the war, while serving under Admiral Thierry d'Argenlieu or General de Lattre de Tassigny, he had been sent on a mission to General MacArthur; that he met Mao-Tse-Tung and Chou-en-Lai; that he had fought in all the campaigns—Italy, France, and Germany—from the beginning until victory. But what does it matter, he is a Gaullist and that alone counts.

He first entered politics in 1952. Introduced by Jacques Soustelle, backed by the Gaullist group in the National Assembly, he became a member of the Assembly of the French Union. When De Gaulle left office in 1954, he continued to work for him, becoming general director of a last-ditch group, the very tiny Republican Social party. In political circles it was known that he edited the blue press bulletins of this small organization, which were read carefully in the corridors of Parliament, by newspaper editorial writers, by foreign ambassadors and powerful political leaders because, so it was said, Frey faithfully reflected the views of the lone wolf in Colombey.

A ready talker, quite eloquent, his hair streaked with silver, the man is serene and friendly. He practices the art of conciliation, has a gift for subtleties and arbitration, for bringing together divergent points of view, plus a certain taste for mystery and secrecy, a tendency to move about in political life discreetly, preferring backstage maneuvers to the glaring light of debate and public confrontation.

With the support of his party leader, Jacques Soustelle, Roger Frey tried his luck several times in the Lyon elections and became a municipal councillor. During the famous days of May 1958, he left Paris quietly right after Soustelle's flight, despite innumerable difficulties boarded a contraband ship chartered at Palma de Majorca, and reached Algiers via

Spain and the Balearic Isles. Later people learned that he was the principal author of the sybilline and alarming "personal messages" broadcast daily by Radio-Algiers to give the impression of a huge organization and a large-scale conspiracy. These messages, he later revealed, had no special significance nor were they addressed to anyone in particular.

As a member of the Advisory Committee which the following August made plans for the drafting of a new constitution, he collaborated with Soustelle in the Ministry of Information; his role consisted in giving the regime control over both radio and television. But above all he masterminded the new Gaullist movement and contributed more than anyone else to the shaping of the framework and structure of the emerging U.N.R. The electoral victory of 1958, apart from what De Gaulle himself did, was due almost entirely to him.

After that the road was clear: Secretary-General of the U.N.R., Minister of Information, Minister of the Interior. In 1960 his rise was temporarily retarded by Michel Debré and perhaps even more by De Gaulle himself. The reasons are not clear, and we can only surmise them—probably friendship and a certain loyalty to Soustelle. And so Frey had to use pressure at the Matignon and above all at the Élysée in order to obtain a promotion after his long stint as Minister of the Interior.

The vagaries of a political career or the fatal evolution of the Fifth Republic were such that Roger Frey happened to hold a position that made him responsible for the maintenance of order precisely when activism was spreading, when the terrorist O.A.S. was first organized, when attempts at murder and rebellion together with conspiracies flourished. Suspected of weakness, even of complicity, by some, accused of treason by others, held responsible for every failure and excess of the police, he lived through a troubled and difficult period. He was threatened simultaneously by the machine guns of assassins, the disloyalty of friends, the stupidity or insubordination of certain agents. Victims of plastic bombs, apprehended suspects, and demonstrators clubbed by the police, all joined the chorus against him as did security officers, activists, the Left, the Right, the ayes, the nays, Gaullists and at times even De Gaulle himself. He not only managed to get out of this extraordinarily dangerous, tight corner but also succeeded in completely rectifying his personal situation, which had been quite compromised. This he did with the aid of the elections of November 1962 that resulted in the U.N.R.'s second victory. As we remarked earlier, if there is one real politician among the Gaullists, Roger Frey is the man.

GRANDVAL, GILBERT, minister, 59 years old
X   *A fraternal year*

He is a charmer—an energetic man of the upper-middle class, courageous, with just enough of a detached manner not to seem overly ambitious, yet persistent enough not to appear amateurish.

There were three key periods in his life, two of them brief and one long. First, the Resistance; he commanded eight regions in the east of France for the Free French, which gave him the unique opportunity of welcoming De Gaulle in the newly liberated town of Nancy and of having a strange conversation with him. He had never met De Gaulle; he only knew his voice which he had heard over B.B.C. on June 18th. Just as he glimpsed him for the first time, all the lights went out—a fuse had blown. For an hour De Gaulle carried on a monologue in total darkness. Grandval listened as if he were hearing him on the air . . .

De Gaulle sized him up and entrusted him with a proconsulate: the Saar. As governor, high commissioner, and ambassador, Grandval remained there for ten years. To his equerry, a Saarlander, who helped him into the saddle when he began riding, he shouted: "Do you know whom you are teaching to ride? A colonel of the cavalry!" To Parisians he seemed to personify the French presence on German soil, and he left when that image started to fade. Almost without any transition he went from one proconsulate to another, from the Rhine to Africa, ultimately ending up as resident-general in Morocco. Arriving at the Rabat airport on July 7, 1955, he jumped from the plane without waiting for the movable stairway to be hooked on. He left on August 27, fifty days later. During this interval he shoved aside all the higher echelons of the Residency, visited without escort both Medina (it acclaimed him) and the French colony (it booed him). He had been selected as the man to guarantee that Sultan Mohammed V, deposed and exiled, would never return to the throne. He asked the Premier, Edgar Faure, "But won't your policy result in the restoration of the Sultan?" Faure answered, "Have you ever doubted it?" Thereupon Grandval resigned.

As Minister of Labor in 1962, he promised a "fraternal year," but unfortunately Gaullism never had as many strikes as it had that year.

GUICHARD, BARON OLIVIER, Commissioner of Regional Planning, 43 years old
X *The victim of ingratitude*

In the very bosom of the Gaullist family, his role is particularly difficult but necessary, for he represents the exemplary victim of royal ingratitude. Each time an opposition leader complains that "they" have all the jobs, that "they"

are given the fattest sinecures, the ready answer is: "Not
everyone. Look at Olivier Guichard, for example. And yet
he . . ."

Yes, "and yet he . . ." In 1951 he assumed a post that
thousands of ardent and faithful Gaullists had dreamed
about—head of General de Gaulle's personal staff. He owed
the promotion to his youth, his future, and not at all to his
work for Free France or his long apprenticeship in the
Knighthood. Imitating his elders who had accumulated
stripes and medals, he became the General's shadow, his confidential agent, his spokesman, even his silences. He represented devotion in its purest form, selfless loyalty, continuity. This lasted for seven years. In the beginning he was
installed in the shabby Paris office on the Rue de Solférino;
here the General came once a week to receive visitors who
grew less and less numerous and attentive as time went on.
And less and less frequently did De Gaulle issue the kind of
categorical diatribe for which he was known but which people had tired of, or utter the bitter remarks that betrayed his
discouragement, his skepticism. Only Guichard knew how
many fits of temper the General subjected him to, and how
much he willingly sacrificed in order to save appearances, at
least, and preserve the myth. When, in 1955, a remunerative
position had to be found for him so that he would not forever
donate his services, the best that could be done was to make
him press officer for the Atomic Energy Commission—one of
the last Gaullist bastions at that time. De Gaulle's return to
power (which occurred during the May thirteenth revolution
but which not a few people had begun to anticipate in February or March and seriously to prepare for around April 15)
was something Guichard had been working at for seven years,
and the success was largely due to him. He participated in
every meeting, made every contact, figured in every conspiracy. He realized that if he went too far he would be

repudiated, but he also knew that it was his duty precisely to go too far because this was the price of success.

In contrast to so many silent members of the seraglio, he spoke readily and often. Because of the nature of Guichard's task, everyone thought his opinions were actually those of his chief. Nothing of the kind was true. Guichard scarcely knew any more than those whom he deluged with opinions, advice, encouragement or interdictions. He simply took chances boldly and with a certain elegance; because of long experience he made fewer mistakes than others might have about what "he" would have said had "he" spoken. Nobody can reproach him for having occasionally tangled the threads; the least one can say is that "the family" is heavily indebted to him. And it is true that Olivier Guichard is eminently popular among Gaullists. They regard this tall stalwart, grown a little heavier since he turned forty, as the inevitable, familiar twin of the great man. Chief of staff during the "desert crossing," it was quite natural that in 1958 he should be named the Premier's assistant chief of staff. His immediate superior, Georges Pompidou, was not only competent but could also claim seniority. In the King's Court, he is thus the number-two man, which is fair enough. And so for the moment there were no disappointments, but they were not long in coming.

In 1959 Premier Michel Debré knew how much he and others owed Guichard. He also looked upon him as a useful link with the Élysée. He therefore wanted Guichard as a secretary of state. The answer was no, a terse definitive no which was repeated at each of the three times Debré reshuffled his cabinet. Well, since acceptance of a ministerial post was prohibited, did he have permission to embark on a parliamentary career? Chaban-Delmas was in Parliament and in the Gironde he could precisely . . . The answer was no, no for deputy, no for senator. Well then, perhaps promotion to chief of staff since Pompidou was gone? No again: he would be a technical adviser like the others, one among many. And soon half of his duties—those relating to Algerian Affairs—were withdrawn, leaving him only domestic matters that were reduced to very little. Not until 1960, and then not too graciously, was he appointed to a technical proconsulate that had not importance and no future—the post of General Delegate for Saharan Affairs, which was abolished two years later at the time of Algerian independence.

Meanwhile a new Premier had taken over. Georges Pompidou was given the kind of gentle treatment that Michel Debré had never received; he had virtually a free hand in choosing his ministers and in promoting those he considered deserving, save in one case—that of Olivier Guichard, whose name was again stricken from the governmental list at the last moment. Secretary of State on the Premier's staff? No. Undersecretary of State? Again no, no, and no.

Today he is Director of Regional Planning, a pretty title, but if you look carefully you will see that seventeen decrees were necessary to define the jurisdiction and duties of this new official. Had the post been really important, there would have been no need to take so many precautions and to do so much paper work.

Granted that this is the way things are, that the last promotion is just another snare, the question still remains: Why such ingratitude and ill-treatment, such sovereign injustice when so many flagrant disloyalties have been overlooked, so many betrayals forgiven and even erased by promotions? And what if the answer should be, it pleases His Majesty? What if the amiable baron from the Gironde finally ceased to please after having pleased for too long, during that long period when courtiers were rare and the Court depopulated? What if it fell upon him to be the living symbol of royal ingratitude? This lesson (like La Fontaine's fable) is doubtless well worth a piece of cheese.

GUY, CLAUDE, 48 years old
✗ *Forgotten*

✝ ⬚ ⬚ ⬚ ⬚ ⬚ 🐪 ⬚

First he was Lieutenant, then Captain Guy. Almost as big as De Gaulle—I beg your pardon, almost as tall—he used to follow him like a shadow. After joining the Free French Air Force in 1941, this embassy secretary served as the General's aide-de-camp from June 1944 to October 1949, from Algiers to Colombey—via London, Normandy, Paris, the Provisional government—from the victory to De Gaulle's temporary retirement. Modest and taciturn, courteous and calm, he continued during the next six years to discharge his task, his curious official title being Director of General de Gaulle's Press and Information Service.

At the time of the restoration, in 1958, he, like so many others, seemed to have swift promotion and a brilliant career before him. It was he who launched the Union to Support the National Action of General de Gaulle, working assiduously, giving everything he had to the task. Alas! His Union was soon taken over by the National Association to Support the Action of General de Gaulle. The former Captain Guy was neither repaid nor otherwise compensated for his protracted and patient loyalty.

HABIB-DELONCLE, MICHEL, Secretary of State, 42 years old
✗ *President of the World Union of Intellectuals*

⬚ ⬚ 🐪 🛡 ♟ ◉ ⬚

Awarded scholastic honors at the École des Sciences Politiques in 1940, then admitted to the bar, he became in 1948 the administrative secretary of the Gaullist group in the National Assembly. Brought up in the seraglio, he knew all its ways and initiated many of his young U.N.R. colleagues when he entered Parliament in 1958. One by one he climbed the rungs of the Gaullist hierarchy and finally, in 1962, he was given a ministerial position.

He collected several presidencies along the way, notably the presidency of the National Association to Maintain Purchasing Power, the presidency of the European Center of Documentation and Information, and the presidency of the intellectuals' World Union—nothing less.

HAUTECLOQUE, NICOLE DE, deputy, 50 years old
✗   *U.N.R.*

In 1962 she finally succeeded in forcing the door of the Palais Bourbon. This was her reward for protracted obstinacy, for unwavering loyalty in the Municipal Council of Paris to which she had been elected in 1947.

A few days after her election, all the female members of the Municipal Council appeared on television. When it was her turn to speak, the female M.C. asked the harmless question: "Madame, do you belong to the U.N.R.?"

"Naturally!"

The answer was like the crack of a whip. How can one not belong to the U.N.R.?

INGOLD, JEAN, general, 69 years old
✗   *Did not judge Salan*

A cultivated military man, commander of colonial troops and writer in uniform, he was Leclerc's companion. He received the highest Gaullist honor in 1958 when he was named Grand Chancellor of the Order of Liberation. Unfortunately, the vicissitudes of the Fifth Republic proved fatal to his career not because he yielded to the temptation of indiscipline but rather because too much was exacted of him. Appointed to the High Court of Justice, he fell ill the day before the start of Salan's trial. A few months later he resigned as Grand Chancellor for reasons of health.

JACQUET, MARC, minister, 50 years old
✗ *Barbizon*

For the last ten years this solid man from Lorraine has held an enviable municipal post as mayor of Barbizon. Almost by chance or because it was convenient—his constituency was near Paris—this delegate to the R.P.F.'s agricultural section decided to compete for election in the Seine-et-Marne and won.

A member of Laniel's cabinet, he was forced to resign in 1954 because an investigation of the newspaper *l'Express* uncovered correspondence showing that he had been guilty of association with the Mendèist spoilsports. He was a long time recovering. During the life of the Fifth Republic's first legislature, he had to assume the formidable task of reporting on the budget to the Assembly; he displayed such good sense, persistence, and shrewdness that he won back his stripes, and received to boot the Ministry of Public Works.

JOXE, LOUIS, minister, 62 years old
✗ *Peace in Algeria*

All things considered, he is a Gaullist. More than once he came close to heresy. Initially considered a dangerous "leftist," this professor of history became the chief aide of Pierre Cot, Minister of Aviation in the Popular Front cabinet of the 1930's. As secretary-general of the Committee of National Liberation in Algiers, he was suspected of favoring General Giraud, whom the Americans preferred to General de Gaulle.

After serving as secretary-general of the Provisional government in Paris after the Liberation, he remained in the service of the regime. It made him director-general of cultural relations in the Ministry of Foreign Affairs, France's ambassador to Moscow, then to Bonn, and finally secretary-general of the Quai d'Orsay. For twenty years he participated in most of the important international conferences. He is clever and discreet and the fact that he worked his way up is not generally held against him. Great stewards of the state with his range and ability are badly needed. Little wonder that he was chosen for difficult missions and thankless tasks. In January 1960, he was given the Ministry of National Education, but he encountered an unfriendly and oppressive atmosphere and resigned after a year. Then came Algeria. He became Minister of State attached to the Élysée and often clashed with the Prime Minister, but he continued to go his own way. The road he followed led to peace, a peace that was largely his own doing; one can only be grateful to him.

Since then he has been in semi-retirement as a Minister of State whose duties are to lay down principles for administrative reform, but this is purely nominal. From time to time he is given a special dossier, sent on an international mission or asked to straighten out some complicated situation. Methodically, politely, and not without success, he devotes himself to his task. But no whisper of his accomplishments will ever get beyond the walls of the Matignon or the Élysée. He craves not popularity but respect and confidence. Does he have ambitions for the future? He says no.

KOENIG, PIERRE, general, 65 years old
Ⴟ   *Resignations*

This man of proven courage, an officer in active service who rose from the ranks, was a commander at the age of forty-two and slated to become a colonel at the most. Four years later he was successively commander-in-chief of the Free French Forces in France, military governor of Paris, an army general and commander-in-chief in Germany. He should have been made a marshal like Leclerc, de Lattre, and Juin. But this veteran, who had served his emperor as well as Napoleon's *grognards* served theirs, made the big mistake of going into politics. As a Gaullist deputy he became a minister in the cabinet of Mendès-France, resigned, then joined Edgar Faure's cabinet only to resign once again. He managed to antagonize both enemies and friends of the regime—orthodox Gaullists and those who belonged to the "System," activists and liberals.

Wisely, though belatedly, he learned his lesson and gave up, retiring comfortably and collecting on the way presidencies and administrative posts in oil, real estate, and steel companies. The soul of his father, Joseph Koenig, a peaceful Alsatian organ manufacturer, can now rest in peace: his son became a marshal—posthumously.

LA MALÉNE, CHRISTIAN DE, deputy, 43 years old
X *Of the Debré side of the family*

As administrative secretary of the Gaullist group in the Senate, he came to know Michel Debré and from then on shared his political fortunes. His Gaullism is primarily "Debréism." He sympathized with the future Prime Minister's hostility to the European Defense Community and the Common Market. He, too, struggled against the Fourth Republic, prepared for May 13 and the recall of De Gaulle. He collaborated with the Keeper of Seals in June 1958 and with the head of the 1959 government, even though he had been elected deputy in the meanwhile. As a member of the National Assembly he sponsored a bill, drafted in collaboration with J.-B. Biaggi, another May 13 conspirator, whose object was to muzzle the press. Belatedly, in August 1961, he was asked to join the government as Secretary of State in the Ministry of Information. He departed less than a year later together with his friend and "boss."

LE TAC, JOEL, deputy, 45 years old

LE TAC, YVES, 43 years old

✗ *Fighting*

On May 25, 1945, a family party took place in Marseilles. The chief physician of the Modern Clinic, Rue Roland-Garros in Sainte-Marguerite, was back with his family. Actually, the three brothers and sister who gathered in their parents' home had been virtually without news of each other for more than three and a half years. The father, André, had been a prisoner in the camp at Compiègne. The mother, Yvonne, had just completed a long and sorrowful trip, a Calvary to be exact, that led from Ravensbrück, to Maïdenec and Birkenau. Her oldest daughter, Andrée, had also been at Ravensbrück, then at Mathausen. Joël had known the camps of Struthof, Neuengamme, Gross-Rosen, Dora, and Bergen-Belsen. Yves had been sent first to La Santé prison, then to Fresnes before going to Struthof, Erzingen, and finally Dachau. Such was the litany of concentration camps. These survivors who emerged from the fog and the darkness are all called Le Tac. Their son and brother, Roger, the chief physician who today is a professor on the medical faculty of Bordeaux, had likewise experienced arrest, the Gestapo, and prison. It is a family blessed by miracles.

Today, almost twenty years later, the two Le Tac brothers

are covered with decorations, which are only their due, but they have also continued to collect battle scars, the results of carrying weapons and fighting.

It is hardly surprising that both of them, indelibly marked by the great adventure of their younger years, have remained stubborn Gaullists. Joël has continued to encounter adventure at every stage of his life, a life often perilous and exciting, which took him as reporter or fighter from the Resistance to Indochina, Korea, and finally Algeria during May 1958. He went into politics in much the way he had become a fighter, at the head of a determined platoon of hearty comrades, breaking through defenses and taking up a battle stance—this time as deputy for a working-class district in Paris. A disciplined, rather modest parliamentarian, he showed his inexperience when he accepted the kind of support he would have eschewed had he been more prudent. But pshaw! You can't make an omelette without breaking some eggs. Joël Le Tac's real stamping ground was not the Palais Bourbon, which was full of sticklers for etiquette and hair-splitters; he preferred the open air, an arena of combat where free, real men confronted each other without worrying too much about the rules.

As for Yves, his life was quieter. From 1945 to 1957, when he lived in Algiers, he returned, he tells us, to "private business." But he had not lost his flair nor had he changed. He proved this when, as head of the Gaullists of Algeria, of whom there were not many, and as president of the Association to Support the Action of De Gaulle, he suffered in the struggle against the O.A.S. This battle earned him first the explosion of a plastic bomb, then four bullet wounds in his back inflicted by a .45 Colt as he was driving his car in the suburbs of Algiers; then, on February 18, 1962, a commando of assassins broke into his room in the military hospital of Val-de-Grâce. He recovered in Paris, just in time to compete in the Marseilles elections against a shipowner, the proprietor and editorialist of a local daily, as well as against Socialist and Communist rivals supported by the press, the apparatus, and the political bosses of their respective parties.

Although he did not win he did not do too badly, coming in second, ahead of the local and influential shipowner. This was a shot in the arm. He readied himself for the next electoral battle, not forgetting that he still had a few accounts to settle.

One rather surprising thing is the manner and appearance of the Le Tac brothers. It would be a mistake to picture them as tough and hardened professional fighters, in spite of all their wild daring, their proficiency in clandestine activities, their tendency to return blow for blow. Their identical and total baldness gives them a certain resemblance to Yul Brynner. Although they seem to be wearing uniforms even when they are in shirtsleeves, they speak softly with a certain distinction, their gestures are measured, their manner calm, poised, and courteous.

LIGNAC, XAVIER DE, pseudonym: Jean Chauveau, journalist, 52 years old
X   *The King's secret*

As a journalist he has the most thankless of tasks—he is the spokesman, if one can call it that, of the Élysée.

His role consists, first, in keeping quiet about what he knows (a good deal) and suspects (everything else), and in allowing only official information to leak out: the daily litany of interviews (save those that must be kept secret, in other words, the most important ones); announcements of presidential trips (but without giving a date or schedule until the very last minute, if at all); the text of speeches, the list of appointments and promotions (after it has been handed out or announced, reread and, if necessary, edited); denials and clarifications (giving planted versions of remarks or news).

Secondly, he has to "orient" the press, and this is not easy. If a newspaper, even if it is anti-government, interprets something in a way that displeases the General; if a friendly paper prints just one column that exceeds the narrow limitations permitted; if the news agency France-Presse and, following its lead, the state-controlled radio or TV, mention or fail to mention something, announce it either too soon or too late, or use inappropriate language—De Lignac is blamed. When he was a newspaperman he could at least comment, approve, criticize, or argue. Since 1958 he has had to keep still, impose silence on others, pretend surprise, erect a screen around the news. He has the passkey to the vault where secrets of state slumber; he is one of the guardians of the King's secrets.

LIPKOWSKI, IRÈNE DE, former deputy, 65 years old

LIPKOWSKI, JEAN DE, deputy, 43 years old

X *Mother-and-son deputies*

Both of them hereditary Gaullists, they served the cause together. At times the fortunes of politics favored them, at others they did not. From 1951 to 1955 the mother, Irène, was a deputy of the Seine. On January 2, 1956, she lost her seat, but her son interrupted his diplomatic career to become a deputy of the Seine-et-Oise. The Fifth Republic, which they had so ardently desired, started off badly for them; both mother and son were defeated. But their success was merely deferred; in 1962 the son returned to the National Assembly. Perhaps both of them will soon manage to enter the Palais Bourbon together.

MALRAUX, ANDRÉ, minister, 62 years old
X *Minister of the word*

★ ⚔ ▣ 📦 ⚑ ▥ ☽ 🐫 🪑 ⅃ ⇥

Ferral (a character in Malraux's *Man's Fate*) was bored in Shanghai:

> Even with the project for a new Chinese Company in each pocket, he thought only of Paris. It was his dream to return to France rich enough to buy the *Agence Havas** or to negotiate with it; to get back into the political game and, having cautiously reached the cabinet, to pit the combined forces of the cabinet and a bought public opinion against the Parliament. There lay the power.

Twelve years after he attributed this project to his character Ferral, André Malraux played a role in government alongside of General de Gaulle. Thirty years later he again became Minister of Culture and Propaganda in the French Republic of silence where one rules by the word. Claude Vannec in *The Royal Road,* Garine in *Conquerors,* Kyo as well as Ferral, Manuel in *Man's Hope,* and above all Vincent Berger in *Les Noyers d'Altenburg* discuss on behalf of the author the daily life of France and of the Republic, De Gaulle, the government, the permanent revolution, and eternal order. All of them together, in a jumble of ideas, a confusion of flights of fancy, a clatter of phrases, share in the historic meditation that parallels public life today just as yesterday it paralleled adventure, fiction, literary criticism, or art—a meditation that for Malraux constitutes a permanent bond between action and thought.

In a quivering, jerky outburst, with the rhythm of that syncopated pathos that blends lyrical eloquence with ellipti-

* The leading French news-gathering and publicity syndicate.

cal moderation, André Malraux seems to be plagiarizing
André Malraux. He observes the present political upheavals
through the spectacles of History or the electronic telescope;
vaults, in three sentences, from Leonardo da Vinci's studio to
the Common Market; moves with the greatest of ease from
the Crusades to President Johnson, from 1789 to the restoration of historical monuments, with a slight aside about the
Kremlin, a detour to the Palais Bourbon, a parenthesis on
the Acropolis, a short stopover at Brasilia, and an allusion
to NATO.

Around him gravitate crowds of people, courtesans or collaborators, friends and admirers whom he has met on the
battlefields of China or Spain, in the Resistance or in Alsace,
and also in less deadly theaters of operation such as those of
Gaullist politics, in the arts or literature, in government or
diplomacy. Above him is the only man on whom he is willing
to depend, who, "for honor and through victory" made a
Companion of the Order of this comrade of the Chinese revolution, this republican fighter in the Spanish Civil War, this
individual who once said: "Any man of action who is at the
same time a pessimist is or will be a Fascist unless he has
some faith to sustain him." Then he casually added: "My
faith is in dynamiting."

The two first met on the Alsatian front early in the winter
of 1944. Malraux was commanding the Alsace-Lorraine bri-
gade. The head of the Provisional government had come to
inspect the French First Army. "Finally I have met a man!"
De Gaulle exclaimed after they had talked. From then on
the nature of this relationship remained fixed. One word
describes it: fascination.

At that time the fascination was mutual. Everything about
them seemed both contrast and affinity: a certain indifferent
grandeur, the same haughty solitude, an identical taste for
power, which in Malraux had been sublimated by imaginary

adventures. On that day De Gaulle thought he had discovered the Joinville or the Saint-Just of his revolution; and Malraux realized that he had met the sovereign for whom he had been waiting and hoping, who for so long he had vaguely conjured up in his mind. He had just written: "It is too late to exert an influence on something; one can only exert an influence on someone." Thereafter the fascination was to withstand the passage of years, disillusions, and many vicissitudes. Another respect in which the two are alike is that they are equally difficult human beings. Responsible for Culture in the presidential cabinet of 1945, then Minister of Information, the writer, bubbling over with ideas, jumping from reform to bold innovation, polishing his phrases and, when appropriate, his criticism, was hardly a relaxing companion. He always behaved as if he were again or still seeking to verify the intuitions and myths derived from his imagination. Had he not gone to China or taken the road to battle in order to find out whether the soldiers, the executioners, and the prisons of Asia or Spain resembled those he had described when he was twenty? Either as minister or revolutionary he had to confront reality with his own way of seeing things in order to be able to say: "The world is beginning to resemble my books!"

Scarcely had the excitement he felt in seeing a Republic created, and in helping to endow it with its initial features, changed to disappointment, than a new event loomed: the R.P.F. This time power was wrested by legal means; the dynamite contained in words would suffice to blow up the "bad regime." Malraux's role was to stir people's imagination, and in this he did not fail: the stamp campaign, reconstruction of the villages in the Landes that had been devastated by forest fire, collecting huge crowds in a Cecil B. De Mille setting—nothing was lacking save ultimate victory. In his book *Man's Hope,* he had advanced this categorical formula: "There are not so many different ways of fighting; there is only one, and that is to win." Also: "Courage has to be organized." But the era of revolution had disappeared. Thereupon, at a directors' meeting of the R.P.F., Malraux made his famous remark: "General, have you taken us to the banks of the Rubicon merely in order to fish?" This led to a split with the party but not with De Gaulle.

The ensuing period was one of tired indifference, followed by a timid, prudent, and hesitant step toward the "liberal" and Mendèsist Left. Malraux voiced his views in *l'Express*, and in carefully hushed tones conducted a discussion with François Mauriac and Mendès-France behind the scenes. He went from Crans-sur-Sierre to Teheran, from Taormina to Boulogne-sur-Seine, carrying with him his manuscript on imaginary museums, the text of which was supposed to comprise fifty pages and to be written in six months; it swelled to over five hundred pages and took three years. The interval was a long one, interrupted by bitter exchanges on the Rue de Solférino and by discouraged comments during his rare visits to Colombey.

Finally the star returned to its zenith. With the same enthusiasm that he had displayed as Colonel Berger of the Southwest underground in 1943, as the Minister of 1945, and as the propagandist of 1947, the writer again undertook to bear witness and to bring the good word. He held a sensational, an unforgettable press conference, urging the three Nobel prize winners, Roger Martin du Gard, François Mauriac, and Albert Camus, to come to Algeria and see for themselves that there was no longer any torture; he announced that their guide would address the people of France from the historic square "to show it that we are not enemies." Thereupon he received his marching orders, was suddenly removed from Information and assigned to Culture. Here he has stayed ever since, frantically scraping the Paris monuments to restore them to their original whiteness, demanding the execution of the O.A.S. leaders, offering his arms to queens and the Jocunda to a smiling American woman, blending, in his private life, the Furies and servitude.

He hardly showed resentment when, three days before the October 1962 referendum, the Palais de Chaillot and the television screen, both of which he had planned to use the next day to launch the election campaign of the ephemeral Association for the Fifth Republic, were suddenly denied him without explanation or discussion. Few people remarked that he did not belong to the new Gaullist party, the U.N.R., or took part in its demonstrations. Nor do many today notice —they are surprised when they do—that he is still on Pompidou's staff, as he was on Debré's yesterday, and on De Gaulle's the day before.

No longer is he a burning, magical genius, seductive yet alarming, the *enfant terrible* of Gaullism; today he is an elderly uncle whose whims are tolerated with amused indulgence because in the eyes of the neighbors he lends prestige to the family.

MARETTE, JACQUES, minister, 41 years old
X   *Happy husband of Marie-Claude*

His record: a little Resistance, a little journalism, a little commerce, and lots of Gaullism. As for the Resistance, he cannot be reproached for having played a relatively modest role in it, since in 1940 he was only eighteen. His official biographies indicate that he "participated in the Resistance." As for journalism, on which he embarked after studying law and political science, he did not stay with it long. But he worked ardently for Gaullism, was active in the National Council among representatives of professional and labor groups, and slowly earned his stripes. He looks like a professional boxer, has a tough air about him, an unlimited capacity for devotion, and a heart as big as himself. After having held down third-rate jobs for quite a while, he finally had his chance. In 1959 he succeeded Edmond Michelet, who became a minister, as senator of the Seine. And a year later it was his turn to become a minister in Pompidou's cabinet. At his side is a new figure, his wife Marie-Claude, a young woman with mischievous eyes, blond hair, and a ready giggle. Gracious and determined, she works for her husband on election handbills and propaganda when he is busy campaigning. She is the youngest wife of a minister in this Republic, as well as in those of the recent past.*

MARIN, JEAN, pseudonym of Yves Morvan, journalist, 54 years old

ꓫ *From B.B.C. to A.F.P.*

キ ◲ ⬙

Although he is not well-known to the larger public, he nonetheless occupies a key position, one of great importance to the regime. Since 1954 he has been general director of Agence France Presse (The French Press Agency), a post to which he was first appointed and then elected by the board of directors.

The initials A.F.P. appear on thousands of wires every day throughout the world. This French press service compares favorably with the American Associated Press and United Press, to say nothing of the British Reuter. Abroad, the A.F.P. reflects the life and thinking of France. In France it is an essential source used extensively by every newspaper, newscaster, or illustrated magazine, even when other sources

---

* Marette visited the United States in 1960 to study Kennedy's election campaign, and was very impressed with American political techniques.

of information are available. The A.F.P. is the bread of all the French daily papers; it sometimes looks gray, may be hard or even a little moldy, but is indispensable.

All this goes to show how much the A.F.P. and its director are watched, supervised, and guided. Fortunately Marin is a sailor and therefore used to stormy weather. Nonetheless he is very much in need of all the good will the regime bears toward a former member of the 1940 B.B.C. group which unhesitatingly rallied to Free France from the very first.

MASSU, JACQUES, general, 55 years old
X *The charge*

Everything is summed up in the famous and probably apocryphal exchange that took place the day before the barricades were erected:

"Well, Massu, are you as —— tough as ever?"

"As Gaullist as ever, General."

The rest has been told and retold a hundred times. He would have been a wonderful leader of men during the Empire, he would have led the charge and been made a marshal. But what could he do under the Republic, with its revolutionary wars and all its political subtleties!

MAURIAC, FRANÇOIS, 78 years old
X *Bard*

People have said of François Mauriac what he himself once said of André Gide, that he needed to offer himself fully. Probably because of this, Mauriac turned to journalism, since it brought him in contact with the masses. As a novelist, poet, memorialist, and Christian moralist, he had of necessity

a limited audience. Newspaper work became for him a vo-
cation of sorts and led, through successive commitments, to
Gaullism.

Excitable, sarcastic, often irritable, at times violent, always
touchy, he is above all a polemicist—without any doubt the
best of his day. But he is too high and mighty to be a militant for any cause, or to be dependent on any political party.
Nonetheless, his seniority in the Knighthood apparently as-
sures him of good standing; according to the unwritten rules,
it is easily worth as much as membership in the Free French
movement.

On the eve of the Liberation, his enthusiasm, which nothing had as yet dampened, did not prevent him from exercis-
ing his critical judgment or displaying the extraordinary
courage he has never lacked. There is ample evidence of
this in his persistent efforts to save not only Robert Brasillach
but many others—and how many more since then!—from
the public executioner. The R.P.F. aroused in Mauriac a
tense expectation that soon gave way to uneasiness, then to
innumerable and serious doubts. Little by little, as hope returned, his faith was restored. Mauriac hailed and acclaimed
almost unreservedly the beginning of spring in 1958; on more
than one occasion he expressed his confidence in the movement.

His allegiance, like his commitment to Gaullism, stems
solely from his feeling about the General himself. It has
never embraced the dukes and barons of the Court, whom
he considers both poisonous and stupid. Some of the faithful, the prime ministers especially, he holds to be of no account at best, or extremely dangerous at the worst. This
prince of letters pays homage directly to his sovereign.

This homage, rendered without intermediaries, is likewise
characterized by intransigence and capricious sensitivity.
Should the grandeur or life of his hero be threatened, Mau-

riac at once, like the polemicist that he is, flays the assassins, anathematizes their instigators, thanks God that a tragedy has been averted, damns all heretics, and inspires the fainthearted. When bulls announcing some dogma are issued at the ceremonies that pass for press conferences, the novelist is present, seated in the front row. He nods his head at the right moment, bursts out laughing when others merely smile. Then, suddenly, his manner changes. Serious, concerned, he reacts sharply to some biting phrase or obvious bit of propaganda. When the historic figure strikes a pose for posterity that goes unappreciated by contemporary chroniclers, this journalist, in the grand manner he reserves for state occasions, hastens to give it pith.

"General de Gaulle! There's a man who is sure of immortality!" François Mauriac once wrote, perhaps not without envy. Between the two men there has never been any true intimacy, any intrigue. Although both of them, thanks to an imposing destiny, have eluded the rules of a similar social background, one fructifies and the other submits with annoyed reverence. This creates—the very words make it plain—natural bonds of an almost carnal character. Yet the first, firm in his convictions, gives but a passing thought or glance to the second, who, deeply feeling and tormented, praises, interprets, but also hesitates and questions. De Gaulle acts, decides, dictates. Mauriac offers himself fully.

MAURICE-BOKANOWSKI, MICHEL, minister, 51 years old

✗ *Paid vacations*

✝ ★ ◉ ◻ 🐫 🪑 ◉ 🦎

This sailor, son of a minister under the Third Republic, began political life at the end of the war and joined the R.P.F. as soon as it was founded. Secretary-general for the

Paris region, a deputy since 1951, mayor of Asnières since 1959, he has personal reasons for his devotion to Gaullism; a member of Debré's cabinet, he was in the first batch of officials to serve the Fifth Republic. He was given the formidable honor of an appointment to the Ministry of Industry under Pompidou. He soon realized that this was a mixed blessing when the four-week vacation caused a controversy because the Renault Company had granted it with Maurice-Bokanowski's consent, although his colleagues only learned about it from a newscast. Then, in March 1963, he had to contend with the miners' strike.

"He is the first Minister of Industry out of more than twenty I have met in the last fifteen years who, when I come to see him, can never decide whether he knows what firm I represent." Thus spoke the all-powerful secretary-general of the employers' federation of an essential branch of heavy industry.

MICHELET, EDMOND, member of the constitutional Council, 64 years old
✗ *Jesus Christ and De Gaulle*

The same words always come to mind to describe him: nice face, generous heart, firm Christian, good-natured grandfather, and what a true, faithful Gaullist!

Everything is clear and aboveboard about him. He can claim a rare seniority in the Resistance because he departed twenty-four hours before De Gaulle on the day prior to the June 18th appeal. Always militant, he proved this in the First World War when, in 1917 at the age of eighteen, he joined the army. He was a member of the extreme Right, but left it quickly for the Catholic Action party. When he was twenty-three he became president of the local Catholic

Youth, which was closely connected with the newly created Christian Democratic party. His home in Brive, where he practiced his trade as a grain broker, became the meeting place for groups in which middle-class youths, who were not yet called "Progressive Christians," rubbed shoulders with priests who had not yet become workers, with rural militants, intellectuals, and Parisians who had come to help organize. It was from his house that the famous tract was sent on June 17, 1940, that was inspired by Péguy's remark: "He who does not yield is in the right against him who does." This was simple and clear.

His bravery in the Resistance won everyone's respect. He commanded the regional echelon of the Combat movement, then the M.U.R. (Mouvements Unis de Résistance), until February 1943, when he fell into the hands of the Gestapo. He spent six months at Fresnes, then at Dachau where he was stamped with number 52,579. Incorrigibly, he continued to act the Saint Bernard even on "Liberty Street"— the deportees' name for the central alley of the concentration camp—about which he wrote a very moving story. Upon his return he was introduced to De Gaulle and at that moment his political career began. Here, too, everything would go smoothly for him. His reasoning can be summarized in a few words: "It was the General who summoned me and made me what I am; he can therefore undo his handiwork, send me where he pleases, deprive me of everything he has given if he so chooses; I am a soldier and he is my leader." He is not just an unconditional Gaullist but more than that, he is a mystic. If Jesus Christ appeared before him and ordered him to betray De Gaulle, he would suspect Him of being tempted by Satan.

Like all believers, he sometimes suffers some anguish or irritation in the face of his god's weakness; but he quickly rights himself, makes excuses, convinces himself that the

General must be, can only be right, and concludes in all humility that probably he himself is not clearsighted enough to understand his reasons. The Lord's ways are impenetrable.

In 1945, when De Gaulle wanted to bring the generals to heel, Edmond Michelet became Minister of the Army. General de Gaulle quit the government. But since he expected to return, he decided that *his* Minister of the Army must remain. So remain Michelet did, first under Gouin, then under Bidault. When De Gaulle founded the R.P.F., Michelet was with him; he failed to win re-election as deputy, but did get into the Senate. For the entire duration of the "desert crossing" he was in active opposition, refusing portfolios time after time. Came May 1958 and he did his best to pave the way for De Gaulle. He was put in charge of Veterans' Affairs and then, under Debré, became Minister of Justice.

He soon learned that it was not easy to be the "liberal" guarantor of Gaullism in this post without actually becoming a hostage. The treatment of Algerian prisoners, the lawsuits against clandestine networks to help Algerians, modification of the procedural code, recasting of the press laws—everything became a pretext for friction, incidents, outbursts between the Keeper of the Seals and the Prime Minister. The General was the arbiter, decided in favor of the head of the government, berated his submissive Minister of Justice, and hauled him over the coals. But one fine morning he no longer pleased His Majesty, and was told so in no uncertain terms, whereupon he immediately offered his head on a gold platter, since this was the will of his leader.

In the same quiet way he joined the Constitutional Council. There he was somewhat bored, but this did not matter: he was in the second reserves, and, like an old disciplined soldier, waited for orders. Didn't the General impose peace in Algeria, against the will of the Prime Minister, just as he, Edmond Michelet, always said he would? Vive de Gaulle. The General is always right.

MIRGUET, PAUL, former deputy, 52 years old
✗ *Subamendments and "La Mirguette"*

Excerpt from the *Journal Officiel,* National Assembly debates of July 18, 1960:

> *Paul Mirguet:* At a time when our civilization, trailing dangerously in an evolving world, is becoming so vulnerable, we must combat everything that will lessen its prestige. In this domain as in others, France must set an example. That is why I ask you to adopt my sub-amendment.
> *The President:* M. Mirguet has appended to amendment No. 8, proposed by the Commission of Cultural Affairs, a sub-amendment No. 9 that reads as follows:
> "Insert the following paragraph No. 4: All measures to combat homosexuality." What is the opinion of the Commission? (Laughter.)
> *Madame Marcelle Devaud,* reporter: I don't think it's so funny! This is a situation that you know about, and I too know about . . . (more laughter) . . . I will merely say to M. Mirguet that Paragraph No. 3 of my amendment dealing with the means provided by the convention against white slavery and prostitution is not aimed solely at women, but at human beings generally.
> *The President:* What is the government's opinion?
> *The Minister of Public Health and Population:* The government refers it back to the Assembly.

(Sub-amendment No 9, put to an oral vote, is adopted.)

A fine Resistance fighter, a disciplined deputy, Paul Mirguet was known in Parliament for other ingenious innovations. He is the author of a miracle reform for taxes which consists in replacing all current taxes with a single tax of 1 percent, known as "la Mirguette," on all settlements, checks, transfers of funds, etc. He also proposed a huge plan to reform the state which he had to introduce alone because his Gaullist colleagues refused to support or endorse it. The ungrateful voters, unaware of the reformist ardor of their deputy, did not re-elect him in November 1962.

MIRIBEL, ELISABETH DE, embassy attachée, 48 years old
X From secretary to the Carmel convent and back

✝ ◻ ◻ ◻ ◻

She was twenty-six in 1941 when she was chosen in London from among all other women. She was to live in the shadow of the General, forever at his side, answering the telephone for him, taking down and transcribing his words, opening doors and windows and, if necessary, making tea. From 1941 to 1945 she was General de Gaulle's private secretary at the Carlton Gardens (London), at the Palais d'Été (Algiers), and at the Matignon (Paris). When she left in 1945, she was given a position at the Quai d'Orsay as embassy attachée. Was it her separation from De Gaulle that made life lose all its appeal? Three years later, after having bade a protracted farewell to the world, she entered the Carmel Convent. Was it the cloistered life that changed her? When she left five years later, for reasons of health, she joined the staff of Pierre Mendès-France. Now repentant, it is said, she is prepared to burn everything she once adored and is inclined to be very critical of the Gaullist faith of which nonetheless she had been a high priestess.

NEUWIRTH, LUCIEN, deputy, 39 years old
Ⅹ *The stranger of May 13*

Lieutenant Neuwirth suddenly appeared in the news during the course of the May thirteenth revolution in Algiers. He was the spokesman of the Committee of Public Safety, the Camille Desmoulins of that "revolution." Within a few hours all of France knew his name as well as Léon Delbecque's. But no one knew who he was.

Several weeks later it was learned that he was not a career officer of the "young army," a professional activist or a "pied noir" in revolt, but a peaceful businessman, a former member of the Resistance, a Gaullist municipal councillor who had represented his city ever since 1947. It took several more months to realize that Jacques Soustelle's permanent representative in Algiers—that was his title during the summer of 1958—was not an extremist like his chief but a disciplined Gaullist.

As a deputy, he worked with the Moslem officials, trying to steer them away from European activism and toward acceptance and even support of the regime's Algerian policy, despite its fluctuations and uncertainties. Today he is a quaestor of the National Assembly, a coveted and relatively important post.

NOËL, LÉON, president of the Constitutional Council, 75 years old
Ⅹ *From Laval to De Gaulle via Pétain*

He had been France's High Commissioner in the Rhineland, prefect for the Upper Rhine, director of the *Sûreté* (the Police), chief of staff in Pierre Laval's cabinet, and minister at Prague. As ambassador to Poland during the five years preceding the war, the thankless and painful task of negotiating the 1940 armistice with Germany and Italy fell to him. Pétain appointed him his delegate in the occupied territory, but he resigned ten days later. In September 1943 a constitutional decree promulgated by Pétain named him, along with Admiral Auphan and General Weygand, to the college of seven "empowered to govern provisionally in case of emergency."

No matter. It turned out that he was a Resistant and a Gaullist, and as such a member of the governing board of the R.P.F. In 1951 he entered Parliament as a deputy. Then came his eclipse. Léon Noël was almost seventy. Would he retire? Not at all. During the summer of 1958 he helped to write the new constitution and was entrusted with the delicate mission of presiding over and inspiriting the Constitutional Council, a body empowered to ratify the royal edicts. In actuality, however, the "Supreme Court" of the regime became merely a registry of records, and this was unfortunate. Léon Noël experienced at least one moment of rebellion: in October 1962 he made known his disapproval of the referendum procedure, declaring that it was entirely unconstitutional. His resignation and departure were announced, but it must have been one of those false rumors.

NUNGESSER, ROLAND, deputy, 38 years old
X *Navigation*

A nephew of the aviator who disappeared in the Atlantic along with Coli, he belongs to that generation of Latin Quarter militants who were too young to fight in the Resistance and who entered politics via those typical *"Boul' Mich' "* student demonstrations. He won his stripes one by one at Nogent-sur-Marne, where he has been municipal councillor since 1953, mayor since 1959, and deputy since 1958.

While others wore themselves out trying to make politics a livelihood and a profession, he succeeded in forging a maritime career that runs parallel to politics: he is general commissioner of the International Nautical Society and vice-president of the Nautical Labor Exchange.

OLLIVIER, ALBERT, writer, 48 years old
X   *Television*

He was an editorial writer for the daily *Combat* during that grand post-Liberation period when this paper, inspired by Camus and Raymond Aron, moved from "Resistance to Revolution," (its motto). With great enthusiasm he joined the R.P.F., directed its paper *Le Rassemblement,* and at the same time embarked upon a career as a political historian. In 1946 he had published—premonition or mere coincidence?— *Les Fausses Sorties (False Exits).* In 1954 he wrote *Saint-Just,* a brilliant and solid piece of work, whose subtitle, *Or the Inevitability of Things,* was typically Gaullist in tone. In 1959 he worked on a book entitled *Dix-huit Brumaire,* which of course made no allusion to General de Gaulle . . . In 1958 the General opened a new avenue to the writer, entrusting him with one of the regime's key means of guiding opinion: he was appointed assistant-director, then director of Information, and finally director of television programs. He has become an expert in this new technique, bringing to the small evening screen the kind of culture that raises the entire level of TV entertainment. For example, when Aeschylus' *The Persians* was shown in a single performance, it captivated, moved, and delighted the largest audience it had had in two millennia.

PALEWSKI, GASTON, minister, 62 years old
X *"Number 5 bis"*

✟ ◻ ★ ◻ ▦ ♦ ◫ ♪ ♠ ○ ✪ + ◻

He was one of the oldest and closest companions during the crucial years—the Grand Duke of De Gaulle's reign. His first "boss" was Lyautey, his second, Paul Reynaud. As the head of the latter's personal staff in 1934, he became acquainted with the great man and has shared his fortunes ever since. In August 1940 he joined De Gaulle in London and carried out a difficult mission that took several months— rousing and wooing East Africa. From 1942 to 1946, in London, Algiers, and Paris, he never left De Gaulle's side. He was the General's faithful, discreet, indispensable chief of staff. Worldly, amiable, some say even charming, he is a confirmed bachelor who has turned many a head. "Gaston" weathers tempers, covers up blunders, explains away awkward silences, smoothes ruffled feelings.

In his memoirs, Jacques Dumaine, former chief of protocol, wrote that when the rules of etiquette were revised, the President's principal aide was designated by the number "5 bis."

In the R.P.F. he played a role that was both casual and effective. Not one to toss a stick of dynamite or start a revolution, he is less at ease in opposition than in office. But his place is in Parliament where, after all, arguments are settled politely, with little bitterness. The Gaullists are exposed to both the evils and the blessings of the system: Didn't the General give them back their freedom, dissolve the R.P.F., and abandon the struggle?

One day, Gaston Palewski, who was not having an easy time of it, and who was beginning to feel the weight of his years, succumbed, as others had done, and joined the government. He remained there for eight months, resigned, and lost his seat in Parliament. Two years later, he accepted the ambassadorship to Italy, one of the finest and most enviable posts in a career of this kind. De Gaulle, so the story goes, obtained it for him. After all, the General couldn't really blame him or bear a grudge. Yet apparently De Gaulle was resentful; Palewski was left to cool his heels in Rome during the first four years of the reign. When newspapermen ventured to suggest his name, De Gaulle merely shrugged his shoulders.

Purged by his four years of exile, Palewski was appointed Minister of State and entrusted with responsibility for atoms and rockets—those precious, gaudy jewels of the magic future. The prodigal was forgiven his eight-month lapse and welcomed back to the family table. But only as a guest—he is really no longer a member of the family.

PASTEUR VALLERY-RADOT, LOUIS, member of the Constitutional Council, 77 years old
✗ *"Le Tout-Paris"*

Early in 1963, a Parisian columnist, who knows the ways of his world, sat down on a bench at the entrance to a new and fashionable nightclub where an orchestra of women was playing and stayed there for a whole week. Every evening, from the dinner hour to closing time, our man counted the comings and goings of habitués known as *"Le Tout-Paris."* From his observation post he compiled instructive and detailed statistics, noted the arrivals of a well-known actor who came each night with a different woman, witnessed curious and embarrassing encounters, the flaunting of clandestine re-

lationships, observed faces one would not have expected to
see. The French academician and member of the Constitutional Council, Pasteur Vallery-Radot was on the list, with
several marks after his name to indicate that he was a frequent visitor.

There is scarcely an elegant party, a grand ball, or the
kind of reception everyone talks about at which he is not
present. He attends every gala evening, often dines in town,
and sups at some fashionable place after theater. He is the
most worldly of the Immortals, the most stylish of the austere
guardians of the constitution, the youngest of the great physi-
cians. He has been a Gaullist deputy but resigned after
eleven months, believing that this was not the right slot for
him. This incursion into politics, and even the formidable
honor of being named to the Supreme Court of Justice in
1962, affected neither his Gaullism, which remains steadfast,
nor the friendly envy De Gaulle feels for the amazing vitality
of his senior.

PERETTI, ACHILLE, deputy, 52 years old
✗   *Neuilly-sur-Seine*

✝ ★ ● ◨ 🐴 🪑 🐾

Baron of a Parisian suburb, he administers the fief of
Neuilly, whose residents enjoy the highest average wealth
and comfort. It took a good deal of know-how and shrewdness for a Gaullist to retain such a desirable constituency
through all the vicissitudes of the "family." And for a Corsican (former police commissioner in Tunis until 1942, then
assistant general director of Police for the government at
Algiers, vice-president of the general council of his native
island in 1951), it took a good deal of obstinacy to impose himself thus on the Paris bourgeoisie, so sure of their power, so
imbued with a sense of their own importance. The U.N.R.

swept him into the National Assembly, where he consolidated his position while apparently confining himself to the role of administrator and municipal management expert who doesn't fool with politics.*

PETIT, ANDRÉ, general, 54 years old
Ⅹ *five years of criminal detention*

He is a typical officer of Gaullist origin who rebelled precisely because of his Gaullism. There are many in his situation today, and they people the Tulle prison as well as other places of detention.

A magnificent Resistant, an escapee from Gestapo prisons, he followed De Gaulle, De Lattre, then Ely. In their service, particularly in De Lattre's, he was the trustee, the political head, the emissary during difficult moments. To save French Algeria he, together with Michel Debré, an enthusiast like himself, and Jacques Soustelle paved the way for the 13th of May.

On the morning of that day, before the explosion, he reached Algiers as Ely's representative and, more significantly, as General de Gaulle's delegate to the army. When the army supported the pronunciamento and directed it in favor of De Gaulle, it was his vigorous and persistent efforts that were largely responsible.

In January 1959 he became the head of the Prime Minister's military staff, while General de Beaufort (also a Gaullist and animated by the same desire to establish a strong regime that would save Algeria) served in a similar capacity under the President of the Republic. General Petit's oldest daugh-

* A very active man, interested in American community problems, as mayor of Neuilly he runs probably the best public school system in France; a relatively large number of American children attend. He speaks perfect English and often addresses the American Chamber of Commerce in Paris.

ter married General de Beaufort's son. The two men worked hand in glove. But during the course of the next few months they realized that they had been deceived. De Gaulle accepted independence for Algeria. The promise made to so many fighting comrades had been broken.

Beaufort left the Élysée in May 1960 and Petit, heartbroken, resigned in December of the same year. He was in Algeria as commander of the Seventh Light Mechanized Division in April 1961, at the time of the putsch. He had no faith whatsoever in the success of this absurd and poorly organized operation and severely criticized the rebels. Nevertheless he agreed to command their army in Algiers. By this gesture of solidarity he cleared himself of what he regarded as a blot on the record, a sad mistake: to have given his promise because he himself had been fooled, to have believed De Gaulle, to have been one of the rare Gaullists in the army.

He paid the price—five years of criminal detention. A rebel in spite of himself, a victim of Gaullism, he is not alone.

POMPIDOU, GEORGES, Prime Minister, 52 years old
X *Patience*

In the ordinary course of events a professor does not become a judge, a banker does not frequent the poets, the cultivation of roses does not lead to the prime ministership. And yet Georges Pompidou, according to his biographers, was a professor. Later he gave his opinion on legal matters as a member of the Council of State and the Constitutional Council. At the same time he apparently was the manager of a commercial bank. In addition, he authored a recent book that revealed a passion for Baudelaire, a warm regard for Apollinaire, a taste for the verse of Eluard. And some people claim they have seen him pruning rose bushes in the garden of a white house at Orvilliers, near Houdan. This is the man who, in April 1962, became Prime Minister of the Fifth Republic.

The key to this mystery is obvious: there are three Georges Pompidous, inseparable yet identical, whose destinies diverge.

The first is the professor. He was born, as a matter of fact, to the teaching profession; it is said that his father, a teacher, curbed his students no less closely than did Professor Henri de Gaulle, the father of the General. A brilliant student at the Albi Lycée, he went from there to the Lycée Louis-le-Grand. Upon becoming a professor, he immediately became affiliated with a lycée in Marseilles where he began his carefully mapped-out career. It brought him to Paris where, according to the immutable logic so luminously exposed by Giraudoux, the entire administrative climb began which inexorably led the lucky man to his point of departure, the capital.

Thanks to the long university vacations, the professor was able to devote himself first of all to a study of Racine's *Britannicus*. Then he edited two small "illustrated classics" for secondary school instruction, choosing passages from Taine and Malraux and providing introduction, bibliography, documents, course questions, and subjects for exercises in French composition. In 1961 he produced an anthology of French poetry—which certainly proves that there is no connection between all this and the man who only a few months later was to become head of the government. The anthology, despite the generous amount of space given to Nerval, Baudelaire (but the "accursed poets" whom justice has absolved, have become quite acceptable to people of good family), and P. J. Toulet, can be safely put into anyone's hands. In his spare time, when he was not correcting dissertations or giving private lessons, he worked in his garden. Tired but smiling eyes topped thick, heavy brows, a debonair joviality, the measured gestures of a man who knows the importance of each day and season—this robust Auvergnat has the physique to push a wheelbarrow and dig with a spade.

His twin brother, the second man, is altogether different. Every morning he leaves an apartment on the Quai de Bethune that reveals his love for ancient architecture and fine furniture. His destination is the spacious, dark-paneled office on the first floor of the Rothschild Bank on the Rue Laffitte. Here he is general director, although the usher in morning coat and striped pants who reigns over the august and thread-bare armchairs in the antichamber sometimes forgets this title, created especially for him, and inadvertently addresses him, according to the firm's tradition, as Mr. Director.

To arrive at this high office, which future premiers had occupied before him, he graduated, as was customary, from a great school—in his case, the École Normale Supérieure. Thereupon he began collecting presidencies and administrative posts all the way from Penarroya to Francarep and from West Africa to the Rateau Company. Presiding over an investment firm in the north of France, he made a point of specializing in the economy of the region. He proved to be as competent on the board of a management and army weapons firm as in the handling of a railway transport company which he also administered. However, he was eventually to quit business.

As for the third Georges Pompidou, he chose politics. To do so he took a diploma in political science. At the end of the war and the Resistance, in which he had served brilliantly, he was appointed head of the provisional government's personal staff. Twelve years later, in 1958, when his "boss" returned to power, he was made director of the presidential cabinet in another Provisional government.

Meanwhile, he frequented the Council of State, tried his

hand at running a tourist agency, and finally left the Council with an honorary membership and no intention whatsoever of returning to it. Although his talents lay in quite a different direction, in 1959 he resumed his juridical duties on the Constitutional Council, to which he had been appointed for a nine-year term. When he carried out confidential assignments that paved the way for the Algerian peace, it was rather as an emissary and official councillor than as one of the "wise men" of the regime. He had learned the virtue of discretion and the advantage of immobility.

And so in power, his golden rule was silence; there were times when he was seen to hesitate over perfectly innocuous questions at the Palais Bourbon, or even at less official gatherings. A political leader, he knew, will be blamed for his every act, decision, or reform, but it is more difficult to reproach him for having neglected to organize the structure of the state or the economy or for having quietly allowed some burning issue to slip unobtrusively into the wastepaper basket. He thought of reforms as fruit that would fall to the ground on its own whenever it became ripe. He saw to it that the regime got its second wind. Someone else had been signed to the thankless task of endowing the regime with its most unattractive, its harshest features. Pompidou was content merely to steer clear of danger—too much expansion could be as dangerous as a recession and, of course, to be too active, to talk too much, was harmful. Such was his method, and it was said to have been inspired by old-fashioned Radicalism. But why care what people thought? His only concern was for the General's esteem, and everything suggested that he had won it.

But, one might well ask, how did such confusion arise between the banker, the high official, and the writer? Were these different individuals or one and the same man? Which of these became General de Gaulle's Prime Minister? If one had to be a lawyer to preside over the high courts, a business-

man to become the director of a bank, a diplomat to negotiate, and a parliamentarian to run the ministry, there doubtless could only be one Georges Pompidou, probably the
professor, perhaps the gardener, certainly the Gaullist. It
was his ambition that proved his undoing: to the dazzling list
of successive or simultaneous offices which already adorned
his visiting card he wanted to add the still unsullied title of
Former Premier of the Fifth Republic. He wanted to impress Montboudif, his native town, whose mayor and general
councillor too, he had long hoped to be. Tomorrow he
might wish to succeed De Gaulle so that his fame would
reach beyond the frontiers of Cantal. But beware—he is
perhaps not the only man who harbors such dreams.

PONCHARDIER, DOMINIQUE, pseudonym: Antoine
Dominique, writer, 46 years old
X   *The Gorilla*

He is the Gorilla. Head of the Secret Service and member
of the governing board of the R.P.F., he has written about
fifty mystery stories in the *Série Noire* under his pseudonym,
and one book, *Les Pavés de l'Enfer* (*The Pavements of Hell*),
under his own name. In his official biographies two things
are always mentioned, one of them quite touching. Under
the heading "relative and kin of," his brother, Admiral Pierre
Ponchardier (1909–1961)—a Gaullist and Companion of the
Order. The other item is reassuring; under the heading of
"hobbies," small-scale models and the harmonica.

But he also knows how to use less inoffensive, less musical
toys. He has been in all the tough fights and in the special
services there exists something called the "Pompon team,"
a solid, aggressive and highly envied group.

Only once did he allow himself to write a book on politics.

It was entitled *The Gorilla in Revolution (Le Gorille en Révolution)*, and appeared in 1959 but did not attract the attention it deserved. For the Revolution of the Gorilla was the 13th of May. The plot was exposed to the full light of day, the insurrection proudly displayed in all its secret motives, the landing called "Operation Resurrection" deprived of its mystery. The actors were even given their right names: "Cousin Jules," or Soustelle, De Gaulle or Pflimlin, even Pondom, the organizer of the Southwest insurrection, "a chap who carried weight." Committees of Public Safety, machine guns that went off by themselves, secret codes and messages are all described. The people who count are those who had "a few small antecedents as killers in 1941–42." This was a new Resistance with its clandestine members and its collaborators—but where was the occupier? Well, it is quite instructive—a slice of life. "You have to see it to believe it," says the Gorilla. You can bet that he was one of them!

SAINTENY, JEAN, minister, 56 years old
✗ *Vietnam and the tourist trade*

There are two important facts in his life. Captured by the Gestapo during the occupation when he was a leader of the Resistance network Alliance, he had been in peacetime a tranquil insurance agent who was better known as Albert Sarraut's son-in-law. He escaped, resumed the fight, became a leader of the Allied landings in Normandy, crossed the lines several times to bring General Patton the information that enabled him to beleaguer Paris.

Two years later, on December 19, 1946, as the Republic's commissioner in Tonkin and North Annam, he intervened between the Vietnamese insurgents of Hanoi and the French who were threatened with massacre, succeeded in saving the lives of many of his compatriots, but himself fell into a trap and was gravely wounded. In his *L'Histoire d'une Paix Manquée* (*The History of an Abortive Peace*), he recounted his 1945 mission in China, the struggle against Japan, the re-establishment of French authority in Vietnam, the negotiations with Ho Chi Minh that resulted in the accords of March 6, 1946, then the eruption of revolution. He returned to Hanoi after the 1954 armistice as general delegate of France to North Vietnam. Upon his return in 1957 he took part in the founding of the National Association to Support the Action of General de Gaulle, and became one of its presidents. General Commissioner of Tourism in 1959, deputy for a Paris constituency in 1962, he attended only one session of the National Assembly, being promptly appointed Minister of Veterans' Affairs in the Pompidou cabinet.

SANGUINETTI, ALEXANDRE, deputy, 50 years old
X   *Honorary member of* 🦊

◻ 🚜 👤 👤 ⟋

His is one of the noisiest voices of triumphant Gaullism, although he joined the Knighthood quite late and after many detours.

Chief Surgeon Sanguinetti had a magnificent war record. A volunteer in the infantry as early as 1939, then a prisoner, he escaped in 1942 and joined a French unit in Africa, fought in Italy and Corsica, lost a leg on the Island of Elba, received the Legion of Honor, the military medal, and an imposing collection of other decorations. He was not a member of Free France, but he is a tough man whose courage has never been in doubt.

His debut in political life was modest and strangely oriented toward the Left, or almost. Three years later he suddenly veered to the Right and had a short-lived career in business. From then on his enemies, in attacking him, repeatedly alluded to his failures, even his bankruptcy.

Having entered on the Left and exited on the Right, he remained faithful to his new friends and even enlarged his circle. He was in the first row of demonstrators at the Place de l'Étoile when Pléven, then Minister of Defence, was pushed, losing his glasses and his hat. Above all, showing all the fire that characterizes him, he joined the clandestine fighters who were most active in 1958; he was thus one of the organizers of "Operation Resurrection."

In 1930 Sanguinetti played on the Saint Stanislas rugby team. One of his teammates was Roger Frey. Twenty-eight years later, during the birth of the Fifth Republic, they were once again on the same team—in the U.N.R., at the Ministry of Information, and at the Ministry of the Interior. Neither the absentminded nor the initiated ever quite knew which man occupied which post at the Place Beauvau, nor what game was being played; everyone realized that the possible plays one can devise with the oval ball vary infinitely.

Having definitely chosen, as his campaign leaflet proclaimed, "peace, progress, confidence in the future, order and stability," Alexandre Sanguinetti received his reward. In November 1962 he entered the Palais Bourbon. The devil became a hermit: the burden of his first speech was the need to suppress compulsory military service. Success carries its own burdens.

SCHMITTLEIN, RAYMOND, deputy, 59 years old
X *Belfort*

✝ 🛏 🦔 ⚚ 🎴 ☉ + 🔷 🪑 🐿

Haughty, biting, bubbling over with jarring, contradictory ideas, he jumps from Lithuania to Germany, from Napoleon to Mérimée, from Fénelon to Caesar, finally ending with De Gaulle. In a position of responsibility under Laniel during the Indochinese War, then director of the Merchant Marine under Mendès-France, president of the France-U.S.S.R. Society, and managing editor of the *Intellectual Review of Lexicography,* a university professor and former embassy secretary, a colonel in the reserves, a doctor *honoris causa*—his biographical sketch is an unbelievable compilation.

It would take too many pages to recount his adventures as a clandestine agent for Free France in the Levant; his diplomatic mission to the U.S.S.R. when he obtained not only the recognition of Free France from the Kremlin but also the freeing of the Alsatians and Lorrainers enrolled in the *Wehrmacht* and taken prisoner by the Russians; his campaigns; his career as Proconsul for Cultural Affairs in occupied Germany; his Homeric battles with Dreyfus-Schmidt, a Communist fellow-traveler, for the mayoralty of Belfort, for that city's representation in Parliament and on the General Council; his court cases on defamation and his political caprices.

A minister of the Fourth Republic, he had to be content with a vice-presidency of the National Assembly under the Fifth. He is champing at the bit—but in morning coat and striped pants—while awaiting the propitious moment to hurl himself once again into the fray.

SCHUMANN, MAURICE, deputy, 52 years old
X   *Spokesman*

╪ 🏛 ★ ♟ 🎴 𝄞 ☉ + 🗇 🪑 🗡 ⌐

"Here is London! Honor and Country. Here is General de Gaulle." During the dark days these words, preceded by five knocks—three and two—which meant that the B.B.C. was broadcasting, spelled hope. These words were usually uttered by the spokesman of Free France, Maurice Schumann. He was the most eloquent, the most ardent, the most popular of the broadcasters. He was almost completely unknown save to former employees of the *Agence Havas* where he had been editor before the war. His name, for those in the know, was associated with the Religious Information Service that he directed when he became converted to Catholicism, a service known by those in the firm as the "Clergy Special."

After the Liberation the spokesman turned out to be a Christian Democrat; he became a deputy leader in Parliament, president of the party, Secretary of State for Foreign Affairs, Minister, and a leader of the Fourth Republic. His quarrels with certain Gaullists are too numerous to count, especially his violent altercation in 1945 with Colonel Passy. And yet he has his place in this compendium.

For if there ever was a Gaullist it is he. His career began at the Carlton Gardens. He never forgets it, nor does he allow anyone else to do so. He has always been torn between two loyalties; the name "party of loyalty," which for a short time after De Gaulle's departure in 1946 was given to Christian Democrats, is one he coined. He always seems to be personally bearing a piece of the true Cross—the Cross of Lorraine . . .

And with it all, he is all smiles, confidential, warm and sensitive, overflowing with vitality, involved in numerous things simultaneously: deputy, president of the Commission, party leader, omniscient journalist, adviser for a thousand undertakings, essayist, belated novelist, good father and husband, good Christian and good Gaullist.

SERVAN-SCHREIBER, JEAN-CLAUDE, newspaper director, 45 years old
✗ *The family spirit*

He is the Gaullist in the family, because *Les Échos* is a rather moderate newspaper and *L'Express* is Mendèsist. This has caused not a few quarrels, and he has even been accused of trying to hand over the family daily to the U.N.R. We all know that nowhere do people tear each other apart so much as within their own family circle.

Yet nothing is more alien to his nature than Machiavellian plots or.devious paths. He is a man who goes his way openly and whose primary virtue is courage. He proved this in the Resistance and in the Second Motorized Division. He too is willing to expose himself to danger, and, although he has not pushed himself to the fore recently, he certainly did in May 1958. Co-founder of left-wing Gaullism, he brings to the political family a little of that human warmth and confidence which he apparently does not find elsewhere, in the more intimate circle of his newspaper family.

SOUSTELLE, JACQUES, former minister, 51 years old
✗ *Brutus and Seneca*

He surpasses in seniority many front-rank Gaullists; he joined De Gaulle in London as early as the summer of 1940. In 1943, during the crucial period in Algiers, he held an essential and key position as director of the Secret Service in Free France. After the Liberation, when Debré and Pompidou were mere members of the presidential staff, he was Minister of Information after Malraux, then Minister of the Colonies. He was officially the No. 2 man in the R.P.F., after

De Gaulle, its secretary-general. When, in 1952, the President of the Republic, Vincent Auriol, tried a diversionary maneuver and for the first and last time asked a Gaullist to form a cabinet, it was Soustelle who was sounded out and who refused.

Others, with or without approval from Colombey, were active in the Mendès-France government; Soustelle was given an African proconsulate. And what a proconsulate it was!—Algeria, where rebellion had just broken out. Upon his return he became the "destroyer of ministries," bagging as his prey the two last constitutional governments of the Fourth Republic, those of Bourgès-Manoury and Felix Gaillard. And it was also to him that everyone looked during the troubled days of May 1958. His belated and clandestine departure for Algiers did not give as much political leadership to the revolt as had been expected, but it emphatically confirmed the general belief that this time De Gaulle had entered the lists in the person of his lieutenant.

In short, until the dawn of the Fifth Republic, Jacques Soustelle appeared on many counts to be the No. 1 Gaullist. To be sure, a few of the initiated occasionally seemed pleased to emphasize the fact that, among his Knighthood titles, one was lacking—De Gaulle stubbornly refused to grant him the Cross of the Liberation. Of all those who rallied to the cause from the start, of all the members of the French committee at London or Algiers, he was and remained the only one who did not wear the medal with the black and green ribbon. Jacques Soustelle is perhaps the No. 1 Gaullist, but he is not one of General de Gaulle's Companions. Is this punishment for something most people do not know about, or merely the consequence of an instinctive distrust? In any case, ever since May 1958 Soustelle bent all his efforts toward justifying this strange premonition. There were too many shouts of "Vive Soustelle" early in June in Algeria when the presidential parade went by. This was not easily forgotten. Not of course because the General fears competition—at the most he is annoyed and irritated by it—but rather because the cry is seditious, meaning "Down with De Gaulle."

When he turned up again Soustelle was nonetheless made a minister, but not enthusiastically, and he was given a place at the very bottom of the table. He helped to found the U.N.R., but he did this with others, he was only one among many. In the cabinet as well as in administrative matters he never concealed his hand, pleading in favor of Algerian integration, in favor of those who, like himself, believed in it. One thing followed another; he became the defender of civil and military activists, soon their spokesman, then the liege man of extreme rightist groups.

Having failed in his attempt to gain control of the U.N.R., he was degraded, rejected. For a long while he hesitated, reluctant to become an enemy of the regime and especially of its leader. But the logic of his position, his friendships, his personality, pulled him irresistibly toward convulsionary anti-Gaullism, toward neo-terrorism, toward armed clandestinity. The prisoner of his own nature, he wandered from country to country like Bidault, hiding behind pseudonyms which strangely enough he selected from the arsenal of Stoicism; thus one day in Italy he was identified under the name of Seneca. He terminated his strange wanderings by making anguished appeals in favor of French Algeria that reached all the way to America, using the same formulas—and this is quite revealing—that he employed twenty-five years before on behalf of the Vigilance Committee of Anti-Fascist Intellectuals. He had looped the loop.

Where is the key to all this? "Fat Jacques," placid, stocky, secretive, rarely smiling, very impressed with himself, inclined to be somewhat hypochondriacal, for a long time seemed to be an intellectual who was lost in the arena of po-

litical action. He was said to be soft, indecisive, or rather so
slow to reach a decision that invariably he missed the propitious moment. He was known to be absorbed by scientific
and literary ambitions which were fully justified by his brilliant debut as a scholar. When he was seventeen he entered
the École Normale Supérieure at the head of his class. He
also received a first in philosophy at the age of twenty—and
this record still holds. At twenty-three he received his doc-
torate for a thesis that challenged the basic tenets of sociology:
at twenty-five he was assistant director of the Musée de
l'Homme . . . It is said that behind his stiff and stilted
manner he took great pains to conceal a raw sensibility.
Twice in the course of his public life he was betrayed in a
way by his nerves.

The first occasion, according to this view, was in July
1940. For six years Soustelle had been active in anti-Fascist
organizations. He favored the Popular Front and was anti-
Munich. His friends at the Musée de l'Homme, Wildé and
Levitsky, were among the first Frenchmen to be shot by the
Nazis, and Germaine Tillion was deported. All of them were
influenced by their chief, Director Paul Rivet, who led his
team of young scholars onto the path of revolutionary Socialism and even joined forces for a time with the Communists.
The Union of Intellectuals included Malraux, Guéhenno,
André Chamson, and the entire staff of *Vendredi*. In 1938
Soustelle became secretary-general of the Union. Although
he broke with the Communists, he remained active in the
extreme Left. Some attributed the break to the condem-
nation of Bukharin, others to the Nazi-Soviet Pact.

Whatever the reason, at the time of the 1940 armistice,
Soustelle was on an official mission in South America. It
was from there that he went to London and met De Gaulle
for the first time. The leftist intellectual was promptly se-
duced. It took him twenty years to extricate himself from

the General's charm, from his influence, to forget the over-whelming impression made on him that first day. When, after the Liberation, he met former leftist friends who in shocked astonishment reproached him for deliberately at-taching himself to the fortunes of a single individual, his answer was always the same: "Yes, but what a man!" No matter how calculating or cold he might be, Soustelle was never able to think of De Gaulle with indifference, so trau-matizing had been his first encounter. He was always to feel a strong bond for the General, a fascinated admiration which is equivalent, depending upon one's temperament, either to love or to vigilant, obstinate hatred.

The second shock that indelibly affected this No. 1 Gaul-list and determined his destiny was his glimpse of a horrible mass of mutilated cadavers—those of French workmen in the mine of El Alia, massacred by comrades of the Moslem work-yards. Eight months before Soustelle had arrived in Algeria as governor-general—he was the last to hold the title—a post to which he was appointed by Mendès-France with De Gaulle's blessing. He was spared nothing: *L'Aurore* de-nounced him as a "crypto-progressive," *Figaro* as a dangerous "neutralist." None of the French elect, with the exception of the liberal Jacques Chevalier came to greet him when he landed. Immediately a powerful campaign was launched against him with the aid of two traditional weapons: isola-tion and defamation. As an intellectual he was suspect, as a Gaullist he was detested by the feudal Pétainists, as a federal-ist he was hated by the Colonialists, as a *"Frangaoui"* * he was despised by the officials—everyone wanted to cut this man down. He was left to his own devices and everyone and everything that mattered in Algeria—high officials, par-liamentarians, agricultural chambers, political movements

---

* Word of contempt used by French Algerians for newly arrived French from the mainland.

led by the elect, veterans, newspapers, important colonizers, and powerful businessmen—tore his private life apart, disfigured his past, vilified his every act in an attempt to injure him regardless of cost. In the administration he no longer had his hands on the controls. Wounded, bludgeoned, calumnied, he decided to gain time. And so he locked himself in his office at the Palais d'Été, devised his plans, wrote interminable reports to Gaullist friends and Mendèsist leftists who answered his letters. Months went by.

Doubtless in the secret recesses of his conscience he had already changed his course when the "revelation" of El Alia occurred. Doubtless his nerves had already given way without his being aware of it. But the fact is that on August 19, 1955, Jacques Soustelle was still the "liberal" governor who threatened to resign if, in less than a month, his plan for reform was not ratified by the government. On August 21 he was the most determined champion of French Algeria, the stubborn partisan of integration. His program took into account all reasonable objections. To make it persuasive he adduced all the favorable considerations his quick intelligence, reinforced by ethnological erudition, could muster. Slow to decide, he manifested as always a terrible obstinacy once his choice had been made. He had become a different man, one whom his former detractors, the Algerian feudalists, now supported with the same ferocity that only yesterday they had displayed in opposing him. The *Aurore* published the full text of the speech he gave on the day of his departure, devoting a front-page story to "the remarkable words of a remarkable man." A hundred thousand citizens of Algiers turned out to honor and cheer him. They were present once again during those memorable May days when he arrived somewhat belatedly to assume the leadership of a rebellion in which, incidentally, he failed.

In July 1940, at the age of twenty-eight, he about-faced

for the first time, forsaking Marxism and the Left in order to follow De Gaulle. After fifteen years of passionate loyalty, he again veered about at El Alia; his sudden and definitive identification with French Algeria, while it did not immediately precipitate a break with Gaullism—the rupture became effective only four years later—replaced his first love with a new and no less passionate loyalty. This became plain when, called upon to choose between discipline of the Clan and his own deeply rooted convictions, he slipped inexorably in his slow, hesitant way from mere criticism into political opposition and then into a subversive struggle against the man whose first lieutenant he had been for so long.

STÉPHANE, ROGER, pseudonym of Roger Worms, writer and journalist, 46 years old
χ   *Gaullist in partibus*

Notice how few symbols appear after his name! Actually, he ought not to be included in this compendium at all. And yet if "Captain Stéphane," a leader of the Resistance and of the Liberation of Paris, had stayed on the beaten path he would be today a minister or ambassador of De Gaulle's Republic. But this ardent yet skeptical individualist had really no inclination, save for two things that were part of the adventure and of which, after Malaparte, he had become the theorist: the machine gun, with all its power, and secret societies. Today the machine gun is rusty; and all that remains of secret societies is a kind of occult allegiance, a fluid bond that weighs but lightly and is acceptable because, directly involving the sovereign, it is neither binding nor official.

Consequently, as an aesthete and enlightened amateur, Roger Stéphane could admire the fortunes of Gaullist polit-

ical action without taking part in it. Can you imagine him
on the platform of a congress, between two dignitaries of the
party? Or can you visualize him, so irreverent, so prone to
argue, so eternally in search of his self, keeping silent, be-
having modestly at the council table or remaining quiet and
docile among the unconditional elite of the regime? There is
no place for a Rossel in this Republic, nor for a Talleyrand at
the Court, nor even for a Lawrence of Arabia among the
"barbouzes."

And so Stéphane remains an interested but private spectator of the reign, waiting perhaps to become its historian.
Meanwhile he has carved out a principality for himself in the
empire of television.

THIERRY D'ARGENLIEU, GEORGES, admiral, 74 years
old
X   *In religion the Father Louis of the Trinity*

✝ ⬜ ★ 🏳 ⚕ ◫ 👂 🐎 ⬛

The Kings had their Court prelates, men who either
plotted or fought—Napoleon his Cardinal Fesch and Robin
Hood his chaplain. The adventure of the Knighthood had
to include one of these churchmen who would willingly exchange the priestly garb for the uniform, who would wear
boots beneath his cassock, who would be ready to give absolu-
tion to the enemy with one hand while parrying blows with
the other.

But Gaullism, more cultivated, would not have known
what to do with a sermonizing, frocked soldier; moreover, it
is hard to imagine a priest at the end of a parachute or at the
head of a bombing squadron, strewing death and desolation.
In Thierry d'Argenlieu it found the uniquely qualified individual: an admiral-prelate.

What a strange destiny was his, son of a Brittany sailor,

brother of a general killed in 1940, and himself a student at
the École Navale at the age of seventeen! After having served
in the army for eight years, four of them in wartime, he left
it in 1920 to enter the Carmelite religious order. As a major-
superior who represented the Paris region for his order,
he reentered the army in 1939, was taken prisoner, escaped,
and on June 22, 1940, joined De Gaulle in London, where
he immediately enrolled in Free France.

For he was no musical-comedy admiral. In September
1940 he was wounded at Dakar, where he headed a mission
charged with wresting from Governor Boisson the allegiance
of the High Commissioner of the A.O.F.* in the Pacific; then,
as commander-in-chief of the Free French naval forces, he
never hesitated to involve himself to the hilt. His enemies
called him the "naval Carmelite," but he was too big a man
to bear them a grudge for this.

After the Liberation he returned to the monastery, but
not for long. In September 1945, he was named high commissioner in Indochina and commander-in-chief. He arrived
with good intentions and liberal views. But soon surrounded
by officers and officials whose task it was to assist him, he
changed his mind within a few weeks. One can hear him
say to General Valluy, two days after the Sainteny–Ho Chi
Minh accords of March 6, 1946: "I am amazed—yes, General,
that's the word for it—amazed that France has such a wonderful expeditionary force in Indochina and that its leaders
prefer negotiation to fighting." It is altogether understandable that when the Ramadier government shelved him early
in 1947, it found nothing better to offer him than a military
medal. From then on his activities were divided between
monastic life and the Order of the Liberation, to which he
devoted two days a week; he had been made Grand Chancellor of the Order in 1941, the year it was founded. He

* Afrique Occidentale Française.

thus continued to function with equal ease in priestly garb and in uniform until 1958 when, for reasons of health, he was obliged to give up his public duties. He remains nonetheless a dignitary of the regime.

TRIBOULET, RAYMOND, minister, 47 years old
X *For the amusement of the Sovereign*

Is it because of his name? (The famous king's jester under Francis I was named Triboulet.) He has always enjoyed the Sovereign's amused tolerance and has been readily forgiven "deviations" which have caused others, and still do, a stern rebuke. A subprefect of Bayeux, the first major town liberated after the landings, he has been at the Palais Bourbon since 1946. Only once under the Fourth Republic did he yield to the temptation of a portfolio, but this was not held against him as it was against others. Actually his is a unique case: he served in the same ministry—Veterans' Affairs—in 1955 and after the "restoration" from 1959 to 1962.

When he let it be known that he had had enough, that he was tired of cemeteries, monuments to the dead, wounded veterans, and mausoleums, he was not dismissed but given another job and promoted.

Sometimes he is irritating, and then he is told so plainly, even in front of the entire cabinet. But the storms do not last long and leave no bitter aftermath.

VALLON, LOUIS, deputy, 62 years old
X *Gaullism with gaiety*

When a newspaperman reporting on Parliament between 1951 and 1955 recorded a biting or witty remark that fell from the lips of a person either too lowly or too highly placed

to be named, it was automatically attributed to Louis Vallon.
Only the rich are lent money. A keen sense of humor, a
horror of boredom, of conventional ideas, a naturally irreverent and nonconformist nature, have made this graduate
of the École Polytechnique, this former trade unionist who
entered politics via the Resistance, a kind of Alphonse Allais
or Tristan Bernard of the Chamber of Deputies. It is quite
true that he has not always felt at ease in the Gaullist camp,
with all its solemnity and stiffness. And he has often had to
pay for his irony, for telling in his inimitable way a few
slightly malicious stories or making some puns in dubious
taste.

His career has followed a zigzag pattern. From assistant
director on the General's personal staff in 1944–46 he went to
a department that seemed to have little relationship to the
post he had left—that of Money and Metals. The Fourth
Republic, which was certainly good-natured, no matter what
else people might say about it, allowed him full control over
coins bearing its name. He used most of his time preparing
its overthrow by the Gaullist party, which he represented in
labor and professional matters. He left Money and Metals
for the Palais Bourbon and, after five years there, became the
government's Commissioner to the Bank of Madagascar and
the Comoro Islands . . . By a stroke of luck all these build-
ings are on the Left Bank, not far from Saint-Germaine-des-
Près. He was to become more austere and even a little more
morose when he had to cross the Seine to sit on the Economic
and Social Council as a consequence of having failed to win
re-election in 1958. Returning once again to the National
Assembly in 1962, he fell heir to the heaviest and most thankless of responsibilities, that of general reporter on the budget
for the Finance Committee.

Leftist Gaullism, the association of capital and labor, the
social doctrine of the U.N.R.—in each of these there is a
kind of hidden antimony, an underlying contradiction. To

take charge of the administration of finance under De Gaulle
was never a very tranquil job; to carry out his social policy
was even more thankless. It required all the basic optimism
and natural good humor of Louis Vallon to hold the fort.

VENDROUX, JACQUES, deputy, 66 years old
X   *Brother-in-law*

At the sale of a village grocery store, an indiscreet person
discovered dishes that had been distributed for advertising
purposes a half century earlier by the Vendroux Biscuit
Company of Calais. He felt he should congratulate Madame
De Gaulle about this (her maiden name was Vendroux), but
was coldly received and not thanked for his pains. And yet
the General's brother-in-law is not ashamed of making bis-
cuits. He knew better than most that when the hero of June
18 left power with no hope of ever returning, he would be
forced to live on his modest colonel's retirement pay. He
also knew that De Gaulle made it a point of honor to refuse
all promotion or subsidy, wishing forever to remain a brigadier-general with temporary rank, but realizing too that bis-
cuits would be useful and enable him to hold the line.

As for the rest, he is a man whose advice is good; he is
thoughtful and liberal, willing to discuss with common sense
and simplicity the things he knows: the food industry, Calais,
his port and native region, the state of public opinion in the
north, the problems of the average deputy. Occasionally he
has been drafted to take an active part in politics, or asked
to present plans for global strategy. He accomplishes his task
as best he can without losing the respect of his friends or
even of his enemies. He is a deputy, a mayor, a general
councillor. Such is the reward of kinship. But these lingering rays of glory have never turned his head.